Critical So ... te ethnographic an ... students
and resear ... ng on the
role of lang ... e authors
walk the re ... mposing
research q ... alysis and
writing ac ... t types of
social acto ... examples
from the a ... sequential
stages of a ... of practical tips an ... e methods
courses in ... umanities
and social ... ly text for
investigati ... lives.

Monica Heller is Professor at the Ontario Institute for Studies in Education and the Department of Anthropology, University of Toronto, Canada. A Fellow of the Royal Society of Canada, she is also a Past President of the American Anthropological Association.

Sari Pietikäinen is Professor of Discourse Studies in the Department of Language and Communication Studies, University of Jyväskylä, Finland. She is also Director of the Jyväskylä Discourse Hub.

Joan Pujolar is Associate Professor in the Arts and Humanities Department at the Universitat Oberta de Catalunya, Spain. He is also Director of the Research Group on Language, Culture and Identity in the Global World and President of the Catalan Society of Sociolinguistics.

Critical Sociolinguistic Research Methods

Studying Language Issues That Matter

Monica Heller
Sari Pietikäinen
Joan Pujolar

Routledge
Taylor & Francis Group

NEW YORK AND LONDON

First published 2018
by Routledge
711 Third Avenue, New York, NY 10017

and by Routledge
2 Park Square, Milton Park, Abingdon, Oxon, OX14 4RN

Routledge is an imprint of the Taylor & Francis Group, an informa business

Every effort has been made to contact copyright-holders. Please advise
the publisher of any errors or omissions, and these will be corrected in
subsequent editions.

Library of Congress Cataloging-in-Publication Data
Names: Heller, Monica, author. | Pietikäinen, Sari, 1968– author. |
    Pujolar, Joan, 1964– author.
Title: Critical sociolinguistic research methods : studying language issues
    that matter / Monica Heller, Sari Pietikäinen, Joan Pujolar.
Description: First edition. | New York : Routledge, 2018. | Includes
    bibliographical references and index.
Identifiers: LCCN 2017020812 | ISBN 9781138825895 (hardcover) |
    ISBN 9781138825901 (softcover) | ISBN 9781317577577 (epub) |
    ISBN 9781317577560 (mobipocket/kindle)
Subjects: LCSH: Sociolinguistics—Research—Methodology.
Classification: LCC P40.3 .H45 2017 | DDC 306.44—dc23
LC record available at https://lccn.loc.gov/2017020812

ISBN: 978-1-138-82589-5 (hbk)
ISBN: 978-1-138-82590-1 (pbk)
ISBN: 978-1-315-73965-6 (ebk)

Typeset in Optima
by Apex CoVantage, LLC

Printed and bound by CPI Group (UK) Ltd, Croydon, CR0 4YY

Contents

Illustrations

Figures

Tables

Acknowledgements

We have tried out bits of this book with a number of colleagues and students, who have all given us extremely helpful feedback. In alphabetical order, we thank: Alexandre Duchêne, Pedro Garcez, Jere Hokkanen, Helen Kelly-Holmes, Marina Massaguer Comes, Anna-Liisa Ojala, Anne Sophie Roussel, Maria Rieder and Umesh Sharma.

We are also grateful to Caroline Kerfoot and the students of the postgraduate seminar at Stockholm University for their contributions in a workshop on data analysis as part of the EU COST Action IS1306 network entitled "New Speakers in a Multilingual Europe: Opportunities and Challenges."

We also would like to acknowledge the funding agencies which have supported the research on which we have drawn in this book: Office de la langue française (Government of Québec), Social Sciences and Humanities Research Council of Canada, the Spanish Ministerio de Ciencia e Innovación (Ref. FFI2011–24781), the Department of Universities and Research of Catalonia, The Academy of Finland (Ref. Cold Rush -project) and the Department of Language and Communication Studies, University of Jyväskylä.

Introduction

What is it all about when people on buses in Australia and Canada tell immigrants to "speak white"? Why do courts across Europe hire linguists to help determine if asylum seekers are lying about where they are from? Why did 20th-century residential schools in North America and Scandinavia punish indigenous children if they spoke their own language? Why do people work hard at changing their accent? Why are there debates about how many, and which languages to teach in school?

It is these kinds of puzzles around language, power, and society that we are interested in. We see in these examples, and the many others we encounter, evidence that language matters. It is connected to how we construct social differences and how social and political life is organized around them. These differences (whether understood as national, ethnolinguistic, racialized, gendered, sexualized or anything else) are bound up with the processes through which we make and rationalize inequality. We conceptualize and make sense of the world around us through language, and we negotiate our relationships with others through language. Who we are considered to be, and who we can become, are language matters. And who we can become is all about our access to things that matter: political power, economic resources like jobs, education, social status or cultural resources like stories, songs and art.

This book is about how to investigate language issues that matter. Research is one way to engage with these issues, to make a contribution to understanding what they are and how they work, and what consequences they have for whom. It therefore lays the basis for other forms of possible engagement. Because language issues matter, lots of different kinds of people care about them. Research is a way to get into conversation with them on the basis of new and helpful knowledge. This book is about how to do that.

You will find many different voices in this book, and this was the main reason why we take the liberty of addressing you as "you" from the start, essentially to make sure that we make clear who the participants of this conversation are. "We," or "us," are therefore the authors, in alphabetical order by family name, Monica, Sari and Joan (at least most of the time), and not an abstract universal know-it-all speaking from the depths of the temple of science. The idea of a *conversation* is, as we will show, critical to what we understand doing research to be about. Producing knowledge, as we see it, is fundamentally about participating in one amongst the many conversations that are now taking place within the social and human sciences. The main goal of this book, then, is to provide a guide to participating in the conversations about language that matter to you.

We use a *critical ethnographic sociolinguistic* approach.

- By **critical** we mean that we put questions of power and inequality in the centre of our inquiry. We ask what resources are important to whom, and how the social processes we examine have consequences. (Here our focus is mainly on consequences for people, but many scholars are also interested in consequences for organizations or communities, specific social practices, animals or the environment.) Second, a critical stance applies also to ourselves: we use our understandings about the role of language in social processes of power and inequality reflexively, that is, by applying them to how we undertake the social activity of doing research (as socially constructed and traversed by relations of power), and to how we make sense of the data we generate as a result of the research process.

- By **ethnographic** we mean in-depth, situated explorations of how these processes work and why, and what they mean to people and why (seeking to both describe and explain), using representative or telling cases to illustrate broader processes. By "situated," we mean we attend to the specific conditions and contexts in which the processes we are interested in unfold.

- By **sociolinguistic** we mean two things. First, that we situate this book in a conversation about how language matters, although we think it can be useful to anyone undertaking critical ethnographic research (and which can draw on converging traditions that go by different names, notably *linguistic anthropology, discourse analysis* and some domains of *applied linguistics*). We are aware that *sociolinguistics* can mean different things to different people; here we opt for the term as an umbrella covering all kinds of investigations into how language matters, socially, politically and economically.

We feel that issues of social inequality can be investigated from a variety of starting points. As these phenomena are interrelated in complex ways, researching them and talking about them becomes web-like in terms of the thought processes, data gathering and dialogues required to understand them. To us, they are best represented as fields or webs where many different things are linked up across time and space. They are organized around the things—resources, stakes—that have value for people. Language is connected to how they get produced, circulated, consumed and valued, and by whom, through what kinds of activities. In Section 0.4 we will develop the metaphors that we use in this book to conceptualize what we think this web is and what its dynamics are. We will often refer to it as a rhizome, an organic entity in which threads cross asymmetrically, forming nodes or nexus that are particularly dense intersections of multiple threads.

But it is hard to follow a story about (how to do) research that is organized like a web, so we are going to attempt to do this in a partly linear fashion. We have organized the book around the sequence of key moments in the research process:

- **Moment 1**: Formulating your research question.
- **Moment 2:** Drawing up your research plan.
- **Moment 3:** Generating your data.
- **Moment 4:** Analyzing your data.
- **Moment 5:** Writing up your story and your claims.

Although we present these moments as a sequence, along the way we will show you how they often project forward and loop back a step or two, allowing for reformulations, adjustments and deepening along the way (this is called *recursivity*).

In addition, we have allowed ourselves some non-linearity. We have assembled all the practical tips connected to each moment in a separate section called the *Shop Floor*. This allows us to address the central aspects of what happens at each moment of the research process in the body of the text, without overwhelming you with details. Our idea is that once you have read the body of the text, and grasp how to think about this moment, you can find out more about the practicalities of undertaking it by looking at the corresponding section of the Shop Floor, where the nitty-gritty of the work gets done.

We provide ample concrete examples for each moment, mainly from our own work. Examples from Monica's work are in red, from Sari's in blue and from Joan's in green, either in the text or marked with a correspondingly coloured sidebar. In addition, we have also provided two story threads which track actual research projects from Moment to Moment. The green thread is based on Joan's research on language and power in Catalonia; the blue one is based on Sari's research on discourse, identity and power in indigenous multilingual Sámi areas of northern Finland. Because Catalonia and francophone Canada share many features, we have opted for two rather than three story lines, though in this chapter we will give you the background of all three so you can follow the examples provided along the way.

You can read these threads in any order you like, and before, after or during your reading of the main body of the text. Our idea here is to show you how some of the ideas we present in the main body of the text actually play out in real life. Put the other way around, they show you the research experience that has led us to formulate the research process the way we do in this book. We do this to show how we have dealt with these particular questions in our own research, and to express our commitment to the idea that research is a personal and socially situated experience.

In order to foreground the material issues that have motivated us to become researchers in the first place, we start this chapter with how language matters, and why it matters now, at this moment of social change. We then turn to what it means to research language from a critical ethnographic sociolinguistic perspective. We then discuss the research process as we envisage it: as a series of five moments, rhizomatically and recursively interconnected.

0.1 Why Language Matters Now

This book is meant to help scholars deploy their resources and ingenuity to understand how linguistic processes are consequential for people, for the ways in which people relate to other people, and also for the ways in which people seek access to the resources that they need in order to live. We understand societies as primarily structured around the processes through which individuals and groups strive to produce and access resources. Our point of departure and our objectives remain in the materialities which are part of how language is constructed and in which language participates, and in language's role in constructing objects and social categories, delineating boundaries and reproducing or changing relations of inequality. We draw on a strand of linguistics that has historically kept branching back into sociology and anthropology, and has arguments to make about how language figures in key social processes such as identity construction, boundary making, the nature and scope of human action, ideological struggles and symbolic violence. In short, our research is **not** about language per se. It is about the **conditions and consequences** of language for people, which is what justifies our title "language issues that matter."

Our aim in this book is to show how to examine this critical potential and relevance of language, within an understanding of language as social practice. We thus aim to speak to both sociolinguists and to other researchers in the humanities and the social sciences who are sensitive to the role of language in the types of processes that they study. But to do that, we must strike a balance that ensures that non-sociolinguists do not feel as if they are venturing too much into foreign territory and vice versa. As scholars in the social sciences and the humanities have become increasingly aware that language and discourse play a central role in the phenomena they study, sociolinguists and discourse analysts have increasingly realized that their own object—language—cannot be understood as separate from the social processes that it shapes and that shape it. So the former have been attracted to discourse and the latter to social theory; but the crossing of disciplinary divides has presented difficulties. We hope that this book helps address these difficulties at least in the procedural and methodological aspects of empirical research, although it will most often address readers who come from language-centred traditions.

It is important for us to make very clear what we mean when we write about language. Mainstream linguistics, particularly since Saussure, was long successful in arguing that language should be studied independently from other social, cognitive or natural phenomena, thereby separating the discipline of linguistics from other social sciences. During the 20th century, social scientists got accustomed to either dropping language from their agenda or simply treating it as a separate *variable* amongst others. In our view, this has been a very unfortunate agreement to lead separate lives, publish in separate outlets and work in separate faculties and departments.

It has also led linguists to examine communication in very narrow terms, as if people only produced meaning when articulating words or phrases. In fact, it has led linguists to worry more about form than meaning, as if language was basically about the shapes and combinations of words, or sounds or units of meaning. To us, this formalism has even led most of semiotics (a discipline for which meaning is supposed to be the object) to search for theories of meaning in which the social embeddedness of communication is not adequately addressed.

Generally speaking, the split between the linguistic and the social has prevented the development of powerful theories and methods to investigate **meaning** from a social and historical perspective, i.e., how meanings are produced in social interaction, under particular material, political, economic and social conditions. This separation has therefore also prevented us from examining how the production of meaning is part of the making of social organization, that is, the production, circulation and consumption of resources, and therefore central to how things work out for people. It makes it difficult to address, let alone answer, the kinds of questions with which we opened this book, that is, to understand why language issues matter to people, and therefore how we should feel about them and react to them.

We build on the work of many key scholars; but this is not a book about theory. So we won't delve into our intellectual genealogy in detail. We do provide a few key readings in the bibliography from the three—white, male, European—theoreticians who have influenced us the most: Mikhail Bakhtin (1981,1986), Pierre Bourdieu (1982, 1991) and Michel Foucault (1971). But read their critics, and in particular look for the ways in which imperialism, colonialism and capitalism have worked to create intellectual traditions which shape us just as they lead us to reflexively ask how our own positions of power create blind spots, relations of power and erasures and marginalizations of other ways of being and knowing. As authors of this book, for instance, we present a gender balance of sorts, and can claim ties to different minorities and peripheries; but we are also all white European or North American, a position from which our response to imperialism, colonialism and capitalism cannot be the same as that of people coming from elsewhere.

There are three main aspects of our position that we want to emphasize.

First, when we talk about language we refer to any form of meaning making that humans make available for fellow humans to pick up: speaking and writing, yes, but also gesturing, posturing, drawing, photographing, painting, sculpting, moving, singing, dancing or shouting, even failing to do one or more of these. Social life is about an unresolvable entanglement between the material and the symbolic; when we observe an inert landscape we do not just grasp it with our senses, but we also work out what it means for us. From this perspective, we believe that researchers who define their object as "discourse," "communication," "communicative practice," "interaction," "literature" or "semiosis" fall within the purview of what for us is "language."

Second, meaning is a constitutive product of social interaction that is embedded in power relations. Meaning derives from how people use linguistic (e.g., discursive, semiotic) resources in their dealings—and struggles—with each other. This amounts to saying that social life is basically made up of language, but also that meaning is not the simple result of the operation of an abstract symbolic system of phonological, morphological, lexical or syntactic rules. At the same time, meanings have histories; they carry echoes from previous encounters. While meaning is "situated," i.e., it is bound to its moment and place of emergence in the singularity of each situation, it is also one moment in a web of encounters that stretch across time and space, beyond the capacity of any single social actor to grasp. This is why we see ethnography as a necessary way to address how social actors act upon each other and the world in specific and singular moments, while tracing the consequences of these moments for the sedimentation of the categories that organize the distribution of resources, and of the activities where they are produced, circulated, consumed and valued. To us, ethnography is central because it directs our gaze towards social life and its meanings as they unfold in specific times and spaces, and links them to the concrete consequences of what happens in the moments of everyday life for the ability of people who are differentially positioned to gain access to key activities and to the resources found there.

Third, contemporary social changes are linguistically inflected in profound and complex ways. We argue that we are living in times in which the role of language is both extended and intensified, as we try to manage globalized networks, develop niche products and niche markets, and engage increasingly in communication-centred service and knowledge work. Late capitalism and its emphasis on flexibility and mobility has also disrupted communities and created wealth disparities; reactions to these problems often focus on the contesting, making or maintaining of social differences linked to inequality through and about language. This is why it is especially crucial to study language critically now. We see important changes in the ways in which social actors have until now drawn on their linguistic resources in their struggles to collaborate and compete with others for access to symbolic and socioeconomic resources. Sociology, geography, and anthropology produce compelling accounts that help understand the deep social transformations that we are presently experiencing. However, all these seminal works and many comparable ones have rarely addressed the important linguistic components and consequences of these transformations, which have to do with the fact that **communicative, discursive and symbolic practices have moved into the centre of what are now the key sites of economic production and often, concomitantly, of political struggle.** Language is a political, economic and social resource attached to high stakes.

The reason for this is that contemporary ties between economic activities, language and communicative practices have increased, largely through *tertiarization* (the extension of economic activities based on services and information). In the core capitalist countries, economic activity has moved away from manufacturing industry into what is commonly defined as the "service industry," a heterogeneous amalgam of activities such as education and training, administration, planning, marketing, sports, (tele)communication, hospitality, entertainment, tourism, care of many types, transport, retail, design and creation, computing, consultancy, finance and so on. Most of these activities are either instrumentally performed through communication or are simply communicative acts or products in themselves. Linguistic, communication and discourse skills also become central for workers, whether in the form of multilingualism (to be able to speak, read and write in one or more languages/standards), or as the ability to master a wide and flexible range of resources for communication (performative skills, genres, registers, communication styles) or both.

Globalization disrupts the control of the nation state and national élites over language in multiple ways:

- Mobility diversifies the languages and the accents present in the marketplace (e.g., in workplaces, at schools).
- Online communication escapes the controls that a linguistic élite formerly exerted over who published and how.
- The service economy turns to language as a means of production for myriad economic actors and as a key element for the division of labour.
- Language practices are taken up as potential commodities, as is the case in many areas of social life formerly considered "public goods."
- What counts as valuable linguistic capital, and who has access to it, shifts, leading to increased competition and struggle over social boundaries.

The field of linguistics (or language studies) as a whole is itself under considerable tension over what constitutes the object of the discipline (indeed, in a way, this very book is a symptom of this tension). The key idea of what language is about from the perspective of mainstream linguistics gets laid bare: the idea that languages are coherent structural systems, one fully separate from the other, the expression of human cultures neatly divided in territorially bound cultures. Such assumptions are not only challenged by the mounting empirical evidence of multilingualism and linguistic hybridity in contemporary societies, and the value and role of language in political and economic life. They are beginning to clash with the everyday experience of citizens living in our contemporary, diverse and multi-connected societies, for whom subscribing to a single language and identity with fixed boundaries is not really an option, or whose formerly stigmatized linguistic resources are now valued, or on the contrary, whose formerly valued linguistic resources now fail to produce what they were supposed to. There are more and more people, practices and experience that do not fit into the pre-existing categories, and we see consequences of communicative behaviour our current approaches ignore or deal with poorly.

These changes need to be understood if we are to grasp what is occurring, and what differences they are already making to how we lead our lives: to what we want to and need to learn, to how we can make a living, to who decides things for whom, according to what criteria. Language is not the only thing that counts here, of course; but it matters in ways we are only beginning to understand.

0.2 Research as Socially Constructed Knowledge

A constructivist position basically posits that knowledge is a human creation and that it takes place in social contexts where persons interact with each other to achieve specific ends; hence our emphasis on research as "experience." This is not the place to engage in a full discussion of *ontology* and *epistemology* (that is, the nature of knowledge and how we know it) or on the philosophy of knowledge; but it is necessary to be aware that this is not a point of consensus in the social and human sciences, and even less in the natural sciences.

There are continuous debates and discussions concerning what scientific knowledge is about, and there are different schools of thought and perspectives on these issues. For example, there is a strong tradition, supported by ordinary common sense, that posits that knowledge is about uncovering aspects of how reality works that somehow remain hidden until a clever individual comes along and produces evidence that demonstrates how things "really" work. This is called a *positivist* approach, and it is commonly used in the natural sciences, but also in some social sciences. However, we prefer a *constructivist* understanding of knowledge, holding that knowledge is a social, historical and political animal—one raised, tamed and produced by us. So one important thread in this book is to undo the confusions and contradictions that the long dominant position of positivism causes to novice researchers, and which are very deeply inscribed in academic life and academic language.

However, it is worth clarifying that Sari, Monica and Joan are not *relativists*, as people who believe that all representations of reality have some form of legitimacy are often called. We believe that there is a material world out there that needs explaining, and that some descriptions and explanations are more plausible and adequate than others: they cover more ground, they make more accurate predictions. To get there, we need to:

- formulate a question that makes sense in the discipline,
- work out a strategy to answer it,
- negotiate access to the evidence needed,
- process the evidence,
- devise the best possible answers and explanations to our question that make sense to the scientific community in which we are working.

Therefore, we see doing research as a fundamentally social experience, in which everything we do is for interlocutors: our close colleagues and the wider academic community in which our work is inscribed, and all the other stakeholders for whom these language issues matter also. We have written this book according to this idea, not as an all-encompassing recipe book, but as a set of recommendations on how to participate in what is, after all, a **conversation**.

One further aspect of this position is that we see social life as produced by people as they engage with each other. This view lies in opposition to some social scientists who consider that social meanings, behaviour or social phenomena are the expression of underlying structures, laws, norms or symbolic systems that operate at an abstract level. To us, on the contrary, any social phenomenon is "located," i.e., any form of organization, idea, role, norm, conflict, text, must have been produced by people at some moment and at some particular place (or may have been reproduced by many people at many different moments and places). Whatever is "social," including language, stems from social practice. We express this idea through the concept of *situatedness*, and this is what justifies and explains our main methodological choice: ethnography. Ethnography is fundamentally about examining social practice **as it unfolds**, while it happens.

It also follows from these positions that this book focuses on research methods that are conventionally called *qualitative*. The term "qualitative" is generally applied to research that is primarily attentive to any aspect of the social **world as it is engaged with, perceived or explained by the people** that we study. Qualitative inquiries seek to see things as they are undertaken, experienced and narrated by people. Thus it focuses on how people see the world and how they make sense of it. To find this out, it is obviously useful to talk to them and hear what they say in an explicit way, but it is also crucial to observe what they do and say in different contexts when they deal with different people, so that we can find out how they see the world implicitly through their conduct.

For us, ethnography constitutes the canonical research method for approaching the social world as it unfolds in social life and is experienced by social actors. Ethnography commonly involves what is called "participant observation," which in simple terms means taking part in what people do in their ordinary social habitat. However, this form of observation is generally combined with other forms of access to people's views, such as interviews, focus groups or even the consultation of documentation of any kind. These forms of data are usually analyzed through careful attention to their communicative form, not just their content (or through what is usually referred to as conversation analysis, interaction analysis and discourse analysis).

Ethnography constitutes a very specific form of experience for researchers. It is time-consuming, emotionally very demanding and requires people to develop very specific skills (many of which can really only be developed while doing it). Moreover, ethnography is in practice quite incompatible with non-constructivist, positivist conceptions of knowledge (as we discussed above). Positivism places contradictory demands on ethnographers: to preserve "objectivity," to keep a distance from research subjects, to avoid "influencing" the situations we observe, to stick to our pre-defined categories, and to avoid changing your plans. However, novice researchers very often set themselves benchmarks that only make sense from a positivistic perspective, and which are often detrimental to the possibility of gathering good data. Through this work, we do not mean to minimize the challenges involved in doing ethnographic research; but we hope to make the experience more rewarding with guidance that we consider to be more consistent with a constructivist viewpoint.

Throughout the text it will emerge again and again that research is not socially and politically neutral, and neither are the methods and theories that we draw upon nor the knowledge we produce. This is the part of the critical aspect of research. It is not the place here to discuss in full how social science is inscribed in the political and the economic, but we do believe that it is essential for us as scholars to accept what this implies: that our work is the product of specific socio-historical conditions that affect what we study, why, how and how it is received by others. This position is basically antagonistic with the position of many scientists who believe that social research aims at providing objective, value-free representations of reality.

We do not even go along with the platonic position that research is "ideally" neutral, but inevitably "biased" because it can never be made airtight from the personal and the political. On the contrary, we believe that social and political interests at all levels (personal or institutional) are actually **constitutive** of any social research in all its components. Those interests are what make research meaningful, bestow the rationale for the questions, guide the deployment of procedures to formulate truth claims and provide interlocutors for them, i.e. the people who actually participate in the ongoing conversations in which the research is inserted. And when we want to engage with other people and institutions about our research, we unavoidably speak within a discursive formation that conditions our talk and shapes the ways we interact and are understood. The ramifications of this position are going to be felt throughout this book, as we present researchers and objects of study as always inscribed in complex webs of relations and interests, in which ethical and political considerations are just as important as those that can be presented as primarily methodological or theoretical.

This position leads us to *reflexivity*. It has to do with the question of who the researcher is, and why the researcher is entitled to produce an authoritative account of the social practice that is being analyzed. After all, the researcher is a just another person with personal views and perceptions, just like the people who are investigated. There is also a certain circularity in the notion that research is aimed at understanding social practice, but that this is done through a research process that is, after all, social practice too. Indeed, when we posit that social life is constituted in social interaction, what we mean is that it happens as people talk to each other or engage in some form of coordinated activity. But it so happens that ethnography is, in principle, the same thing: talking to people and doing things with them. Actually, the term "participant observation" expresses the fact that the researcher is often one more component of the social practice under analysis. How can one be, at the same time, the subject and the object of observation? And how can the phenomena studied be essentially the same as the instruments used to study them?

The simple answer to these concerns is that there is nothing intrinsically and fundamentally different between the perceptions and accounts of our research participants and those of our own as academics. There are, however, differences in terms of their social standing and the type of conversations in which they take a part. In any case, this not only raises methodological issues, but also political and ethical ones, as it raises the question of what legitimizes the researcher to determine a specific research agenda, i.e., to produce knowledge that can potentially be used by other people and organizations to perform changes in society that may or may not affect either their research participants or other people. The principle of reflexivity requires that we be the first to examine and explain the position from which we speak both as social scientists and as persons of our times and places and histories. It involves owning up to our theoretical and political affiliations, which inform the topics that we choose to analyze and the perspective from which we analyze them.

0.3 Research as Experience and as Conversation

This book is meant to be "practical" not so much in its focus on procedure but in its attention to how researchers confront the experience of doing research. It is not a user manual or a self-help guide with a list of general principles and instructions meant to provide the solution for each problem or the "correct" way to do a study. Rather, it is meant to help students and colleagues to open up their own path and adapt their own approach to the research questions they pursue, in a context characterized by personal and institutional constraints as well as ongoing social change.

To do so, we have attempted relatively novel ways of writing that draw on different layers of the practical personal experience of the authors of this book, simply because our lives are our most accessible source of examples to situate and discuss the issues addressed. We use our experiences as material to exemplify (and reflect upon) how research gets inserted in the personal, social and professional lives of those who participate in it. And we also see autobiography as one more way to express our commitment to an epistemology of the situated, so that the ethnographic gaze is not only directed to the object we intend to study, but also to ourselves as researchers.

We have tried to choose examples of our own experience as researchers in a way that illuminates a range of ways of doing research on language issues that matter (as there is no one single way to do this). But we have also tried to explicate moments of choices, detours and interrupted research paths that all are part of ethnographic, critical qualitative research, in an attempt to talk about the things that are often left out in our academic articles and dissertations, and by doing so to demystify the process of ethnography.

The formula we have found to write this is to combine two main voices throughout the text: (1) that of a relatively conventional author (such as what you are reading now) and (2) that of the separate autobiographical threads of the authors that appear regularly in all the chapters. The main authorial voice is the norm, while the autobiographical threads get distinguished by a sidebar assigning different colours to each author. Just to underline the issue of voice, Joan's thread at the end of each chapter is narrated in the third person, while Sari's is narrated in the first person.

Most of the examples provided come from real research projects done by the authors in the past. For narrative convenience we have also narrowed down the range of projects that we use as examples, so that we do not have to spend time providing too much contextual information. Most refer to either Joan Pujolar's (1991, 2001) early investigations on how young people use their bilingual repertoire in Catalonia, or Sari Pietikäinen's (2013, 2015) research on dynamics of language and identity in multilingual, indigenous Sámiland/Finnish Arctic North. Joan's examples mainly present a research agenda that addresses linguistic and discursive issues centrally; Sari's exemplify a project that addresses political and socioeconomic issues in which language and discourses about it arguably feature in a central way. We also use at some points in the text Monica Heller's (e.g., 2011, Heller et al., 2015) experiences of doing research on the politics of language in Canada, especially francophone Canada.

Joan's story mainly develops the thread of how a researcher invests in sociolinguistics out of the experience of participating in minority language advocacy, in this case, the process of "normalization" of the Catalan language. The concept of normalization refers to a political commitment to use the apparatus of the state and civil society to transform Catalonia into a canonical, linguistically cohesive nation state, in part through extending the use of Catalan into all areas of social life. Through his thread, we illustrate how a specific strand of sociolinguistics is inserted within diverse movements in which political mobilizations draw in complex ways on nationalism and the articulation of cultural institutions.

Sari's story illustrates research on intertwined relationships between economic development and cultural transformation on the terrain of tourism in the Finnish Arctic North, especially in terms of the stakes for indigenous Sámi involved in economic change (of which the introduction of tourism is an element). Her story is as an example of a research area in which social, cultural, economic and political concerns are paramount, and which can be usefully illuminated by the use of a combination of ethnography, sociolinguistics and critical discourse analysis.

Monica's story concerns the ways in which French/English bilingualism is a central terrain for struggles for political and economic power in Canada. It illustrates how institutions like workplaces and schools are important terrains for the production and distribution of linguistic resources, in the context of ideological conflict regarding the role of ethnolinguistic categories in the making of citizens.

We provide more context for each of these threads at the end of this chapter. Through them we aim to make it easier to grasp how and why our research approaches need to be historicized at many levels. At the end of the day, each piece of research—like any form of social interaction—is performed by specific people who have personal histories and conduct their work within specific historical conditions, and hence constitutes a unique experience.

Thus, our central concern is to engage in a dialogue with the reader, presumably a researcher who has a life trajectory and specific interests that she needs to articulate into a research project, and who needs to cope with the challenges most typically encountered in the process. What we have to offer to those who seem tempted to follow us in some way, or in part of the way, is the **experience** of dealing with change and uncertainty, a frank depiction of how doing research has really been for us and what we have learned from it.

We hope to help readers figure out a way to join the conversations that matter to them. Novice researches cannot (normally) hope to redefine the conversation from scratch; but neither are we going to help sustain the pretence that nobody is pulling the strings, even when the pulling may be done for legitimate reasons and with reasonable criteria.

0.4 The Research Process: Sequencing, Recursivity and Rhizome

We have chosen to organize this book into chapters that reproduce the trajectory of a conventional research project, five "key moments": question, design, data/fieldwork, analysis and writing/knowledge sharing. Here we will begin with a reminder of what these moments are, and then explore how we want to nonetheless see them as more complicated than a simple linear sequence. We will discuss the concepts of *rhizome* and *recursivity* as keys to understanding the actual dynamics of the research process.

As a result, these five moments serve as signposts to organize our account and to present the research process extended in time in which decisions have to be made and actions need to be done. We have settled for these because we believe that they work in a general fashion if interpreted very flexibly, because they seem easy to grasp and help guide readers throughout the book, and also because they tend to coincide roughly with how research is institutionally organized in doctoral programs, grant schemes and evaluation procedures.

0.4.1 First Key Moment: Formulating Your Research Question(s)

The process of deciding what issue we wish to understand more or better and formulating it in concrete words. Although formulating questions is in principle easy for anyone, it is much more difficult to turn one's academic interests into a question that is researchable and that makes sense in the context of the specific community/ies in which one is working.

0.4.2 Second Key Moment: Drawing Up Your Research Plan

The process of devising and writing down a strategy to fulfill our intent to build knowledge. Here we focus especially on the experience of writing research plans or projects and sharing our research agenda with various audiences.

0.4.3 Third Key Moment: Generating Your Data

The multiple ways of gathering information and pieces of evidence about the social world that are supposed to support the argument we wish to make or the hypotheses we wish to test. For us "data" is primarily made up of evidence of, or resulting from, social practices.

0.4.4 Fourth Key Moment: Analyzing Your Data

The multiple ways of making connections between our data and our research questions or hypotheses. We discuss mapping, tracing and connecting data, and how to make claims on the basis of our analysis.

0.4.5 Fifth Key Moment: Writing Up Your Story and Your Claims

Writing the research results. We discuss this step as a complex, and often emotionally difficult, moment, when the consistency of arguments is tested, and authors find their voice in a variety of conversations.

Now think about these moments as entry points into a complex, dynamic web of people, resources, discourses, activities and things that relate to each other in ways that you wish to understand. To talk about this web, we employ several concepts and metaphors throughout the book. The concepts are *recursivity* and *rhizome*, and the recurrent metaphors are *forest and trees*, *roadmap*, *node*, *nexus* and *a skein of multi-coloured wool* and its *knots*.

The reason why we complicate the neat sequence laid out above is that in real life researchers encounter repeated moments of crisis that threaten to subvert it. For example, you may find yourself in the middle of fieldwork and suddenly realize that some aspects of your research questions and research design need reviewing. This is something that habitually anguishes novice researchers, but it is important to realize that it really comes with the ticket, and is in fact necessary. This is how we constantly check our hypotheses, and adjust according to what we learn. These apparent setbacks are in fact constitutive moments of the process of producing knowledge, and so we need to plan for *recursivity*.

The concept of *recursivity* has a long history in linguistics, particularly in generative linguistics, to refer to grammatical structures that can infinitely recreate full replicas of themselves at lower levels (as a prepositional phrase can have more prepositional phrases inside). Here we use it in a more metaphorical sense. For us, recursivity means that you must be prepared to go back to square one (or maybe two or three) and retrace your steps whenever necessary, though hopefully more or less within the same territory. Definitions must get refined, implications must become better delineated, connections more apparent. Research questions may well change at different stages of a project, because you encounter problems or opportunities in the fieldwork, or new data you need to explain.

Research design involves imagining the whole process (state of the art, methodology, fieldwork, analysis, even writing) without actually doing it in the real world, so we shouldn't be surprised when the real world reframes our design.

Can you really separate fieldwork and analysis? While you do ethnography, you see two people talking about something interesting, or you find a new interesting document. Can you really take account of them without considering how they connect to your question? You write down a fieldnote. Does it contain "only data," or is there something of your interpretation in it too? You are analyzing someone's interview and you realize that you still need to interview someone else. Is this acceptable? Your analysis raises new interesting issues that were not strictly in your research design. What do you do with these?

Finally, when writing and disseminating your research, you realize that you keep analyzing and reanalyzing your data, and often as a reaction to how other people respond to what you say. Is this acceptable? And people (other students, professors, politicians, social workers, citizens, your family) come up with other questions that are connected to your research. Should you refrain from addressing them, responding to them just because you had not thought about it that way earlier?

So it is important to read the book layout and the whole text with the awareness that each "moment" of the research process may potentially contain elements of the other moments, or each stage impact or feed onto the other stages and thus transform the whole process more or less as a consequence. In a similar way that the research design projects fieldwork decisions into the future, the fieldwork or analysis or writing can make us retrace our steps to issues that we had earlier (provisionally) closed.

We also adapt Deleuze and Guattari's (1980) concept of *rhizome* as a way of depicting our research processes as networked practices in which each decision is conditioned by previous decisions and impacts on the future ones. And like a rhizome, research has multiple entry points and unforeseen connections. Let's take a close look at the use of the metaphor of rhizome in research and knowledge production, and at some of the connected metaphors we use at various points.

The basic image is that of the components of organisms that keep growing and interrelating, very much like the webs of roots formed in the earth by plants or the neurons in our brains. Thus we see the rhizome as an epistemological metaphor for a dynamic, non-linear system of knowledge production, located in a multiplicity of connected processes. The concept is a provocative critique of modernity's dichotomic "facts" and fixed boundaries and binaries (e.g., true/false), and provides a starting point for researching the complexity and connectivity of social phenomena. The rhizome is a representation of knowledge that can account for resilience, heterogeneity, interconnectivity and multiplicity among the nexus in a network. It offers a way to map the complexities and multiplicities encountered in research—the ways in which processes, changes and practices connect to each other in emergent ways. Along with rhizome, we adopt a family of terms such as *nexus* (the meeting places of multiple processes and dimensions), *dots* (the elements constituted by a web of relations), *interconnections* and *knots*; these all help depict positionality within processes characterized by movement. The rhizome, to conclude, lends a metaphoric physicality to complex processes, enabling us to envision a system of dynamic changes that are never complete.

With the backdrop of these concepts related to the ontology of scientific knowledge and their implications for how to do research, we use three additional metaphors that we hope will be helpful to discuss how to conduct a dynamic, open-ended research process. They are the forest and its trees, a roadmap and a skein of multi-coloured wool. These interrelated concepts each try to guide you where to look and what to do when navigating the rhizome of your research.

The metaphor of a forest and its trees may help you think about scope. The topic of your research is the forest that you need to know well enough to be able to navigate across in order to find the particular questions, key moments or data (the trees) that you will focus on. Once you have investigated your trees more closely, you will need to take a look at the forest again in order to put your trees into a bigger picture: what are they part of? Where do they belong? Are the trees in this forest typical, telling, exceptional? What do they tell us about other forests, or about the notion of "forest" more generally?

The roadmap similarly marks interconnected roads and railways, air hubs, towns and seas. It is your research design. Once you set out on your journey, though, you may find that the lake that looked so attractive on the map is now a swamp, that the river that looked easy to cross is actually quite swift and rocky, or that in fact to get to the town the first road left, not the second, is more scenic.

The image of a skein of wool that a cat played with captures the idea of interconnecting and intersecting processes relevant to your research project. Each research project, question and piece of data consists of several processes or elements, each of which you can investigate. What you need to do is to choose one or perhaps two threads in that skein that you then follow more closely (ethnographically). You see where they lead you, and what other threads they connect to. You discover the nexus where the most threads are tangled up, or where the knots are tightest. Those knots then may lead you to a different-coloured thread, which appears more closely linked to your research question. Throughout the book we argue that the interdependencies of language, power and identity require such a networked way of thinking.

0.5 The Authors as Your Guides and Conversational Partners

This book is written by researchers who carry the conventional label of "sociolinguists," which sometimes can include or be included in related labels like "discourse analysts" or "linguistic anthropologists." Language is therefore our privileged object of scrutiny and we study people's language practices through qualitative methods, primarily ethnography but also through discourse analysis. We are interested in the ways in which human communication structures social life in a wide sense, and vice versa, how social life structures the ways we can use language. Hence we see our research agenda as standing at a crossroad between the language sciences and the social and human sciences.

In our stories we lay out how we came to ask the questions we asked, the way we did, at the particular historical juncture we found ourselves in. Our stories are largely about ethnonational, ethnolinguistic categories as they intersect with gender, race and class, at particular moments in struggles between nation-states and the minorities and peripheries they create, at particular moments in the development of capitalism. Your stories will be about other things, but we are likely to share the concern for issues of social organization, social difference and social inequality, the conditions that make contesting or reproducing them possible, and the role of language in those processes.

0.6 Summary

Here is what this introduction has covered:

- This book is addressed to novice researchers in sociolinguistics and in other disciplines in which language issues are important to understand the phenomena they study.
- We identify our approach as centred in critical ethnographic sociolinguistics, with a central concern for how social difference is harnessed to the contesting, making or maintaining of social inequality.

- We identify our position as constructivist, by which we mean that any account of how society works is socially constructed by the researchers.

- We consider that research is a form of social practice that can be described as a conversation within a specific community organized around the production of knowledge.

- We argue that meaning is situated, i.e., that it emerges out of social practice and cannot be abstracted from it.

- We see ethnography as a privileged research practice to address the situationality of social practice and discourse.

- An important aspect of this experience is the awareness that research is intrinsically political and we must critically address its implications and consequences, including the relationship of the researcher with the process and people involved.

- To illustrate the situatedness of research and its character as **lived experience**, we also incorporate plenty of biographical material into our account.

- To illustrate the social and political positionality of research, we argue that our perspective derives from and responds to current sociolinguistic changes brought about by late capitalism.

- We adopt a roughly chronological approach to the research phases: question, design, fieldwork, analysis, writing, dissemination.

- We point out that research is recursive as it routinely forces the research to query its bases.

- We think of the research process as a rhizomatic experience in which complex interconnected elements are in constant movement.

Keywords: critical, ethnography, sociolinguistics, discourse analysis, language, reflexivity, recursivity, rhizome, nexus, research, knowledge production, situatedness, late capitalism.

The Politics of Language in Catalonia

The focus of Joan's research developed out of his experience with the politics of language in Catalonia. During the 1970s and 1980s, the revitalization of the Catalan language evolved from a social movement to official policy, and Joan felt part of this development. This constituted a program for social change, and one that required some kind of sociological or sociolinguistic expertise to formulate the program, to imagine the possibilities, to set up the goals, to carry out the necessary actions and to evaluate the results.

In the late 1970s, Spain reconstituted its political system from that of a military dictatorship to a parliamentary democracy. During the thirty-nine-year-long dictatorship, the Spanish government had consistently banned the use of the Catalan language in all official proceedings, in education and the arts; it had replaced public signage, and kept control of private language use through the administration of censorship. During the 1960s, it had gradually allowed the publication of books and newspapers in Catalan, as well as some radio and television broadcasts, as long as their circulation was limited. In this context, the Catalan population continued to speak their language, but mainly just orally, as the new generations were unable to learn the written language at school. Catalans interiorized a sense of when and where it was appropriate or risky to speak the language.

The Catalan language politics of the time must be understood against the backdrop of social and political transformations in Europe and North America. The booming sixties had brought about rapid industrial growth and millions of migrant workers from other areas of Spain. In this context, Catalan activism found the support of an emerging middle class that had experienced remarkable success in their entrepreneurial projects, even as the industrial workforce that fed the ranks of opposition trade unions became largely Spanish-speaking.

The politics of language in the Catalonia of the 1980s were the product of the meeting of these two different strands that coalesced in the political movements for democracy, workers' and civil rights, and national autonomy. In this context, organizing underground trade unions and attending clandestine Catalan language classes were seen as closely connected activities. As a Catalan government was re-established in the 1980s, the revitalization of Catalan was hailed as one of the unanimously supported national agendas, Spanish speakers included. Not only was the 1983 law of "linguistic normalization" approved unanimously in parliament, but the first education provisions met with the disagreement of the main left-wing parties because the initial idea was to create different language streams for speakers of each language. At this point, Spanish-speaking left-wing activists refused to have the children separated and demanded that their children attend Catalan schools too. This was how the widely known Catalan immersion programs started.

In 1980s Catalonia (and even later), this was an issue that made up what could be presented as a big conversation or as a set of closely related conversations. In other words, it had a large and complex constituency: people wrote about it in the press or debated about it on TV and radio, municipal and national authorities made decisions and launched campaigns, and the general population responded in multiple ways to the call to redress the historic aggression and offence to the language and the community.

Joan's research trajectory was initially inscribed in this project to turn Catalan into a fully functional language for government, business, entertainment and public life in general, at a very specific historical juncture. His first study after graduating was a survey about the use of Catalan and Spanish amongst the businesses of his hometown. For his postgraduate studies he turned his attention to questions about how young people used the two languages, as the new generations were seen as anticipating what patterns of language use and linguistic allegiances were going to rule the future. Most of his examples come from an ethnographic study amongst two friendship groups of youth in the city of Barcelona. Later on, after Catalonia received a new wave of migration, mainly from Africa and Latin America (in the period 1998–2008), he also studied how Catalan and Spanish figure in immigration-related debates about identity and social integration.

Discourse, Identity and Power in the Finnish Arctic

My research trajectory can be traced through a rhizome of discourse, identity and power. It is the intertwined relationship of these three concepts that I have tried to figure out when navigating my studies on social policy, communication, journalism, critical discourse studies, sociolinguistics, linguistic anthropology and applied linguistics. It has been a central focus in my research on media discourse and ethnicity, multilingualism in minority and indigenous language contexts, and on language, economy and identity in expanding Arctic economies.

One of the threads that mark my research is the ways in which different kinds of boundaries and categories around people and languages are discursively constituted and contested. This interest has led to different kinds of research projects, including studying the discursive construction of ethnic difference in newspaper texts (my Ph.D. dissertation); the empowering potential of minority language media (my postdoctoral research); discourses, practices and experiences around multilingualism in indigenous Sámi contexts (a project on northern multilingualism); contestation and creativity of language and identity boundaries in minority and indigenous language contexts (a project on peripheral multilingualism) and dynamics of language and identity in expanding Arctic economic hotspots (my most recent project, called "Cold Rush"). All these various projects, many carried out as teamwork with a group of researchers (including Monica and Joan), share a critical perspective on studying language issues that matter: how language figures in social, political and economic processes, especially in terms of inequalities, access and participation. Much of this work is framed by an overarching interest in exploring identity and language boundaries and categories that are discursively constructed and situationally taken up, defended, managed and contested.

Much of my work explores the geographical area of the Arctic North, especially the region that is known as Lapland, Sámiland, North Calotte, Northern periphery and Ultima Thule. Already this variety of names indicates that this area has been—and continues to be—a space of multiple, interconnected and overlapping discursive struggles over meaning and definition. And with each label comes a particular proposition of what is at stake. For example, use of the term Sámiland emphasizes indigenous Sámi issues, foregrounding the idea that it is the land of the Sámi people, where particular indigenous rights apply. In contrast, the Northern periphery label emphasizes the view from the Southern centre, for which the North represents a marginal, repository wasteland. The area is a multilingual and multicultural contact zone of boundaries and categories related to language, ethnicity, citizenship, region, and history. Moreover, the boundaries around people and languages are under construction, more or less visibly, according to the historical changes of nation state borders, political and economic shifts and people's mobility. All this means that this area is a rich point for examining conditions and consequences of boundary-work.

How I came to study this particular area is a result of several things, including research interest and coincidences. Until I met my husband, a Finn from Lapland (from the multilingual region of Torneodal), I had the same contact with Lapland as many other Finns: I went there once for a skiing holiday. However, over the last two decades, I have been travelling and stayed longer periods of time in villages across the Arctic North. From my very first visits, I was intrigued by the complexity and multi-layeredness of this region, not only in terms of multilingualism, but also with its different, still relevant stories and accounts of past and present boundaries.

For example, I was told how one particular village had belonged to the Swedish Crown, to the Russian Empire and to the republic of Finland. In each period, the ways in which people have been categorized has varied based on their livelihoods, or (one of) the language(s) they spoke, or the name of their houses, or other criteria that made sense to the rulers, though not to the locals. These historical categories still matter under current changing conditions, in which the category of indigeneity is under continuing legal and political debate. I was also struck by the intense and rapid dynamics of boom and bust cycles of various kinds of business ventures, linked to wider economic shifts as well as to the restructuring of services and resources provided by the welfare state of Finland. So for example, I saw a small village school closed down and left abandoned for years, until it was reinvented as a major fishing resort. Or a village motel losing clients after a mine nearby was closed down at the same time that tourist consumption practices changed towards more high-end or more autonomous experience-based tourism. After years of decline, a short-term boom came through, turning the hotel into a refugee centre with new conditions and consequences for economic profit and local legitimacy. All these transformations impacted the ways in which categories of belonging, access and legitimacy are tied into rhizomatic processes of discourse, identity and power.

Language and Nation in Francophone Canada

Monica entered the field through processes similar to those of Joan, though her position has been different. Her work has centred on the politics of language, nation and State in Canada, and in particular in struggles around French and French-English bilingualism. She was drawn into it simply by virtue of growing up in Montréal in the 1960s, a time when francophones, historically economically and politically marginalized, collectively mobilized to better their life conditions and life chances. As in Catalonia, speaking the minority language (French in this case) was understood to be linked to this effort.

In the 19th century, francophone North America had been constructed as an organic nation, with ties to the soil. Its goal was "*la survivance*" (survival) as a Catholic francophone nation. In the 1960s, the strategy changed to accomplish social and economic mobility through modernization, including the adoption of secular state-territorial nationalism focused on Quebec. The rest of francophone Canada had no choice but to respond with their own similar movements, though out of necessity through seeking autonomy over institutions (notably schools) rather than politically-bounded territories. More recently, the conditions of late capitalism have destabilized the dominance of nationalist discourses, introducing the idea of French and of bilingualism as added value (rather than a set of rights), and of mobility as the rule, not the exception.

Though Monica does not provide a separate thread at the end of each chapter (there are only so many stories about minority language movements it makes sense to tell), her work provides a number of examples in the body of the text. They are largely drawn from work done in the 1970s, '80s and '90s. One set comes from her first ethnography, conducted in 1978 and 1979 in an industrial brewery in the city of Montreal. This project set out to examine a key element of Québec nationalism, which was the effort to facilitate francophone access to the anglophone-controlled private sector through legislation requiring businesses to make French the language of the workplace. The centrepiece was a law passed in 1977. Monica chose a site typical of the kinds of businesses the law aimed at, and set out to find out what was going on. Another set comes from a series of school ethnographies conducted between 1983 and 1996 in French-language minority schools in the province of Ontario, where Monica has lived and worked since 1982. These schools are the canonical form of institutional nationalism referred to above, that is, spaces meant to operate only in French, in order to facilitate francophone educational success. They are, of course, much more complicated than that; as sites both of social selection and linguistic and cultural reproduction, they show what kinds of ideologies and values of language (kinds of French, kinds of multilingualism) are connected to the making and contesting of "francophone" at the intersection of class, race, gender and religion. Other projects have examined the life experiences and mobilities of people on the linguistic boundary, and the effects of neoliberalism and globalization on francophone nationalism; you'll get an example or two along the way from these other data sets.

1 First Key Moment
Formulating Your Research Question

1.1 Research Questions as (Hi)Stories and Conversations

The entire enterprise of putting together a research project hinges on the question you are asking. Everything else flows from there: what kinds of evidence will count as relevant to answering your question, how you will put it together, how you will make sense of it; all these subsequent steps flow from what you are asking and why you are asking it. Research questions are not always given the attention that they deserve. They take very little space in research reports and are often obscured by or combined with other notions such as "objectives," "hypotheses" or "justifications." However, they are the bedrock of your project, and both require more work and take more time than we generally expect. For these reasons, we are taking the time to fully examine what it means to ask a research question here.

Research questions have their own stories. They take different shapes, and we get to them in different ways. Then we try to answer them, and the process of answering brings up new questions. In this chapter, we reflect on how we choose and formulate our research questions. We emphasize four points:

(1) Research questions are part of complex and ongoing conversations with different stakeholders.

(2) Critical research questions leave room for the investigation of not just what, who, when, how (description) and why (explanation), but also for discovering their consequences, that is, what difference things make and for whom.

(3) Research questions are pivotal for your choice of methods, theory and site.

(4) The formulation of research questions typically evolves throughout the research project.

Points (1) and (2) involve ethical and political considerations that we will address in detail in Section 1.3 from page 30. However, research questions do not take shape in a vacuum.

They derive first from our own inner conversations with ourselves about the world around us. You are therefore bound to have some kind of emotional investment, more or less marked, in these questions. More importantly, they take place in the conversations we have with other people who are part of that world too. Some of those people will share your interests and your questions, and some will not; some will share your perspectives, and others will disagree. No matter what, though, your conversations with them help you frame and sharpen your questions. (They will also help frame and sharpen your analyses and your discussions of research results; we will take those issues up when we discuss Moments 4 and 5, analysis and writing.) One way or another, our research questions emerge out of the stories of our lives and of the lives of the people whose paths we cross.

In the academic world, research questions may originate from very diverse circumstances. In some parts of the world, in some disciplines or fields, your research question may be decided by senior professors, or determined by the logic of the field. For example, if you wish to participate in the conversation about language revitalization, you will need to address at least one of the strands existing at time of writing (say, education, standardization, language ideologies, values) or else explain why you are asking a different question. In other fields, you may have more room for choice, at least within the academic conversation. However, you still need to be aware that research questions always have a complex (hi)story behind them which includes a broader range of participants in the conversation beyond academia. Your questions will connect with the interests of a variety of social or political groups, and with past and ongoing debates. This is always the case, but particularly so for critical research, which formulates questions around things that make a difference to people, that have value for them, that affect them emotionally and materially, and that they may struggle over.

These conversations may be explicit and evident, or implicit and hard to identify. They may be concentrated in specific areas, or they may be diffuse and distributed across a range of discursive spaces. Whatever the situation, you enter into ongoing conversations that were there before you arrived (and that you join as a special kind of participant as it continues to unfold). You need to map out its contours, and identify its participants. Here we provide some examples of how our own research has been shaped by political developments around us:

Monica arrived at her questions about language choice in Montréal by virtue of living there at a time when people were arguing about what language, English or French, to use in public. Clearly, this mattered a lot to people; they argued about it in the street, over dinner, in the media. What was this conflict about? What was at stake?

Joan was drawn into his research question in much the same way. However, when he met Monica he was intrigued by the differences between the Québec context, where the tensions were constructed largely in economic terms, and Catalonia, where the use of languages in public space and public institutions was explicitly linked to alignment with Fascism or democracy.

As a Finn, Sari could not help but be aware of the tension around the marginalized position of indigenous Sámi and the struggle for their rights that emerged at the same historical moment as the one that saw movements for minority language rights around the world. As elsewhere, many of these struggles focused on gaining autonomous control of what had been dominant language-using state institutions: schools, the media, health care, the law, government. As someone interested in media, she could see that the Sámi-language institutional world was distinguishing itself from the Finnish-language one, and this became something to explore.

In conclusion, we need to be aware of what research questions mean in the context of our own lives, and in the context of how we have learned to understand the world around us, whether from our own experience or from previous research, or both. Research questions have a history, both for us and for others. Our ways into our research questions cannot be separated from the ways in which the issues we address matter in our lives and in those of others. It might be less direct for you than it was for us. It almost certainly involves issues other than the minority language movements that emerged so strongly in the 1960s to 1980s. But we will assume that you are attending to a topic for some reason connected to how it matters to you, and it matters to you because it matters in the world around you. Let's examine different ways into formulating research questions about it.

1.2 Different Ways to Get to Your Research Questions

No matter what the history is of the issue you pursue, or the types of people who feel that they can voice a view about it, if you address it as a researcher you are entering into a field where your statements and your procedures will have to follow specific rules and criteria. This is what sets apart research from arguments derived and knowledge produced from other areas of life. In other words, you are entering into a specific kind of conversation, one in which you have to make **explicit** your assumptions, expectations, commitments, argumentation procedures and all your other ways of working.

In this section we focus on the process of formulating the research question in critical language research projects. For convenience, we assume that research projects derive from a single question (although they may have more than one), though to be answerable in practical terms, the overall research question gets commonly broken down into smaller, more specific, questions.

1.2.1 The Forest and the Trees

Let us then assume that you are entering into a field because of your own biographical trajectory, and that you are entering a conversation that has already started, although that conversation can take a number of different shapes in different contexts inside and outside academia. Your experience and that conversation may have given you some initial ideas about what is going on, how and why. We will loosely call these *hypotheses*, that is, candidate accounts of things we see and experience, which are always called into question (supported, contradicted, modified) by new observations and by new experiences. In everyday life, these frames are usually implicit, or do not require much investigation or empirical confirmation. For example, people tend to believe things like "multilingualism is confusing and bad for your children," or "multilingualism is enriching and improves your cognitive abilities." We do not tend to bother to look closely at whether these hold up all the time, and we take them as true.

In research, you have to take the position that your formulation of the question is open, although it is based on a set of hypotheses drawn from your own experience, from the research literature and from your conversations with other stakeholders. That is, you are asking a real question, one that requires careful formulation, systematic and explicit investigation and analytical procedures, as well as explicit negotiations of position with other stakeholders. You do not yet have the answer to your question—otherwise, doing the research would be a waste of time. However, at the end of your research project, the results of your research lead, in turn, to new hypotheses and generate new research questions, as we describe below.

Put differently, **your topic is not the same thing as your research question**. Rather, your research question captures one aspect of your research topic—the one to which you are interested in finding an answer. In this sense, you ask a research question of your topic. Every research question has to have resonance beyond the particular setting or group of people it involves. It needs to set the scene about some particular way in which language matters, and then explain why a focus on some place, some period of time, some people, some activity, will shed light on that bigger question. It needs to translate, or transpose, the larger question onto **things that are actually observable**, generating questions specifically about those things. One way to test this is the "so what" question: think about the potential impact of your research. Does the question you are thinking of put a new spin on an old issue, or does it try to solve a new problem? What happens and to whom if you are able to find answers to your questions? Who will also care deeply about what you have to say? Will you be able to use it to decide for yourself how you feel about something, and what, if anything, you want to do about it?

There are many different ways of arriving at your question. (Practical tip: keep notes as you go along; they will help you develop the explicit formulations and procedures that you will eventually need.) One major aspect of these paths has to do with the continuing relationship between *the forest and the trees*. Any research project must have both. You might start with the forest (or even a set of forests): some big questions that have theoretical, methodological, social, political or economic importance. You might, for example, want to know about the making of social difference and social inequality—the big question that motivates much of our own research. You might want to know how and why language changes, or how racism and racial discrimination works or what categories of gender and sexuality are important to people today and why. Put in those terms, however, it is practically impossible to construct a research project that would answer those questions. They are so large as to constitute a long-term research agenda for many people. At the same time, they are good questions; starting from any one of them, your job then becomes looking for a way to render addressing that question feasible. You need to identify the trees, and pick the ones worth looking at, that is, the ones that help you see racism at work, or processes of construction of categories of gender and sexuality, or struggles over language that connect to access to education or employment.

However, because the biographies of researchers can be very diverse, it may also happen that their starting point is a set of trees. If that is the case with you, then your job is to find the broad question that makes some of the smaller ones meaningful and helps to see the connections between the small dots and the bigger pictures. The goal in the end is to explain the trees as a function of the forest, and to illuminate the forest through what you can discover about the trees.

1.2.2 The What, the Who, the When, the Where, the How and the Why

There are several different ways of encountering trees, or coming up with smaller questions, and using them to map out the forest, or to build out to a broader question. You may have to start with a "what" question, that is, to figure out what the thing is, how it works and who is involved before you can ask why. Linking what, how, and why can then lead you to discovering what this tree has to do with the forest.

One way to encounter a tree is to identify a **gap** in the research in your field. Here are some examples of the gaps we saw when we were starting out. When Québec passed a law in 1977 that said French must be the language of work, most research on language policy focused on investigating the policy documents, or used survey data, but no one looked at what actually was happening in the process of implementation: did people actually speak French and only French in the workplace? How did language choice actually happen? Similarly in Catalonia, during the 1980s, people investigated language proficiency using large-scale self-report data, but did not look at what people actually did. Sari saw that much attention had been paid to legal and political definitions and debates about Sámi indigenous rights, but not so much to how they affected people's lives or how people made sense of these debates. Such gaps are not only interesting just because we can fill them. It is also productive to ask oneself why there is a gap at all: what were the interests of those who set up the previous research agenda? Are some issues taboo for some stakeholders? Are some issues methodologically easier to address? These questions may well help you significantly in establishing your position and justifying it.

A second way to find trees is to notice a **puzzle**: something regularly happening around you that seems odd, mysterious or different, and that you want to describe and explain. For description, the question is "what?" One good example from our own experience is when, later in our careers, minority communities started getting involved in heritage tourism. Monica sees an ad for French-language summer theatre in an area that has never had tourism or any kind of cultural industry: what is the theatre, what is the play? Joan notices an old house in a small town has been turned into a museum honouring a 19th century Catalan literary figure: what kind of a museum is it? Sari notices a new crafts store has opened up in the Sámi village she has been working in: what kind of store exactly is it? From there you can get to the "why" questions. For all three cases, such a question could be formulated like this: Why would a linguistic minority region, defined as such in political terms, and long devoted centrally to fighting for political rights, shift its attention away from politics and towards economic development—and in particular, of all the economic activities one could potentially imagine, why would they invest in heritage tourism?

However, on its own, a question like why a linguistic minority region is investing in tourism is not terribly important or interesting. Nor is why some schoolchildren speak French or English in some playground in Canada, or why some people answer in Spanish when spoken to in Catalan, or why Sámi journalists carefully think about how to deal with Finnish-speaking interviewees in a radio program. The "why" question in itself can be very abstract or vague if we do not deploy it through the details of who, where, when and how. Put differently, to figure out what forest these trees are part of, you need to ask questions which lead out to the trajectories of the people, the place and the resources involved. The goal is to describe what the phenomenon is, who participates, how things work, and why all this is happening. What kind of tourism are we talking about? When and how did this particular minority region invest in tourism? How did it get started? What are the tensions and strategies around this development? Are there people who always speak Spanish no matter what, or does everyone use Catalan sometimes? Who does what? What happens when they do? Is Joan the only person who cares about this or is there a broader debate involving lots of different kinds of people with different opinions? When did Sámi media get started? What are its goals? Who wants to work in that field? Who funds it? What audience does it reach? What do they think of it?

Finally, no matter what your way into the topic is, one of the challenges in formulating research questions is figuring out what the right level and scope are. What questions are too narrow to yield any interesting insight on anything that matters; what questions are so broad that no human being, nor even a team of human beings, could ever hope to answer them? Here we would like to suggest that the goal is to figure out the linkages between the narrow and the broad, and to construct your actual research project around the feasible.

In this context, feasible means that your research is manageable and "do-able" within the normal constraints that you will experience, such as access to the data, time constraints, skills you may need or any ethical or safety considerations. It is also connected to your own position: how people read you, where they think you belong, what your networks are, and what resources you can muster. Thus one important task for you at this point in the research project is to make the choices necessary to achieving what can reasonably be done within the time, expertise and resource constraints under which you are working. The making of a good research question means making lots of (often difficult) choices.

Still, in every case, you need to be able to say what broader questions the specific ones relate to, and conversely, how you might transpose the big questions onto sites and phenomena that can illuminate them. You can ask the big questions about language, difference and inequality by looking at the social activities where difference and inequality are created or resisted. French-language schools and Sámi media are sites where speakers of minority languages try to gain some measure of power. Language choice in public is a struggle over ownership of public space. You can get to the big questions by identifying what is at stake when people argue about what language to speak, or how to speak a language: what are they really struggling over?

1.2.3 The Research Question, That Moving Target

It is necessary to be aware that the process of exploration and investigation might cause your question to shift substantially, and more than once. This is actually a good sign, because it means that you are discovering things that you (and your readers) did not know before. Of course, you always have to start somewhere, whether for a thesis proposal, a research grant proposal, or a job interview. This is not making do with imperfection: it is a necessary and normal part of every research project.

However straightforward the process of formulating a research question might be at one point, then, it always involves some messiness, and indeed may do so from the beginning—more like following the yellow thread in the skein of multi-coloured wool your cat has messed with, and discovering that actually the purple thread it is knotted up with is much more interesting. Or to use one of our other metaphors, it is like following one branch of a rhizome, only to find that it is a dead end, and the things you are interested in are in another branch. So let's say Sari was first interested in whether Sámi journalists worked the same way as big-city Finnish ones in producing news (the yellow thread). Once she got to see them in action, though, she discovered that there was a difference in the way language mattered, and actually working in Sámi languages structured their work and relationships in many ways (the purple thread). As you can see in the account of Sari's research in the blue section at the end of the chapter, she realized that the question of what it means to speak/write Sámi at all, anywhere, was a more consequential question to ask, and that was the thread she then chose to follow. Joan discovered that the young men and women he was working with on language choice in Barcelona acted not only differently from each other, but also differently depending on their gender orientation. At first, he had thought of gender as a peripheral issue of his analysis; but it became a central one as he asked what (class-located) masculinities and femininities might have to do with ideologies of language and identity. Monica was told that "all the students in French-language minority schools spoke English outside the classroom." Her question was why, but first she needed to establish whether or not that was actually true. It turned out that some did, and some did not. Now she had a new research question: who does, who does not and why?

In sum, research questions are actually not closed and specific things. They come out of a history of thought and experience, and they take the form of a set of hypotheses that are interlinked. That process itself is not simply linear; one thing doesn't lead to another and then to the obvious next research question to pose. Questions too are embedded in rhizomatic processes and entangled in complex relations.

Broad social, political and theoretical questions must be addressed through more specific questions focused on observable phenomena that can shed light on the bigger picture. But all those questions need to be checked against what we see and experience; it is always possible that our initial formulations were based on assumptions that turn out to be wrong, or in any case overly simple. Then we revise, and check again. The more we discover, the more we find out what we do not know, requiring us to make decisions about whether to keep following the yellow thread, or switch over to the purple one. Research questions need to be shaped and crafted throughout the whole research process. This is what the concept of *recursivity* presented in the Introduction was meant to express. We will take up the question of how to design a research project, that is, how to get started on making something feasible that nonetheless speaks to broad concerns, in the next chapter (Moment 2).

1.3 Reflexivity, Ethics and Research Questions

As we discussed in the Introduction, reflexivity and ethics are part of the entire research process. Since your research questions derive from your own experience and of those around you, you need to be aware of how who you are and the conditions under which you live lead you more easily to some questions than to others, and what the implications of that are for the kinds of relationships you can build with participants, and what you can explore with them, or for the kinds of materials that are more or less likely to cross your path.

First, it is important to think about the potential impact on other people of even asking your question, since you are in a field where language issues matter to many people. Your questions might be sensitive; people might worry about what you think the "right" answer is. Minimally, anyone affiliated with a university is likely to be associated with institutional pressures to "speak properly." In areas where certain languages are repressed in an effort to discipline populations, it may be dangerous to admit you know anything about those targeted languages, or to betray that knowledge in how you speak. You need to link the ways in which the language issue you are focusing on matters to what it means for you to ask questions about it (and how), and to build research relationships around it.

Second, your own position, your own stance, generate particular affordances and blind spots. It can be easier to ask questions about languages and borders say, in the Banat, where the borders of Romania, Hungary and Serbia meet, if you speak the relevant languages and perhaps have some familial or professional ties there. At the same time, if you have that kind of knowledge, you might not notice things because you take them for granted. You might not see, for example, how important sports are, because everyone has always engaged in them (or not) without much discussion, and they are not usually related to the question of borders in the taken-for-granted ways of thinking about social difference and territory that operate in the region. You might be used to a particular political stance in this complex corner of the world, where imperialism, socialism, fascism and capitalism have all met. Conversely, if you are an outsider, it is easier to attend to everything equally, but you might not have the background knowledge or network ties to be able to see which trees are relevant in this forest, or how they are relevant. This kind of reflexive analysis is worth pursuing in a systematic way, e.g., to document it and discuss it with your peers. It will help you focus on how your own positioning makes some things more accessible and visible than others, and therefore which dimensions of what you are asking you might make more of an effort to pursue, or conversely, abandon.

Further, your position affects the scope of your questions, and therefore eventually of the claims you will be able to make. If, as a man, you are never allowed to speak to women where you are doing fieldwork, then you would be well advised to take into account how gender, and masculinity in particular, might be important. You would also be well advised not to formulate your questions (and, later, your claims) as including "the community" if you only have access to the male half of it. Positions of class and race are also always relevant; they index relations of power, of which knowledge production is one form. This kind of reflexivity also helps you get straight to the relationship between your own voice, the one that in the end will be telling the story and the voices of the people you encounter, work with and do your best to understand.

Of necessity, we are all situated somewhere in the conversation, and therefore in the field of relations of difference and inequality which characterize all discursive spaces. The questions you ask, and the promise they contain of the kind of knowledge you are likely to generate, have their place in that field. You are staking a claim to being a legitimate asker of such questions, and a legitimate producer of answers to them. As a result, you need to be attentive to the potential impact on other people of asking the questions you want to ask, and therefore to what you must, can or will not negotiate with them. You need to understand who has what stakes in the game. Further, even at the stage of formulating a research question, you may well be involved in gathering information involving others, and so you need to be aware that at some level this is already data collection, and as such requires full consideration of its ethical implications.

Depending on your relations to the field and to others, and on the nature of your question, some people may be wary of you, and others perhaps a little too concerned that you remain utterly faithful to their perspective. Some may ignore you, and others may welcome you. One position is not necessarily better than another; we just have to do our best to be aware of how they affect what questions could or should be asked, how, when and of whom.

1.4 Summary

Good research questions save time, and are therefore worth spending time to formulate. There are lots of different research questions that you could ask about your topic; picking one question over others, guided by a mapping of the field and situating yourself within it, helps you focus, and gives you an angle of approach to your topic. This helps you streamline your research and eventually your communication of results; having multiple different-coloured threads going on in your research is confusing for everyone (except maybe the cat). At the same time questions are often a challenge to formulate. Look at them as dimensions of developing and carrying out any qualitative research project, that is, as a process: they keep evolving.

- Situate your research questions in the conversations you have (with supervisors, academics, stakeholders, students, locals, neighbours, strangers . . .).

- Identify why it matters to you and to others.

- Ask questions to which you do not have the answer.

- Document the process of arriving at your research question.

- Link big questions to specific questions, that is, show how the forest is made up of specific trees.

- Treat your questions and hypotheses as formulations that can be revised as you go along.

- Recognize how your position uniquely allows you to carry off a research project, but also how it limits what you can and cannot do.

- Good research questions can be characterized as interesting, relevant, feasible and ethical.

- Bear in mind that in the end, this is your story.

Keywords: research questions, hypotheses, conversations, stakeholders, reflexivity.

The (Hi)stories and the Conversation(s)

As was briefly explained in the Introduction, Joan's research trajectory was initially inscribed in the project to extend the use of Catalan to all activities of government, business, entertainment and public life in general (usually referred to as "normalization") at a very specific historical juncture. In this context where linguistic catalanization was seen as equivalent to political democratization via autonomy, Joan's first research questions were primarily directed to overcoming the obstacles that seemed to arise in the way of making Catalan the main public language. At the time, the main obstacles were: (1) Almost 50% of the population were not of local origin anymore—they understood, but could not speak Catalan; (2) Most Catalan speakers felt unable to read or write in the language, so their literacy practices were in Spanish both at work and in the family; (3) Most mass media were in Spanish. At this time, a good many research projects in the field involved questions of the following kind:

- How (much) is Catalan used in X context?

Still following some of Joan's earlier projects, X could stand for street graffiti, the signage of shops, the invoices of companies, or the blueprints for machines by industrial designers. And these questions could be subdivided in this way: (1) How many instances of each language do we find? (2) What types of items do we find in each language (which topics, in which shapes, in which locations)? (3) Which reasons or motivations do people bring up to explain their language choices (such as aesthetic preferences, political commitments, emotional attachments, abilities or resources available)?

By sampling graffiti written on the streets of Barcelona, Joan found that most were in Spanish, and that languages were roughly distributed according to content. Spanish was the language of mural expression of workers' strikes and trade union issues, as well as statements connected with youth movements or dirty jokes. Catalan appeared in nationalist graffiti and also in connection with local or neighbourhood political conflicts. In his second study on the use of Catalan by private businesses, he found that the main obstacle to using Catalan was the fact that most people could not write in Catalan, and also that businesses whose clients were elsewhere in Spain and abroad preferred to use Spanish as a language of wider communication.

When he started his postgraduate studies, Joan then turned his attention to spoken language. The reason for this was that Catalan nationalists were concerned that Catalan was becoming less and less present in spoken interaction in everyday life, particularly in large cities. When speakers of either language were in contact with each other, they often settled for speaking Spanish. During the 1980s language planners concentrated their efforts to convince Catalan speakers not to switch to Spanish and conduct bilingual conversations with Spanish speakers (this was possible in theory, because Spanish speakers understood Catalan well). But this was not very successful. Their main hope was that the new generations would adopt other patterns of language choice. At school, everyone was learning the two languages reasonably well and Spanish speakers did not have any obstacle to speaking Catalan. However, by the early 1990s, no significant change was detected and it appeared as if the young generations were doing the same as the old ones.

It is worth highlighting here that the "problem," as it was then framed, was not formulated on the basis of hard evidence. Most sociolinguists and politicians judged what was happening out of their own everyday experience (with linguistic debates, this happens a lot). Most of the sociolinguistic data available at the time came from the national census, in which people were asked what languages they could understand, speak or write. They were not asked how they used the languages, so nobody knew exactly how much more or less Catalan was being used. Sociolinguists called on the authorities for many years to fund complementary research on language use. In the meantime, entrepreneurial individuals were making do with small-scale surveys and studies, and this was very much the frame in which Joan was operating when he moved to England to conduct his postgraduate studies.

So this was a very large and entangled and unexplored section of the forest of Catalan normalization. Spoken interaction takes place everywhere, in very different types of situations and amongst very different types of people. In his M.A. thesis, Joan decided to interview a small group of university undergraduates to learn about their practices of language choice in everyday life and the ways they rationalized them. This is how he phrased his questions:

- Do we find that people adopt different norms of language choice in similar situations?
- How do people evaluate their own language choices and those of others?
- Does the heterogeneity of language choices point to changes in social relations?

Joan would certainly not phrase the questions in this very basic way now, because nowadays much more is known about people's language practices. Moreover, the phrasing was very broad unless one interpreted that it applied to the rather localized context that he was researching (the "trees," i.e., that group of students). Finally, the third question was of particular interest because it betrayed his recent contact with Sociolinguistics and Critical Discourse Analysis outside the Catalan context. Joan was now participating in more conversations than earlier.

The results of this study were very illuminating for Joan, basically because he realized that people of different profiles were managing their bilingual repertoire in noticeably different ways, and were presenting very different reasons to justify it. He was primarily struck by Spanish speakers. The Catalan sociolinguistic tradition had traditionally interpreted their position within the frame of immigration and integration, not social class. So they assumed that Spanish speakers were simply on their way to adopting the local language, but Joan's evidence did not corroborate this.

After this, Joan had to decide on his thesis project and he was facing additional questions. The forest was not exactly working in the way he had thought, and now his question had to do with how Catalan identity connected with social class. To address this question, he needed to explore different trees in a different environment, which led him to focus primarily on young speakers of Spanish of working-class origin and to avoid institutional contexts. This is why his new "trees" would be young people "growing" in what he considered were their "natural" habitat: the leisure activities commonly associated with youth culture (this was, by the way, a debatable choice too).

What is interesting about the thesis questions is that Joan can recover the formulations of his questions at the beginning and at the end of the project. The initial questions were largely the same as those of the former study, though applied in a different context in which participant observation would have more weight. But (attention!), in the final version of the thesis, we read the following questions:

- What are the worlds and the truths of the people I studied?
- What is the position of the Catalan language and culture within them?

Along the way, Joan had decided that he had to operate differently: first to identify what principles and values seemed important for the groups studied, and then to work out how Catalan fitted within them. This was the result of his willingness to do a bottom-up approach, to let the data speak, as it were (again, a debatable concept). In any case, the two main questions were projected onto seven, more concrete, additional ones:

- What forms of gender display were manifested in the groups?
- How did gender identities contribute to the constitution of the cultural forms (i.e., the activities, values and ideologies) obtaining in that particular social space?
- What views of the world were conveyed through the speech styles (accents, slang, argot) that members of the groups used?
- What views and ideas were Catalan and Spanish used to convey?
- What patterns of language choice existed within the groups?
- What connections can be established between the patterns of language choice and the identities and practices described in previous chapters?
- What can we do about it?

Now what these questions tell us is basically that Joan fully reconstructed the story of his research when he wrote his thesis. During the process, issues of gender emerged as important, youth slang became relevant. The traces of his initial questions can be found in the last three, which in a way indicates that they continued to lead his agenda. This is one example of how research questions evolve and get refined and renegotiated during the research process. It is also arguable now that the initial questions were excessively broad. There are lessons to learn here about how a research process evolves; but mainly that it is fraught with debatable choices and decisions.

How I Started to Study Journalism but Ended Up Examining Tourism

The way I got to my research questions about indigenous tourism is an example of how developing your questions is a process which involves many steps, navigation and detours. It can be messy, a bit nerve-racking and yet intensely stimulating. I came to study tourism by following one thread (journalism), which then turned out to be tangled up with two other threads (identity and economics), getting me to wonder what was going on, and forcing me to ask new questions. So my (hi)story of developing these research questions is an account about what happens when you move from one research project to another (from the Ph.D. dissertation to a postdoctoral research project, and then further to a research project); from a research topic to another (from ethnic representations in news discourse to language and identity in economic development); and how these changes also bring about a change in your theoretical framing, in your ways of working and in your own position as a researcher.

As is so often the case in the research process, it is easier with hindsight to notice—or reconstruct—how and when these shifts happened, but the experience always feels much messier at the time. It entails encountering something new; in order to answer the "what is this?" question, it became necessary for me to trace a few leads and navigate unknown forests on the basis of a hunch, often feeling silly and out of place, yet intrigued and forced to come back. So from the point where I am writing this piece of text now, and looking back at two decades of work in the Arctic Finland, and especially in the Sámiland area, it is relatively easy to say now that I was witnessing a shift in discourse from indigenous rights and identity politics to economic development based on these same resources, and that my various research projects on these topics can be located at various points of this ongoing change. However, when I started to work on these issues in the late 1990s in the Sámiland, this change was not altogether clear to me, and I certainly did not start with the questions I have now. This is where I ended up, rather than where I started. To tell you this story of how I got to my research questions on Sámi tourism and authenticity, I will have to trace back to my own trajectory as a Ph.D. student interested in the critical discourse analysis of power, news media and discourses of differentiation.

I first came to Sámiland for research purposes in the late 1990s as a Ph.D. student finishing her dissertation on discourses of ethnic differentiation in the news. At the time, I was working with a critical discourse analysis frame, exploring ethnic representations in newspaper texts, combined with journalism studies (and its focus on the news ideals of equal access, balanced representations and fair reporting). With this project, the overall research question was: "How is the difference between ethnic minorities and mainstream Finns discursively constructed in news texts about ethnic and immigration issues in the Finnish national daily Helsingin Sanomat during the period of 1985–1993." One of my findings was that Sámi, a legally recognized indigenous group in Finland with their own cultural autonomy and representative institutions, received very little attention in the mainstream media, and that attention was typically limited to small number of topics (Pietikäinen, 2000). I therefore sought out a conversation with Sámi journalists to hear their views about (the lack of) coverage of Sámi issues in the mainstream press and to reflect on the conditions for news production that brought about these imbalances.

These conversations led me to develop my research interest in power, discourse, and media as a postdoctoral research project. I chose to focus on the empowering potential of minority language media (Sámi and Russian media in Finland). This project asked to what extent media could function as a resource for their communities: to facilitate civic participation, community engagement and cultural revitalization. I also drew on language revitalization studies from the field of minority and indigenous language research. And I used critical discourse analysis to account for what people did and said about what they were doing and how these accounts were embedded in the discourses in circulation.

So journalism was the door through which I entered Sámiland and Sámi media space as a Finnish-speaking outsider from the south. Once there, I sought to talk with anybody interested in a discussion with me, interviewed volunteer journalists and followed their work in newsrooms, editing rooms, meetings and in the community. It soon became apparent to me that the space was multilingual: people used the three Sámi languages spoken in Finland, both official languages of Finland (Finnish and Swedish) and also Norwegian and English. This entailed a lot of language work, not only in the balancing of community and professional life, but in the exercise of the profession itself; this work was also politically and emotionally charged. In comparison to the majority media spaces that I had worked in before, language choices really mattered here. They impinged a lot on the organization of journalistic work as well as on networks between people; language attracted people's attention and triggered a lot of discussion.

Once I noticed this urgency around the Sámi language (a new tree in the journalism forest), my focus also shifted from journalistic practices to language practices, and in particular ideologically invested discourses around their value and importance. I started to ask new questions: Why it was so important to do all the news (Sámi-related or not) in three Sámi languages? To whom was it important? How did they navigate constraints like varying Sámi competences and constant time pressure? Why do language choices take priority over other concerns prominent in journalism, such as saving time and money, being quick, or making news available to the widest possible audience? I was also curious about the apparent consensus on the urgency and importance of language work; did anyone have a different view?

After examining journalistic practices and language ideological discourses in the minority media context, I wanted next to understand this new thread better (the ways in which Sámi languages mattered), and for this, I needed to move into other spaces, that is, from the journalism forest to another forest. This also meant developing a new project, this time a multi-sited, collaborative project focusing on discourse, practices and experiences of multilingualism in indigenous and minority language contexts. This also meant working as part of a research team. In this context, I followed the leads for this new thread: traces of why, how and to whom Sámi language mattered and what kind of relationships the various language resources had in multilingual practices. Some of these traces led me to other Sámi institutions (schools, Sámi parliament, Sámi museums, Sámi associations), even as I followed other traces into various emerging tourism spots: souvenir shops, local hotels, newly opened restaurants or emerging tourism service businesses. The framing of this project drew on critical sociolinguistic ethnography and discourse studies on multilingualism and language categories.

It was at this stage that the growing importance of the tourism sector in the area became visible. Already when working in the Sámi media, it had been impossible not to notice the growing number of tourists travelling with me up to the small villages in Sámiland, rather than just staying in the big tourism resorts near airports; or getting for the first time a "fully-booked" notice from local hotels that used to always have rooms available, or even closed down in the low season; or having suddenly to queue up with tourists to get service at the tourist office. I saw new hotel buildings rising up, and the first pizzeria opened along with new businesses in crafts. I observed the development of local products turned into indexes of Sámi authenticity, displayed with labels carrying narratives of their origins. In the frequent news coverage in the local papers about the need for economic development of this peripheral region, tourism always figured as a major strategy. And obviously, this context was multilingual with its various ways of using Sámi resources.

My first attempts to explore this new forest, tourism, were rather improvised and unfocused. The terrain was too unfamiliar for me to formulate any useful research questions. So just to get a better idea of what this forest was about, I started to hang around the tourists. At this point, however, I often found myself wondering what on earth I was really learning by trailing these groups of tourists. It was especially hard to figure out what I should look at in particular, or better, what I was supposed to see?

To get a better sense of all of this, that is, to be able to formulate my research questions (to find my trees) without losing sight of my thread altogether, I followed multiple, overlapping and recursive paths, gradually forming my research rhizome. First, together with the team members, I mapped the whole range of tourism activities and their connection to Sáminess. Some of the team members were doing similar kinds of mapping in other minority language sites of the project, and we were able to discuss the commonalities and differences in different sites. Then I started to systematically document spaces and activities in greater detail in the Sámi site I was focusing on, asking questions like: who comes here, how many and for how long? Why do they come here, what is available for them once they are here and what do they do once they are here? (As we will see, this led to a variety of data collection strategies in my research design.)

The move from the journalism forest to the tourism forest also required familiarizing myself with the literature on tourism and economic development, although I noted that there was little work on the ways in which language matters in tourism, and equally little on tourism in economic peripheries. This shaped my thinking about the kinds of conversations that could be developed in the intersection among fields, and what kinds of questions thereby arose.

After several rounds of doing this kind of mapping as part of the teamwork, I was able to construct a tourism trail (a patterned map of activities) documenting the typical stops, activities, questions asked, products consumed, time spent and the seasonal variation of the typical tourist profiles. This trail seemed to be organized around two themes: unique Lapland nature and authentic Sámi culture. Let me show you how we got to that conclusion in the team with colleagues.

My second path was to explore the meaning of tourism for the tourists. I first asked if I could interview them or if they would show their photos, but I soon realized that this was not effective: the tourists were polite enough to accommodate me for a short while, but they were not really interested in spending time with a researcher who was asking all kinds of questions. As a result, I got short, predictable, uninformative answers. The researchers of the team working in other minority language sites had similar kinds of experiences. I needed a new strategy.

Thus my third path was to go back to my tourism trail and map out the local tourism providers. This coincided with my growing interest in the changing conditions of peripheries, sparked by the readings that I had done in tourism studies and economic development, as well as by the discursive focus on tourism business development in the area. So I retraced my steps (again), but now with slightly new lenses: I approached, for example, shop keepers, service providers, guides, restaurant workers and hotel receptionists, to ask about the types of tourists they encounter, things the tourists ask and the activities they want to do. I began to hear stories about the conditions of providing these services and products, debates around them and the sometimes surprising developments they led to; for example, tourists asked about huskies they imagined they would see in Sámiland, although these animals are not indigenous to the region. The demand was so high that husky safaris and visits to husky farms are now available throughout the region; many tourists wanted a refined version of "local food" as part of their experience, so restaurants began to develop various versions of the local culinary experience. There was also a constant demand to see "real, authentic Sámi." The response was the development of various types of "Sámi cultural programs and performances," including traditional Northern Sámi singing (joiking) while wearing traditional Sámi dresses, reindeer lassoing and reindeer herding. Finally, a nexus in the rhizome that I had been tracing!

The performance and production of Sáminess for tourism consumption—to commodify the resources used so far mainly for identity politics—was a clear connection point to my previous work. Here, as in journalism, the key concerns were the conditions and consequences of using Sámi resources: who are the legitimate producers and performers, what kinds of activities are perceived as legitimate? In short, what is at stake here and for whom? After finding this focus (the tree) among the various tourism threads (the forest) available, it was easier for me to decide what to do next: I decided to focus on production and the performance of "authenticity," whether that authenticity was constructed around Sáminess or something else, e.g., the North, Lapland or nature. So finally, after many attempts, I was able to formulate research questions, at least to momentarily help me to design research projects around Sámi tourism and questions of authenticity in a context of economic and political investments.

2
Second Key Moment
Designing Your Research

2.1 What Is Research Design?

The core of the concept of research design is the idea that once you have a research question (or questions) that serves as a jumping-off point, you have to figure out how you are going to answer that question. In that sense, your question really drives your project. And as a result, there can be no one-size-fits-all model for what a research project should look like. Rather, there are a number of ways in which to define and justify what counts as relevant information (otherwise known as "data"), and a number of ways in which to go about pulling it together so you can make sense out of it. There can also be a number of ways of expressing research design textually, although we will focus here on the most common, conventional forms.

Research design is a concept that can be understood as an imagined projection into the future of your whole research project, that is, a working through in your head (and in writing) of exactly how you will go about answering your questions. As a projection, the research design also needs to be understood as a hypothesis or a blueprint that you will need to test in real life. And because in real life things never work out exactly as planned, in this chapter we will discuss both how to best set up your research plan and also how to confront the unexpected, so you can stick to your agenda (unless the unexpected really makes you change your mind). The key tension here is that encountering unforeseen things and adapting your plans is a necessary element of the knowledge-building endeavour (after all, life, including research on it, is by definition unpredictable), but in order to come to a meaningful conclusion of your project you do need to stick to a plan. Remember this: **research design is an ongoing process**. Exactly how this plays out for your specific project can only be for you to discover. However, here we offer some resources for addressing these tensions.

It is important to be clear about the principles or the criteria that you will use to decide what to do, when and how. If specific plans later do not work out, you will be able to go back to your criteria to work out a Plan B. So the **rationales** for your choices, your **criteria**, are more important than the choices themselves, and they are the elements that must survive the reality check (or become more complex and sophisticated in the process). In addition, these criteria will also allow you and your readers to make the link between your questions and how you want to address them. In many ways, these criteria will contain the seed of the actual theoretical understanding that is supposed to constitute the core of your scientific contribution.

A research plan requires you to be very concrete about what will count as evidence for answering your questions and why, as well as where you will find that evidence, and how you will put it together for the analysis (which we will discuss in Moments 3 and 4). It involves putting together (and writing up) something coherent on the particular project you want to undertake; you need to do this by keeping in mind your readership, which may range from supervisors to possible participants, from conference audiences to the readers of your blog, even to journalists. As a result, it is one of the many steps in positioning yourself, in finding your own voice—and it will not be the last.

At the same time, we are conscious of writing this book at a time of institutional change in the world of research, while neoliberal and private sector agendas create still other sets of expectations or desiderata. **Research design is embedded in specific political and institutional contexts**.

In Canada, the major funding body for social science and humanities research has changed their policy twice during Monica's career. Each time, new policies and new priorities were manifested in changes to the requirements for research proposals. Most recently, application criteria and forms were changed to include (among other things) a separate section on "knowledge mobilization." This concept of course requires interpretation, but on the whole it refers to the ways in which what you learn from your research will be shared not only with traditional academic audiences, but also with other interlocutors, from the state to the private sector, and to civil society. In Finland, the policies and criteria have also been changed several times, most recently related to guidelines regarding open access publication and data management, including requiring a plan on how the data will be made available to other researchers upon project completion. This poses several critical questions for ethnographic work and data, as there is also the need to protect confidentiality and to honour specific agreements with the research participants.

The political, economic and social conditions at play underpinning the very possibilities for doing research will invariably materialize in constraints on the time and resources available, on the issues addressed, the audiences available, and the genre of research proposals. But these constraints have material consequences not only for how you imagine or project into the future. They will actually guide you in the making of multiple decisions, to the point of doing things that you might not have thought about doing initially. So if you have to have a knowledge mobilization plan, you will start to imagine doing, say, workshops with government officials, or interactive websites, or even working in other ways (perhaps more collaboratively than in the traditional lone researcher model). Finally, since you yourself are also an actor and a participant in the social world that you intend to observe and analyze, the ethical and political aspects of the process are also constitutive of it; they also need to be spelled out.

Further, institutional requirements oblige us to fix research design into some kind of a text: a research or a thesis plan. Thus, **research design is also a discursive, usually textual,**

genre. It can pop up as a research proposal for a student project, as a grant application or as a request for approval from an ethics board. It will also emerge in the stories we end up sharing about our research to potential participants, to audiences for our papers, books and presentations, or to the media. The exact form of the genre varies across contexts in multiple ways. How we structure it depends on the audience, but different kinds of readers (your supervisor, reviewers of your grant applications or the readers of your articles, for example) want to know different things. Different intellectual spheres have varying genres.

The main body of this chapter will largely focus on the process of projecting the unfolding of your research project into the future, that is, on fleshing out what you will need to actually do in conducting your project. We focus mainly on the initial steps: figuring out what counts as data, finding it and documenting it. While most proposals need to also contain information on analysis and what is alternatively called "knowledge mobilization," "impact" or "dissemination" (that is, once you have a story, with whom you are planning to share it and how), we leave these aside since they are the subject of more detailed treatment in subsequent chapters (see Moment 4 on claims and Moment 5 on knowledge mobilization). Nonetheless, as we will see in Section 2.4, how you organize your data is a function of the kind of analysis you imagine you will be undertaking and of how you think you will tell the story.

Section 2.5 will deal with the ethical and political aspects of the research process. Section 2.6 will examine some aspects of representing your research design as text. To help illustrate these two facets of research design (projecting how you will actually do the research, and how to communicate that to your readers), the two colour streams will divide here, Sari's taking up the thread of imagining how you will actually do your research, Joan's addressing the process of writing this projection into a text of a proposal or a grant application.

2.2 Research Design as Projected Work Plan

Research design is the moment in which you face the tension between what you would like to do and what you can do. In the previous chapter we pointed out that research questions must be practically researchable, so we shall assume that you already have made an effort to bring your initial interests into a workable focus, and that you have already made some sacrifices by dropping aspects that were making your topic too vague or too broad. But now, as you dig down further into what you actually intend to do, what activities you will engage in, where, when and with whom, and you reckon how much time, or money, or resources, or travel or contacts each will require . . . well, doubts are likely to appear again.

Further, a research plan is not just a list of jobs to do or boxes to tick. It is also supposed to have an argument that ties all the parts together. So writing down a research plan actually contains the first structured formulation of the points you intend to make, that is, the first detailed formulation of **your argument**:

(1) your question and specific hypotheses (in the context of state-of-the art research);
(2) your methods (the sites, people you will interact with and the data to collect or construct);

(3) your anticipated results (and how you imagine that you will get them out of the data);

(4) your schedule, and, often, some ideas on how you will write things up (tell your story).

If you are writing a grant proposal, this is a dissemination plan. Also, grant proposals usually require budgets.

It is by writing down your plans that you will find that both the strengths and the weaknesses of your ideas become clearer. (In Moment 5 we will develop this aspect of the role of writing in the whole process of research.) At this point, though, you may start finding flaws in your research question, and consider tweaking it, or rephrasing it or qualifying it; in a way, this means that you are revisiting stage one again. Indeed, as we anticipated in the Introduction when discussing *recursivity*, it is constitutive of the process of researching in social sciences that all stages affect the others, so that you will feel you are constantly made to reconsider issues you had already dealt with before. However, at this point, the practical and procedural focus is to come up with a plan, and the plan may well help you to clarify, delimit, further narrow your research question and maybe even divide it into different aspects or sub-questions.

However, before we plunge into the materialities of research design, it is important to reflect in some detail on what it is for and how it should be managed. In the previous pages we have repeatedly said that the process of doing research is not linear, but rather that it may require adjustments along the way and frequent rethinking and redoing of previous stages. Additionally, ethnographic fieldwork is amongst the most unpredictable of data gathering activities, as it often depends heavily on specific historical circum-stances and the individual characteristics of the participants.

There are a number of different ways in which we can talk about this complexity. To help visualize it, we use three of the metaphors we presented in the Introduction: the roadmap, the rhizome and the skein of multi-coloured wool. The *roadmap* expresses the simple, formally linear character of research plans in which, roughly, one envisages doing one thing after another, but situated in a landscape with multiple possibilities regarding which roads or rivers (and which kinds of roads or rivers) to take, and multiple choice points as roads intersect and rivers flow into other rivers. The idea of the *rhizome* expresses rather the apparently chaotic shape in which social life initially appears to us (like the skein of wool that the cat has irreparably entangled), as well as the trajectory that researchers usually have to follow.

If we think of research as a rhizomatic process, you can imagine multiple entry points. You identify some nexus, enter it and then follow the threads wherever they lead. This often means coming across new nexus, or knots, and switching tack in the process of untangling or navigating them. As if that weren't a strange enough concept, we are adding to that image the idea that this process may also lead you to return back to your original point of entry. You might decide that you actually need a new point of entry, or that in this tangled skein of wool, you need to follow not the yellow, nor the purple but the orange thread in the knot. To go back to the roadmap, you might decide that you should go back up the road to that fork and turn left instead of right; that you ought to have stopped in that big town back there; that you should be on foot instead of in a car; or that you are in the wrong neck of the woods altogether. Or that you have the wrong map. Below you will find an example of this from Monica. Sari's and Joan's examples are in their stories at the end of the chapter.

One such experience for Monica involved a project that aimed at discovering how francophone Canadian élites set up institutional spaces for constructing what it means to be francophone and to speak French in provinces of Canada where French is a minority language (that is, everywhere but Québec). This question led her and her team to focus on contemporary institutions and associations that claimed the right to make such decisions. Along the way, though, she found people often referring to something they called "la Patente" (the "thing") as important in the history of contemporary francophone discursive spaces. After it came up more than once, she started to ask questions; fortunately some of her teammates were less clueless than she was, and put her on the path of a francophone secret society (actually called the Ordre de Jacques Cartier) that had existed between 1926 and 1965. This required her to shift her research design in order to include a historical component, that is, to identify ways into finding out about la Patente and of linking it to contemporary discursive spaces. This could have (and could still) lead to a separate research project with its own focused design.

There is no way for anyone to predict in advance if and when such new discoveries will happen, or exactly what form they will take. What your project looks like when you are projecting it forward into the future is not what it will turn out to be in actuality. Nonetheless, projecting it forward is a necessary step, not only to satisfy program requirements, your supervisor, ethical review boards and funding agencies, but more importantly in order to make sure that your conceptual toolkit is ready for the journey you are proposing to undertake. It allows you to develop the skills that you need in order to think through the various steps from the entry point up till the end of the journey, the baggage that you need for the trip and the pros and cons of alternative routes.

Research design is a starting point, or a set of hypotheses, against which to interrogate what you actually end up encountering. It is a touchstone, a reality check. It can save you time and energy and help you to find hidden paths. If your idea about your project has no shape or substance, you have nothing to guide your explorations and no material to reinforce or modify. That is, if you have no map, you might easily get lost. Your research design has to build in signposts or landmarks so you can once again find the left fork, or the village, you now realize you need to attend to. At the same time, it has to have ways in which you can put boundaries on what you will consider; you can't follow all the threads, you can't attend to everything at once. Further, you will need to anticipate some way to keep a record of what you find so that you can make sense of it later, rather than in the moment, both because of the limits on our ability to focus and remember, but also because it is in the slow piling up of links, connections and resemblances that the contours of a story begin to take shape. Is this the same person I saw last week at the school? Is that the same song I heard three months ago across the border? Where have I seen this handicraft before? We will discuss these in greater detail in Moment 3.

In the rest of this chapter we will examine different dimensions of the kinds of hypotheses you want to consider when giving your project both shape and substance. You first need to think about what you need to know in order to be able to provide a convincing answer to your questions, that is, what criteria you should use in identifying where to go, what to look for, and whom to talk to. That information—or data—has to allow you to do two things: **describe** what is going on, and **explain** why that, why there, why then, why with those participants. Then you need to have some ideas about where you might find that information, and how you might get there—to imagine plausible maps and routes. That includes thinking about the kinds of relations with other people that you will be constructing (depending on your project, you might well want to think about your relationship to the rest of the environment as well).

Once you have projected yourself into fieldwork, that is, into those spaces and with those people, you have to imagine what it is about in what is going on in there that you really need to know, and how you will put it into the kind of shape you will need, in order to be able to return to it whenever you need to. Do you imagine yourself making notes? Videotaping? Would you like to interview people or perhaps you would like them to document their activities with a camera? Or perhaps you will need to trace back in time and use archives, or perhaps map activities across spaces—in which cases you will need to travel to different "nexus." Finally, what kinds of tools will you use in your analysis to check your hypotheses across the information you have gathered together, in all its different forms, over the life cycle of the data collection phase of the project?

Your **touchstones** in designing the data collection are:

- What you need in order to be able to both **describe** and **explain** what you are looking at.
- How to be respectful of the participants in your project (that is, **ethical**).
- How to remain within the realm of what you can actually accomplish (that is, **practical** and **reasonable**).
- And how to take into account the fact that you are an actual person with a personality, a history and a social position (that is, **positioned** in ways that make some things easier than the others, and that will influence how you are read by other people).

In sum: what counts at a specific moment as research design is always part of an emergent process, drawing on knowledge from the past and then further developed as we go along. Having said that, however, we still need to present a workable and realistic design, one that links our questions to our procedures for finding the evidence, that will help answer them in an orderly way. We now turn to some modes of creating such order.

2.3 Where to Start? With Whom?

This issue is usually, in traditional parlance, discussed as *site selection* and *sampling*. By that, people generally mean choosing where to go and what kind of people, how many of them (or farms, or business trips, or newspaper articles) to bring into what then gets constituted as your "data base": the universe of experience and conversations through which you will discover the information that you think you need in order to be able to answer your question. We usually think of "sites" as actual places, and the population constructed via sampling as actual people or institutions (or both). Here we would like to think of them a bit differently: as a choice of entry points into a web of more-or-less spatially and temporally situated experiences, connections and relations.

It is important to keep in mind that we do not study the specific sites or groups of people, but the interconnected and overlapping social processes for which they may provide the scene or the participants. Moreover, how you **name** and **define** the sites and the people is something that should be handled with care, not so much in terms of their content (whether they are defined "accurately"), but in terms of their *genealogy*: you should know where the categories come from and why they make sense to you and/or the participants. Most contemporary critiques of ethnography and discourse analysis caution against simplified and reified notions of group, place, community, and time, or a priori conceptualizations of power relations, recognizing that these are themselves products of specific ideological positions. These critiques stem from the increasing awareness that traditional social science has often uncritically used vocabularies that were part of the contested (or at least contestable) processes they were studying.

In Canada, the question of who counts as a member of First Nations is a deeply contested issue, shot through with colonial and neocolonial relations and the exercise of power by the state. The same is true of the category Sámi in Finland. The categories "Catalan speaker" and "Spanish speaker" are anything but transparent. Historically—Joan would argue—they stem from common-sense ethnolinguistic categories used by people: the politically incorrect terms "Catalan" and "Castilian," which people were assigned to according to whether one used Catalan for "in-group" communication or not. Sociolinguists find the categories relevant when it comes to describing and understanding people's linguistic practices and their likely implications for Catalan normalization. Thus, they maintain the distinction in sociolinguistic research despite the fact that most citizens of Catalonia are bilingual. The criteria for assigning a person to the categories can however vary: they may express a person's "native" language, the language "first learned," their most commonly used language or the one people claim to be their "own language." All in all, the choice stems from the way each researcher wishes to structure the argument; but the categories can never get fully detached from the ideological struggles about national belonging.

For us, there are two main reasons behind wanting to make a shift from a terminology of sites and groups to one oriented to process, which is connected to why we use metaphors like skeins of wool, forests and trees, maps and rhizomes, rather than embedded boxes, flow charts or hierarchical decision trees:

- The **first** is that through fieldwork we realize that the clean boundaries that we thought set apart one community or institution from another turn out, upon inspection, to be made and re-made in everyday life. They are often fuzzy, and social practices end up being more about relations across borders than relations within them.

In real life, it is often not straightforward to tell one identity category from another (e.g., what makes someone a Sámi, a Finn or a Lapp), or one activity from another (is this work or play? Different generations relaxing together or child socialization?). What matters then is that those distinctions are meaningful to people and that there are observable ways in which they make them meaningful. This means thinking through how you will recognize the things that are meaningful to people.

● The **second** is the corollary that whatever is (or seems) fixed can only be fixed in relation to things (and people) that move, so that you have to take mobility into account, even if what you want to focus on is what makes immobility work. You might want to focus on a particular village or neighbourhood, but what is fixed there works because it is connected to people working elsewhere who send remittances, or have trade relations with people in your focal site, or because they live in a site through which fish and game pass. The same logic can be applied to businesses, institutions, clubs, indeed to any social formation, however "local" and fixed it may appear. As a result, you need to pay attention to what allows (or requires) some things or people to stay in one place, and what allows (or requires) others to move around, as well as how the two sets connect to each other.

In our own research biographies, the vulnerabilities of both social categories and the interdependence of what is fixed and what is mobile have been key themes connected with the conditions of late capitalism, as we discussed in the Introduction. Indeed, these latest social changes have destabilized our formerly taken-for-granted ideas about fixed, bounded communities, identities, languages and cultures, drawing our attention more and more to the kinds of processes which may have long existed, but which we now really need to grasp if we are to make any sense of our contemporary world. Concepts such as *rhizome* or *network* also invite us to look into relations among activities separated in some ways, to some degree, by time and space, and at relations and connections between what moves and what doesn't.

This is how we can get a better idea of how social categories are made and put into relation with the circulation of resources—indeed, at how space and time, and people and things gain value themselves. As a result, the kind of design we want to talk about here emphasizes researching *complexity*, *connectivity* and *intersectionality* (overlapping, intersecting identities and related systems), making sense of the interconnected and irreducible multiplicity of ongoing social processes, and enabling us to envision a system of dynamic changes that are never complete. (Much of the literature on this set of problems has been connected to terms like *mobility*, *circulation* and *multi-sitedness*, and we provide some key references to that literature in the bibliography.)

Nonetheless, even if we know that boundaries are constructed and fuzzy, and that we need to understand processes more than we need to understand objects, we still need to start somewhere. Further, even if we know our route will change, we still need to articulate the principles of selection we use to imagine where we might start in order to use those same principles to guide how we might shift direction. Thus, we may use socially contested categories or bounded spaces as starting points or, as we anticipated, as **entry points** into the issues we pursue, provided that we are aware of how problematic and vulnerable they are.

Thinking in terms of entry points, then, involves querying what they give access to, how they can be of use to address the research question. They are supposed to be somewhere in the rhizome, somewhere in the web that we seek to understand.

2.3.1 Finding a Nexus

In many ways, just by virtue of the work that you have done to formulate the research question, you are probably already in the relevant space in some way. Now what you need to do is to look around for a nexus or a node or a knot, that is, a space or a moment or a practice where threads meet, experiences intertwine, resources are produced and exchanged, and relations are made, as relevant to your research questions. It may end up being dense and complex enough that you end up exploring it in detail, or, as we have repeated over and over again, it might lead you elsewhere.

Monica mentioned earlier her question regarding what passing a law making French the language of work in large private sector companies in Quebec had to do with what people were actually doing in the workplace. Clearly, a major criterion for a point of departure would be a workplace in the private sector large enough to actually be subject to the law. Given the law's implicit aim to facilitate French-speakers' access to capital historically in the hands of English-speakers, another criterion was a company that fit that historical profile. Any such company would likely be a nexus where the trajectories of (English-speaking) ownership and management, those of (French-speaking) workers, those of state regulation, and those of the capital, resources for production, the products themselves and the market, would intersect. (Eventually, she chose a large brewery.)

Sari started by looking at discourses about Sámi language and identity circulating in people's talk, in media coverage, and in legal documents. She then started wondering if those discourses were ever contested or played with in any way in specific contexts. A major criterion for this nexus was thus that it should explicitly comment on and challenge the dominant constructions of language and identity categories in a creative, new way in comparison to what she had found so far. Sari started looking at spaces outside the institutional regimes to see if things were different there. She looked at overlapping spaces of tourism, arts and media, and found a "carnivalesque" nexus of subversion and transgression of traditional constructions of boundaries and categories, for example in Sámi media comedy shows on "Fake-Sámi" or "Super-Sámi" categories associated with illegitimate claims to Sámi identity. (The first tend to be understood as people with overly romanticized understandings of Sámi identity, and who want to participate in that imagined world although they have none of the forms of capital most Sámi recognize as legitimate. The second tend to be understood as people who exaggerate those forms of capital, and devote their lives to performances of Sámi identity, especially in political contexts, rather than leading ordinary lives.)

Joan's choices of sites and people in his thesis project stemmed primarily from the idea that the new generations who had attended Catalan schools should use Catalan more. An important population profile were the descendants of former Spanish-speaking migrants living in large cities. This directed his interest towards (1) "Spanish speakers" of working-class areas; (2) young people (e.g., those who had had the chance to learn Catalan at school); and (3) "informal spaces," usually understood as spaces not regulated by the state or other major institutions. He really didn't know much about how he would do this, so he started contacting people working in youth clubs, that is, where at least the right kind of people gathered, to ask them for advice. This led him to friendship groups in working-class neighbourhoods.

The issue of entry point(s) is thus just the beginning of the choices you need to make. One important component of these choices has to do with dimension or scope: how much is too much? How much is not enough? Which is better, breadth or depth, that is, say, less time with a greater number of participants or more time with fewer people? We begin this discussion below by considering that problem in conceptual terms, that is, as a question of where and how you draw the boundaries of the data that you target.

2.3.2 Boundaries and Claims

Even if you have a clear idea of the type of material that would allow you to address your research questions, you are likely to be confronted by the problem that resources are always finite, that not all types of data are equally accessible, and that you cannot fully predict how successful all your plans will be. However, it is obvious that you cannot let your project get steered only by simple practicalities. There are intellectual criteria that we can use for deciding where to draw boundaries, not just practical ones. These criteria are to be used to make decisions within the bounds of the possible and the feasible, they will help adjust the object and the questions, and, finally, they will determine the types of claims that the analysis can eventually produce.

This interplay between boundaries and claims should not be understood as a mere procedural complication that needs to be gotten over and done with, in order to then move on and forget about it. Rather, it lies at the core of the interpretive processes that will define your project (this is why we said earlier that, in the research plan, you begin to form your argument). Notice that the term *boundary* comes up again and again in this text, although it seems to apply to different things: to the definition of the research object, to how specific categories are viewed or experienced by informants, to how we as researchers define the elements that we analyze. Indeed, it is important to grasp that all these processes of categorization or boundary management at different levels are in constant interaction. As we argued earlier, the boundaries that are supposed to delimit our categories are always fuzzy and constructed and problematic, not just those of our informants, but ours as well. Despite this, you will need to draw boundaries for your project, even if you are aware that those boundaries, once you access the entry points or nexus that interest you, will become fuzzy and traversed by the very trajectories whose intersections constitute the nexus, not to mention others you are bound to discover once you start taking a closer look.

Monica's choice of a single factory through which to examine the role of the state in legislating changes in linguistic practice allowed her to limit herself to the site of the building and the beginnings and ends of the working day. This meant limiting her claims to what she could see there, and having less to say, for example, about how work fit into the lives of employees, how the product was circulated to the consumers, or where the money went. It also meant thinking about what could be said about the field of "big companies" in general.

Joan's choice of gathering data in the leisure activities of groups of young people allowed him to examine how people behaved when they were not constrained by formal hierarchical relationships at school, at work or within the family. It provided a perspective on how young people got together to perform specific ways of behaving and relating to each other, as well as how they constructed constraints and norms. As he did not feel that he had the time and the resources to follow his participants into other areas of their lives, he was not in a position to consider, for instance, to what extent what he was witnessing connected, coincided or contrasted with what these people were saying and doing elsewhere. Additionally, because he preferred not to press people on issues that they might consider too intimate, he was not able to bring into the picture dynamics connected with sexuality, such as heterosexual or bisexual relationships.

Sari chose to focus on the few Sámi tourism entrepreneurs located around a village in Sámiland to examine commodification of authenticity for tourism markets; this allowed her to limit her research to the ways in which these entrepreneurs manage the simultaneous political and economic tensions related their business. This meant that she could say less about the Finnish tourism providers elsewhere in Lapland, and that she needed to think about what can be said about tourism in the peripheries and beyond.

The participants in the activities of the nexus will also be busy making or maintaining boundaries themselves, in how they divide up time, space, activities, resources and social relations in ways that are meaningful to them and observable to you. Put differently, since we argue that boundaries are constructed, it must be possible to see those boundaries in operation, and use the signs of their construction as criteria for deciding where to focus or where to stop. In practice, this means looking for how people shift their behaviour in ways that then get routinely taken up as calling into play a whole series of distinct ways of behaving, and of evaluating the behaviour of others. It will be your question that decides whether that contrast is a necessary component of what you need to understand, or rather a good place to draw the line. In the initial stages you probably have to start with a hypothesis about where these boundaries might be, but as you go along, you need to check to make sure you were right. In any case, the indeterminacy of the spaces and networks needs to be understood as normal, and your proposal should recognize that there will be elements that you can decide in advance and others that will need to be discovered.

After Monica's brewery project, she was given a postdoctoral position that required her to design and carry out a project on francophone Ontario. She began by looking for the spaces that mattered the most in terms of having consequences for who would count as francophone and what would count as French (i.e., where boundaries were being drawn). It became clear that schools were a central space: large amounts of money were devoted to them, and they were the focus of public discussion in every discursive space in Ontario related to French and francophones. People hardly talked about anything else. So it seemed reasonable to start with schooling.

But what kind of school? How many? Which ones? At that time (1982), no one had taken an ethnographic look at any Franco-Ontarian schools (or for that matter, any francophone minority school anywhere in Canada). So there was no prior knowledge to build on, only what was reported either by surveys or people's personal experience. She had to use other criteria. There were two kinds of state-funded French-language schools, Catholic and "public" (non-denominational). There were many more of the first variety than the second, and they had been there before the latter historically, making them potentially more typical—and so she decided to look for a Catholic school. There were also many more elementary schools than secondary ones, so that narrowed things down as well. Further, elementary schools were understood in public discourse as key sites of primary socialization; people talked about them as the places where foundations of identity would be laid. So, then, Catholic elementary schools.

Since Monica wanted to do a close analysis of interactional as well as institutional processes, and she had six months in which to do her fieldwork due to constraints of the funded research grant which was the context for her postdoctoral fellowship, one school would be all she could handle. And since she was not in a position to move from Toronto, it would have to be accessible in a trip from home or work to the school and back in one day. Many people felt that she should have chosen a school in eastern or northern Ontario, since that was where the "real" francophone Ontario was; she was thus obliged to think about what difference it might have made, asking why people attached more importance to the east and the north than the south, and what seemed to be actually happening in terms of the movements of the populations whose children ended up in those schools.

She also had to think about how much time she would need within what was possible. Since she could devote herself almost full-time to research, she opted for spending every other day at school, with the time off devoted to fieldnotes (see Shop Floor). This would allow her to experience the full cycle of a school day, and a full range of activities.

Beyond picking a school, it was also necessary to learn what to focus on within the school. Here, having never done fieldwork in a school, but having read a large number of school-based ethnographies of communication, it seemed clear that something in classroom interaction would be relevant to a question about how an institution constructs identity, and what kind of identity performances that produces. But the rest was pretty much a black hole, and so this is where the story of her research design before beginning fieldwork ends.

When Sari started her fieldwork, she was looking for people who either self-identified as Sámi language speakers or were referred to her as Sámi language speakers. However, when she started asking about people's language repertoires, and especially about Sámi languages, she noticed that people tended to shy away from categories such as "native speaker" or "bilingual speaker." Instead, many talked about the various ways they had gained, lost, reclaimed or forgotten their Sámi language skills. They also used situated categories, such as "real Sámi" "Fake-Sámi," "Super-Sámi" or "wannabe-Sámi," that clearly made sense locally in terms of describing various relationships to Sámi resources. This helped Sari to make drawing of boundaries her focus here: she started to trace where, when and who were drawing on these categories, how they seemed to help to make sense of the complex, ongoing processes related to inclusion and exclusion.

When picturing the types of groups on which he would do his fieldwork, Joan started with some key criteria. First, he thought that two groups was best as a target for various reasons: (1) taking groups from different neighbourhoods helped identify what characteristics were specific to one group and which were arguably shared more widely by members of their generational group in Barcelona; (2) it made the project more viable in case something went seriously wrong with one of the groups (a conflict, an accident, repeated problems with access, etc.). Second, he wanted to compare a homogenous Spanish-speaking group with a linguistically heterogeneous one in order to explore how homogeneity–heterogeneity played out in negotiations of language choice. Third, he knew gender was fundamental to understanding youth culture, so he made sure his groups were gender-mixed. Sociolinguistic research at the time was also showing that gender was an important category in understanding linguistic practices. Of course, these choices left out the possibility of investigating men-only or women-only groups, or people more accustomed to going out in pairs or small parties. Although everything largely worked out as planned, in the process of data analysis he eventually realized that categories such as "Catalan speaker" or "Woman" were more fluid than the simple notions he had used to classify the people and the groups. The homogeneous Spanish-speaking group contained people who spoke Catalan in other areas of their lives and members who also spoke both languages within the family. To examine gender issues, he had to give up the man–woman dichotomy and build a more complex classification of people who displayed their gender identities in different ways.

As anticipated above, your choices of which part of the rhizome to address will set the limits to what you can ***claim*** about other parts. In the case of the brewery and the school, Monica was claiming that the specific nexus she chose *represented* a relevant category of nexus. Here *representativity* is based on the knowledge one is able to gather about the field one is in. Who are "Barcelona youth"? What is a "Sámi journalist" and where does one find one? What is a "French-language minority school" and how many different kinds are there? Representativity is one way to explain why you are going for a specific nexus.

In cases like many of those we ourselves began with, there was little such information available, since none of them had ever been investigated in this way. As a result, it was not possible to say whether there might be important differences that one should attend to. Instead, relevant differences had to be discovered later on the basis of what we would find out. It was also not possible to say for sure whether what we found in our specific nexus would definitely apply to all nexus like it. Rather, what we were doing was generating hypotheses about the kinds of conditions under which the kinds of things we observed would be likely to occur, and why.

The type of claims you can formulate are dependent on how much has been researched in the particular area you are working in, so that available studies contribute to delimiting your scope. This is one reason why ethnographers like to read other ethnographies; it is a key way to see what differs and what remains the same, under what conditions. Sometimes you have to do the comparative, hypothesis-testing work yourself, which of course is what also keeps you moving along and around the rhizome(s). But claiming is also linked to your ability to show how things are connected and consequential, that is, how what you see produces specific configurations of distribution of resources, and how people navigate that distribution from the position in the network they find themselves in. This is why it is important to think about what you need to know, not only to get a good handle on what is happening, but also what your theoretical framework leads you to identify as plausible forms of explanation. For us, this has to do with what material and social conditions (where resources lie, who controls them, what market conditions augment or diminish their value) act as constraints on the production and distribution of resources.

This notion that one can engage in an open process of hypothesis testing is obviously in contradiction with the very idea that one must have everything planned in detail beforehand. Ideally, you should be exploring new nexus and processes up to the point in which you reach the state of so-called *data saturation*, by which we mean that new data is no longer leading you to new information related to the research question. Thus, you should stop when you are no longer learning new things, but instead you start seeing the same thing over and over again. However, this is not always possible, and you will most likely have to settle for getting halfway there. Your research plan, in any case, must include your best anticipation as to where and when this point will be reached, because the final decision will have to take place while you collect your data (in Moment 3 we discuss further how we make such "judgement calls").

Another dimension to think about is whether you want to identify a particularly *illuminating, telling* or *important* case. This could be a nexus that is particularly dense, or where conflict and contradiction serve to illuminate the underlying values and conventions at stake. It could also be a nexus with major consequences for the making of boundaries and for the circulation of resources, and thus for the making of social difference and social inequality.

In French-language minority schools, admissions committees decide which students, beyond those which law obliges them to accept, schools actually want to admit; these are nexus where the values of reproduction of francophone identity traverse the economic value of the French language, where inclusion of immigrants encounters fear of assimilation by English-speakers. These are also nexus that actually determine who will gain access to those schools, as spaces of distribution of valued cultural and linguistic capital.

The Sámi Parliament in Finland has a special committee deciding which applications for registering to vote in Sámi elections will be approved. This is a highly powerful nexus for defining legal and political boundaries of the category of Sámi in the Finnish context: a person who gets accepted for this register will be considered a recognized Sámi with all the rights that come along with that status. Conversely, applicants who are turned down will not have such a status or recognition. Another interrelated nexus to this is what is accepted as evidence that your Sámi heritage fits with the criteria set for this purpose and satisfies the reviewers.

To understand how the Catalan language gets associated with Catalan national identity, one revealing site would be the run-up to the 2007 Frankfurt book fair, where

"Catalan literature" was the special focus. The invitation triggered debates on whether "Catalan literature" included only works originally written in Catalan, or also works written in Spanish or other languages by Catalans, or by residents of Catalonia generally seen as not Catalan (such as, for instance, the English novelist Robert Graves). This debate was of concern to the government, as it was in charge of choosing which writers would be showcased; it had economic implications both for the writers and for the publishing companies and the media tended to take sides on these questions. So such a site would help illuminate the interplay between the literary, political and media fields in shaping ongoing debate about who counts as "Catalan."

You can undoubtedly think of many more such consequential sites (or what have been called *key situations*), depending on the question you are asking. The key approach is to **ask where things get debated and decided, and by whom**. The "things" in question link whatever counts as a valuable *resource* (government funding, language learning, tourism business, lumber, book sales) to the boundaries that regulate how and by whom they get produced and circulated. In this sense, doing rhizomatic work can be compared to a connect-the-dots task: When mapping and moving along your rhizome, you are looking for dots (nexus) that are crucial for you to be able to make a dense enough picture that you can claim to be describing something bounded, and that will give you the resources to explain it; connecting the dots is the important work that you, as a researcher, undertake.

Such an approach generates a simultaneous sense that, while there is not a single understanding or "truth" out there that would always hold true across space or time, nonetheless, as complex and ongoing as an activity or process may be, it is not random: there are always regimes and logics that matter more than others, and there are always patterns and particularities as well as important frictions and anomalies. So while you might have doubts as to whether the data or the site or key situations—the nexus—you are thinking about are "enough" (in terms of size, depth, breadth, or their significance), it is important to keep in mind that they all are historically and socially embedded and framed. It is this logic—the line/link—that connects them, and so makes them part of the bigger picture that you try to tease out and trace back and forth (bearing in mind that any bigger picture has to be defined in terms of boundaries you can account for empirically, not as a putative pre-existing whole).

One final footnote: the one mode of selection that we are **not** going to discuss in detail here is random sampling. Certainly, if you have no ethnographic guidelines to help you pick useful points of entry, picking randomly is as good as anything. You'll certainly discover something. Random sampling can be useful, for instance, when one wishes to estimate the distribution of particular features in a population. But be aware that the typical justification for random sampling is that it corrects researcher bias, that is, that it puts to the side the very forms of ethnographic knowledge we have been arguing are central to making choices in research design. In any case, researchers are always guided by their questions and by their assumptions about what constitute relevant units to sample (18–35 year olds? Males? People living in rural areas?), and about what constitutes the universe within which the random sample is selected (people with phone numbers? Computer access? Permanent addresses in a census district?), so "random sampling" is never really random; it is always implicitly embedded in either your assumptions or in the kind of ethnographic knowledge that we have been arguing you should use instead.

2.4 Approaches and Evidence

Once you have decided on your point(s) of entry, and have an idea of whom you will be working with, you need to plan in greater detail exactly what kinds of information you need, and what makes sense as a way to find it, record it and document it and eventually make sense of it. Moments 3 and 4 cover these topics in greater detail, and so here we will only briefly discuss how you might outline your approaches at the research design stage.

The **first** point to be made is that you need to render the conceptual terms of your question and framework into things that are actually **observable**. If you have a question about *language practices*, then you need to be able to say and see what a language practice is. If you have a question about *boundaries*, you need to say what will count as a boundary for you in the context of your research (we gave you examples of how that might be done above). The same holds true for concepts like *identity, discourse, resource, capital* or any of the other items in our conceptual repositories.

Second, once you have done that, you need to figure out how you will see those things—what counts as "seeing" in your case and what kind of "signs" (traces) you are looking for. You have a limited set of choices. If you are looking for things that are likely to be happening in real time, and you can be there yourself, then you can see them more or less directly. If you are looking for things that have already happened, or to which you do not have access, then you can ask for accounts. You can ask for accounts yourself, whether in verbal, written or visual form, and in ways that can be part of daily routines people engage in anyway, or in ways that involve your request for an account as a special genre (this corresponds most closely to our conventional idea of an interview, a journal, or a prompt for verbal or non-verbal expression, as when we ask people to make maps or drawings). Thus, for the first type you may wish to find out whether the people you are working with produce accounts themselves; for example, in organizations, self-documentation is quite prevalent, through reports, minutes of meetings, publicity or other means. In daily life, people engage individually or collectively in many forms of self-documentation, from the old-fashioned diary to social media selfies. And of course, you can see whether anyone else has produced an account, whether a media report or art piece, or a study of some kind.

Third, whatever choices are available and finally made, there is one aspect of observation, accounts and documentation that is **essential** to bear in mind at all times: **all research activities occur in socially situated communicative events.** You must therefore try to understand how the conditions of their production affect the form and content of the data you obtain. Thus, if you engage in participant observation, conditions will steer you towards situations in which your presence or participation is somehow possible; and participants will usually be forced to react to our presence in one way or other, that is, they will need to interpret why you are there and how to address you. Your data will be the product of these adjustments done in specific situations. The same can be said in relation to accounts: accounts must be treated as situated productions and performances like any other. This is an aspect that is very often overlooked in social science research, in which accounts or questionnaire responses are taken at face value, and researchers ignore the conditions that may lead informants or respondents to express a particular view or attitude. **How** something is said sheds light on **what** is said, so both are equally important.

In his fieldwork, Joan had to fit in the leisure activities of two youth cliques in Barcelona. However, he could not simply just turn up when the groups met and drop a few comments or crack a few jokes like everyone. The groups also operated on the basis that each member had some form of personal relationship, more or less intense, more or less close, with every other member. So Joan had to find ways of relating and sharing with each individual. Whether this meant, at times, going with one of them to buy records, or play computer games, or discuss a particular problem or play table football with the guys, it meant bringing the people into his life and becoming part of their own history, so that the data emerged out of Joan's interaction with them.

During an interview, one woman once responded to an identity category question posed by a team member working with Monica by saying "Je suis canadienne-française, I guess" ("I'm French-Canadian, I guess"). In both the combination of French and English, and in the content of the hedge ("I guess"), this woman was signalling indeterminacy around her identity claim, setting the researchers up with a puzzle to be solved—and whose solution would help shed light on what shaped identity categories for her. In a survey, she might just have ticked a box, and the really interesting issues around ambivalence, contradiction and ambiguity would never have emerged.

Similarly, a young boy enrolled in Sámi medium education drew himself as a small plankton under a magnifying class when asked to draw himself as a Sámi language learner, but provided a picture of himself dressed up in Sámi dress when he portrayed himself as a Finnish-language learner. This visual image of his experience of interrelations of language skills and identity categories brought to the surface important meanings and stances that had not come up with other modes of inquiry such as interviews and background questionnaires used in this particular study.

Fourth, people are rarely able to tell you exactly what they do, but comparing what they do with what they say they do can be revealing of their values, their frames of interpretation, and what they think you want from them (people usually are not aware that they use multiple languages in one utterance, for example, and often deny it if it is pointed out to them). This means that it is often good to attend to multiple forms of data, notably the material manifestations of communicative data in conjunction with their embedding in communicative action of multiple kinds, in situated conditions, and how they relate to each other. *Triangulation* is one common term to name this process; the term is a metaphorical extension of the technique commonly used in topography or astronomy to work out a given value on the basis of two interrelated known values. Thus, having different types of data on the same issue may result in information that can be compatible, contradictory or ambivalent, and the exercise of explaining this is likely to be especially productive, indeed, as productive as having to deal with conflicting accounts, which are likely to express contesting social and political stances on the issue studied.

Fifth, in addition to the social and political position of the informants, one important aspect of how different types of data are accessed or elicited is also the (perceived) social and political position of the researcher. The reflections of the sociolinguist William Labov (1966) on the "observer's paradox" made the concept very popular across the social sciences. However, this "paradox" only points at the surface of the unavoidable condition of social research, namely that the data is invariably the product of the researcher's involvement in the topic at hand and with the people who provide the data.

More specifically, given that anthropological work often aims to document the diverse ways in which people construct their everyday sense of social life, "insiders" may have a problem with eliciting particular types of information. Conversely, they may also be able to exploit the advantage of a more complete and nuanced understanding of many aspects. On the other hand, "outsiders" can afford to ask naïve questions; but they may also have a harder time "learning how (and what) to ask" (as the linguistic anthropologist Charles Briggs [1986] put it); they might notice things insiders take for granted, but might have a harder time distinguishing what is relevant from what is not. Whatever it is, researchers of different origins may not be able to plan the same types of activities, and they may well have to approach people, phrase questions or raise issues in different ways. What this means is that how the researcher is understood and perceived in specific contexts matters, and that this is a component of the research process that must be addressed in the analysis as well.

One day, a few weeks into her fieldwork in the Montreal brewery, an English-speaking employee drew Monica aside and asked her if she was a spy for the government, checking to see if everyone was obeying the law. Several years later, when she got off a city bus at a high school in Toronto, a young woman getting off at the same time asked her if she was new at the school and therefore was likely a student; that stopped happening a few years later, as Monica grew older and was assumed to be either a parent or a teacher, with attendant implications for changes in what she would be able to do, see, hear, and ask and how people would interact with her. On the part of her interlocutors, these exchanges must be read as important (and revealing) efforts at understanding who she was, what kinds of relationships might be possible and therefore what could and could not be shared during fieldwork.

Being the strange element on the spot can also prompt people to explain how things are or how they came about: when Sari started to work in Sámiland, as a newcomer and outsider to the Sámi community, people at times provided her their family history not so much in terms of their languages (as Sari was expecting), but rather by showing on the map where their families had lived, worked, moved around and currently were living. This helped Sari to recognize the importance of mobility to them (due to wars, new nation-state borders, changes in viable livelihoods), and the conditions it created for cultural and linguistic practices.

Joan unexpectedly found that some of his interviewees were happy to openly acknowledge aversion against the Catalan language even when he clearly was seen by interviewees as a specimen of "Catalan." This was because the interviews were done after both parties had had the chance to share many other things, not just opinions but also the conventional nightly adventures of urban youth. This had allowed interviewees to feel that Joan would not take it personally. Besides, the interview contained many other items and this was just one of them. Had the interview been held at the beginning of the fieldwork period, interviewees would certainly have dodged the issue. So the very possibility to work with specific material (such as, say, anti-Catalan discourse) was a product of that specific researcher–researched relation and the way in which it found a place in the interview. Another researcher on the same terrain, Kathryn Woolard (1989), an American, on the contrary found that her informants often would provide lengthy descriptions and explanations about language, types of people, accents and stereotypes in ways that they would never do for a Catalan researcher (like Joan), for whom they considered that the information was not new.

So when you design our research, you must bear in mind how **feasible** it is for you (with your age, gender, social extraction, profession) to undertake various kinds of research activities, or whether you need to think about relying, where possible, on others, or whether you should be thinking of a different research design altogether. Hiring people with particular linguistic or communication skills, cultural backgrounds, gender affiliation, age, race, sexuality or other relevant categories is an option often pursued, particularly in large projects. Pulling together a research team is another useful strategy; this allows you to enter multiple nexus of a complex rhizome, or start at different places on the map (figuratively or literally). This often means combining people with different social positions, or associable with different social categories, including insider and outsider. As a novice researcher, you will probably not be able to start by heading a research team, but you might well be part of one. Certainly you might consider what the pros and cons of doing your thesis research alone or as part of a team might be. These could include: isolation versus collective knowledge construction; autonomy versus being subject to the needs of a collective; access to mentoring versus possible subjection to hierarchical control.

Finally, you also need to think about **sequencing**. If your field is a rhizome, or a ball of wool, despite all the messiness and movement they involve, you need to decide which nexus you will enter first, or which thread you will pull. And even though you need to plan for the inevitable moving back and forth that will happen, you might want to plan systematically to enter all the nexus you know exist one after the other, until you find that no matter where you enter, you encounter the same things.

2.5 Data Recording and Documentation

This brings us to another consideration in research design: recording and documenting the information that you gather. While we provide tips in the Shop Floor section, let us introduce some general considerations here. As we have said, sometimes you can identify and collect existing accounts, and so you have to keep them in the form of documentation they come in, though you might want to extract the most relevant parts. Otherwise, with regard to observed and elicited data, you need to think about how important it is to you to retain access to details of form (and hence do audio or video recording during the activities), or whether you will have enough if you just write a broad post-hoc account. Of course, sometimes recording is not possible, and fieldnotes, far from being second best, allow you to analyze as you go along. Multiple forms of documentation and recording allow for different ways into the data, as well as facilitating different forms of contextualization and retrieval.

Most importantly, the way you organize your data needs to correspond to what you think you are going to do with it. It needs to be **conceptually** accessible. Your research design needs to show how you will interrogate your data to answer your question: do you need to know not just what happens, but how often, who does it, with what consequences? Do you need to know both what and how something is done? Whatever the answers to these questions (or to other possible questions), you need to make sure that the relevant information is available. Further, you need reliable ways of making sure that those linkages can be made.

This will require some complex archiving skills that most commonly consist of coding and transcribing. Coding involves tagging your data throughout, i.e., creating your own system of marks or labels, your own index, related to the topics or concepts that you want to explore in your data. It can apply to all the forms of data you construct, whether fieldnotes, audio or video recordings, documents or material artefacts. Transcription turns our audio-recorded data into a format that is easily recoverable for the user and transferrable to others: a written record. Transcriptions in sociolinguistics typically contain a written representation of what was said in interviews, conversations, focus groups or other social events. Both coding and transcribing are themselves acts of analysis, and so overlap with what we have to say both about collecting data and about analysis in Moments 3 and 4. At the stage of research design, though, you need an idea about what kinds of documentation you envisage, what you imagine you will do with it (will you record everything? Will you transcribe everything? Is that feasible?) and why.

You will also have to narrow down the whats and hows on matters ranging from equipment and software, to travel time and time spent collecting data. But let us remind you here that this is another moment for recursivity: in the light of your estimations, you may find that you have to redesign your sample, maybe even rephrase your research questions. Well, better now than later—though it will probably happen later too!

2.6 Ethics and Politics

We took up above the question of feasibility: what you can accomplish given your resources and who you are. We also insisted that your own identity and social position played a role in the process of defining a research project and even in the practicalities of data collection. In addition to this, who you are is also a political and ethical question, and needs to be thought through in terms of the overall position that your research plays or may play in the social contexts in which it may have an impact. We know that conventional positivist researchers claim that scientific knowledge is unbiased, "neutral" knowledge. We argue to the contrary. We could hardly do otherwise, given our insistence that research stems from our (historically situated) experience of social conflict, and given that we aspire to make a difference. Overall, this entanglement of our research in society obliges us to examine these issues as openly and as explicitly as anything else. It is also necessary to be aware that, as experts, we are part of the processes through which individuals and organizations, whether public or private, use knowledge to pursue their goals, whether these be economic profit, political governance or anything else. As such, we have a place in the social hierarchy of power-knowledge.

Further, if you are working on language, chances are excellent that you are working either **directly** with people whose language practices you seek to understand and explain, or with materials that are meaningful to social actors in some way. You need therefore to think through what it means to spend time with people engaged in different kinds of activities; what it might mean to ask for different kinds of information and what your participants deserve to know about your project so that they can engage freely in it.

Indeed, in all our cases, the research projects are a form of political intervention (whether intended to be so or not) that, in itself, requires an interrogation of its ethical principles. One aspect of this is how the project is supposed to, or might, affect the participants, either personally or in terms of the wider social groupings they may belong to. Another is the issue of how the research process can affect them personally, disrupt their activities or have an impact on their social standing. This is why you need to build into your research design how you will handle the relations of power that necessarily traverse the activity, as well as choosing activities that correspond to the ethical principles to which you adhere. We have in particular advocated transparency and dialogue, recognizing nonetheless that ethics and politics are emergent and situated, that is, hard to predict entirely at the research design stage.

Finally, though you always have power as a knowledge producer, your relations with people might be traversed by other relations of power, and with varying kinds of attendant rights and obligations, some of which might make you vulnerable to them, not just the other way around. Your own safety and security need to be taken into account.

The following sections deal with a process that usually, in most academic institutions, occurs after your research design is completed and before you actually start to collect data. It is often called "ethical review," because it covers your preparedness to handle your relationships with the people, things and activities you will be encountering in a responsible, respectful way. For us, the essence of the process has to do with understanding what it means to gain and retain people's trust. We shall deal with the principles first and with issues in connection with the procedure later.

2.6.1 Relationships With Participants

At this stage, as with research design generally, you have to project into the future the kinds of relationships with your participants that you are going to develop. It is worth bearing in mind that building these relationships and the trust that goes with them is an ongoing process that affects not just what you do before or during the data collection; but also after, i.e., how you conduct your analysis and later share new knowledge.

Having said that, let's talk here about the first stage, when you have to imagine what you might need. Of course, it might not be possible to fully imagine what might happen as you carry out your project, but you will be well-served by having made an attempt to think through how you ought to and want to handle your relationships and your actions, so as to give yourself a set of guiding principles with which to handle the often complex and unclear situations you will probably encounter.

We must insist again, (because we cannot say it too often) that ethics, like everything else about research, is a context-sensitive process. This means that the concerns that we raise here need to be treated as guidelines, not as a recipe or a checklist on how to be ethical. In addition, it is a relationship, and therefore centrally about trust, and about mutual rights and responsibilities. It will probably be necessary for you to handle multiple roles, since inevitably you will be not only a researcher, but also a lodger, a friend, a source of valuable goods or information, possibly an employer if you work with paid assistants and other roles that you may not be able to anticipate in advance. Indeed, you may well already have a relationship with people (as a co-worker, family member, neighbour, friend and so on), in which case you will have to work through what it means to add "researcher" to the list. We deal with the key elements of your ethical review proposal in Section 2.6.2 overleaf and in the Shop Floor.

The first key principles in this regard are (1) the idea that research participants should be aware that their conduct is under scrutiny and (2) they should be able to consent or refuse involvement in it. This principle clearly overrules a common temptation of researchers to observe or record in secret so as to get data "unspoiled" by their presence or by the presence of recording equipment. We already argued above that the "observer's paradox" derives from a questionable assumption about knowledge building, which implies that we do not generally believe that observing in secret has any significant methodological affordances anyway.

However, the principle of informed consent may be contextually negotiable in specific conditions, especially as concerns what is considered to be "public" or "private." In North America, for example, it is usually considered that formal negotiations around research ethics are necessary only for cases considered private. The working definition of "public" that Monica was provided by her institution is "any situation in which people cannot reasonably expect to have control over other people's access to them—to what they say, how they look, what they are doing." Needless to say, we know that what counts as "reasonable" is a matter of variable and often ambiguous cultural convention, and that even in public we recognize signs of the making of private spaces by such techniques as orienting bodies so as to use backs as barriers, or lowering one's voice or focusing the range of one's gaze.

A fourth common principle is protection of identity, i.e., that we must disseminate results in ways that our audiences cannot recognize or identify the participants in any way (hence the convention of using pseudonyms). However, it is common to encounter participants who have an interest to have their views or experiences publicized in their name. Sari, Joan and Monica have had such experiences and, in these cases, you will also need to decide whether conditions warrant an exception or not.

A fifth common idea is that it is good to be open to sharing your notes or recordings with the people you are writing about. However, this principle will have to be weighed against the need to ensure the privacy of other participants (which is the reason why institutional requirements to place our data sets in the public domain may actually pose both legal and ethical problems).

All these competing demands and contextual specificities are the reasons why ethics is a process and a matter of making judgement calls in which crystal clear guidelines are impossible. They also explain why even when your data can be considered as situated in the public domain, most ethical review boards want to hear about it so as to decide for themselves whether that is the case or not.

One common concern arises when you are working in a setting where there is an official hierarchy of supervision (as in a workplace, or a hospital or a school). In these cases, you need to make clear at the outset that you will not share your data with anyone other than the people directly involved, and you need to extract a commitment from supervisors to let their employees or supervisees participate freely. You should never share your data with the media unless the participants have given you permission to do so.

The issue is somewhat different, however, when you are working as part of a team, and especially when you are involving participants directly as team members. Team members do need to have access to everyone's data, or else it is difficult to make the linkages that are the strength of teamwork. You may also be asking participants to make their own observations and recordings; in that case, what applies to you, applies to them. You should negotiate carefully with them beforehand and along the way who owns the data during and after the project, who may do what with it and whose work needs to be acknowledged by whom.

2.6.2 Ethical Review Procedures

In some places, you may not be able to legally carry out your research unless you have submitted a detailed proposal that is reviewed by the relevant authorities. These authorities may take several forms, and you may have to deal with more than one. In many countries, there are university boards made up of faculty members, who decide on the basis of your description of your plans whether or not you are ready to begin data collection. These boards are usually staffed by people whose job is to make the process run smoothly. There are usually standardized forms you have to fill out and a specific list of kinds of information you are asked to provide (we go over these in more detail in the Shop Floor section). If the board is not fully satisfied, they will ask you to respond to their questions, make modifications or provide additional information. You may go through several rounds of submission and evaluation until you are all on the same page.

In addition, agencies often wish to discuss with you how you will relate to the people or the material artefacts they are responsible for. Usually, university boards will make sure you have thought through your responsibilities not just with respect to people and things, but also with respect to such institutional interests. You will often find you need to attend to such institutions when they are responsible for the well-being of what are often called "vulnerable populations," that is, groups of people who might be intimidated or potentially abused by researchers. This is frequently the case, for example, with institutions like school boards responsible for children, or institutions like hospitals responsible for the sick. It is also often the case with institutions such as archives and museums that regulate access to socially valuable material artefacts (such as, documents, artworks, archaeological finds or archived recordings). Also, you may have to work with political agencies concerned about letting you (as a citizen or non-citizen) collect information about the people and resources they control and are responsible for. Sometimes, these considerations can be controversial; for example, not all members of "vulnerable populations" appreciate being constructed as "vulnerable." Debates you encounter at this stage are therefore actually often quite illuminating, although they may require you to take a more complex approach to the bureaucratic process than is often anticipated, and you may have some choices to make between expediency and ethnographic complexity.

Some researchers find this process difficult and a bit mysterious. It is true that it can be difficult to communicate with researchers working in different paradigms and establish shared expectations across different traditions. You should approach this process, though, not as an annoying bureaucratic hurdle to be overcome, but as one of the many conversations involved in the research process. As with all these conversations, it forces you to think deeply about what you believe your rights and responsibilities as a researcher are, and why. And as with all such conversations, you should not hesitate to approach concerned parties to try to work things out in ways that might allow for more nuance and negotiation than formalized institutional communication might allow. Further, as bureaucratic as some of these processes might be, we feel strongly that we are better off having them than not. They **do** help us reflect responsibly on the power we inevitably wield as knowledge producers, as it relates to the forms of power our participants have, and also to the risks we ourselves may propose to undertake or to which we might expose others.

In some cases, a major distinction may be made between the kinds of safeguards that are necessary in different kinds of places. Sometimes these distinctions come less from ethical processes and more from legal ones. Some legal provisions have to do with what is often called "duty to report," that is, what you are legally expected to do in cases where you suspect illegal behaviour, such as child abuse. Others have to do with cases where for some reason or another your data are considered germane to a legal case and are subpoenaed. The jurisprudence on this is thin, but Monica is aware of one case in Canada where researchers, with their university's support, were able to resist such a subpoena. In any case, you will need to find out what the rules are in your jurisdiction so that you may be able to fight them. For example, Monica has refused to collaborate with university suggestions that her request for consent letters to participants include a warning that she might not be able to guarantee confidentiality if her data are subpoenaed by the court.

Of course in some places, there may be no institutional process at all. We feel, however, that whether or not you are obliged to do so, this is an important process to undertake in some fashion, and you should prepare yourself in ways that respond to some of the most important points such processes usually point to. Put differently, we feel that whether or not you are required by some authority to prepare procedures for ensuring your work is ethical, you should do so anyway.

2.7 Research Design as Discursive Genre

As Joan's story below shows us, what counts as research design is strongly connected to the conventions of writing it up or speaking about it that make sense to your principal interlocutors at this stage. These interlocutors can be very diverse, so that you are going to have to adapt to many different formats and registers. If you are a student, you will need to learn how to communicate your ideas to your professors, to other students and possibly to scholarship proposal evaluators. You may need to communicate to members of university ethical review boards and to other gatekeepers, such as institutions or organized groups with whom you wish to work. For example, in Canada, many school boards and hospitals have their own research permission and ethical review procedures, as do many First Nations groups. Working in political jurisdictions other than your own can also require other forms of presentation, since you may need authorization from another state, for example. Sometimes these ways of presenting your design are highly conventionalized and regulated (such as applications for university ethical review boards), and sometimes not. Sometimes they are exclusively written or oral, sometimes a combination. You may not always feel comfortable with what is asked of you; you can certainly consider asking review boards directly about what it makes sense to do in your case.

There are a number of ways you can learn the genre. You can ask to see examples written by other people; you can ask people with more experience to read and comment on your drafts; you can explicitly ask for guidance on what is expected. In some competitive environments, people are afraid to share drafts for fear of appropriation or plagiarism. We don't want to underplay this risk, but at the same time, we do feel that collaborative work tends to be stronger and less isolating than trying to do everything on one's own. After all, if we regard doing research as essentially participating in a conversation, you should not refrain from engaging in dialogue from the start. And it makes more sense to think of the other people involved at this stage not so much as gatekeepers who are looking for ways to keep you out, but as stakeholders whose perspectives can help you understand the field of power and meaning that you are seeking to (further) explore.

Of course, you may well be facing gatekeepers as well. Here you will need an analysis of your position of power with respect to them. In some cases, you will be the one with power and privilege, which you will need to understand in order to form the relations of trust that underlie all ethnography. In other cases, it is the gatekeepers who will have the power. In some cases, you might have to argue for the possibly of unortho-dox forms of knowledge production that your minoritized position has led you to value. In others, the structural obstacles may be greater and will require more institutionalized approaches to overcome.

2.8 Summary

We can think of the research design moment as one set of turns in the long, stimulat-ing conversation that is the research process. It is also the first draft of your argument. Research design then is hardly preliminary. It is a necessary step in understanding what your question means in the broader context, and the stakes connected to it. And it is also the first practical attempt to make your hypotheses explicit, and to devise the roadmap that you make for yourself as you set out on the next step of the journey.

It is useful to think of research design also as a place to go back to when you are in the middle of your journey and encounter difficulties, or just lose your way. Part of recursivity will involve figuring out what to make of new phenomena you encounter, and that you could not have planned for, or new frames of reference that might call your design into question. At such moments, it can help to go back to your original plan, to remind yourself of the reasons why you set out on a particular path in the first place, and to clarify against what hypotheses you need to evaluate and interpret the new informa-tion that you find. Your original ideas may well hold up, and serve as a guideline for deciding which forks in the road to take, and which, however fascinating they might be, you need to leave unexplored for the moment. Your research design can also help you at the very end of the process, as you think about exactly what journey you have been on, and where it has led you.

In this chapter, we have addressed how you might think through these first steps in your project: deciding what counts as relevant information, figuring out where to find it, and developing your ideas about how to pull it together and make sense out of it. We have also addressed some of the ways in which research design may need to be revised along the way, with examples based on the authors' experience. We have insisted that all these steps need to take into account what is feasible and what is ethical. We will talk in greater detail in Moments 3 and 4 about what pulling information together (data gathering) and making sense of it (data analysis) might actually look like and feel like when you are in the thick of things.

Here is what this chapter has covered:

- Research design involves putting together your questions and hypotheses and an anticipation of your argument.
- It contains a projection into the future of all the activities you intend to carry out to pursue your question.
- It allows you to assess the means and resources at your disposal for your project.

- It requires figuring out what counts as relevant information for answering your question, that is, what criteria you will use to make choices about where, when and how to do your research.

- Use prior ethnographic knowledge (including from secondary sources) to identify boundaries and linkages.

- Choose as starting point representative or telling cases that constitute rhizomatic nexus from which you can begin pulling your threads.

- Be prepared to change tack as you go along and as your hypotheses are tested.

- Attend to multiple ways of identifying where you can find information.

- Distinguish practices from accounts of practices.

- Decide how to document the information you are looking for.

- Be aware of how feasibility, your social position, relations of power and ethics delimit the claims that you can make.

- Take into account the ethical and political dimensions of your relations to others and of theirs to your research subject.

- Take into account the discursive conventions that your interlocutors will be expecting, so you can communicate your intentions in ways that make sense to them.

Keywords: rhizome, nexus, web, map, triangulation, feasibility, process, saturation, positivist, interpretive, ethnographic, multi-sited, discourse analysis, projection.

Research Plans and Identity

Joan's first experience of writing research plans was primarily connected with applications for grants to do postgraduate studies. In one of his first grant interviews for a two-year M.A. in the US, one interviewer asked him what topic he had decided to study for his thesis. He answered that, at present, he simply needed to deepen his knowledge of sociolinguistics because it was a very peripheral subject in the philology degrees at home. He did not get the grant.

Since this was his first experience at conveying research design to someone else, the question stayed engraved in his memory. He concluded that he needed to have a thesis project at least to be able to present a convincing case. So Joan built an account in which he was going to explore how young people chose to speak Catalan or Spanish in face-to-face interaction with each other. Indeed, in the coming months, this account would travel in different formats through applications to multiple types of institutions: five-page plans, 400-word abstracts, one-page descriptions, 1,000-character summaries, three sets of keywords, and two main and two secondary study areas. Most applications were unsuccessful or only partially successful: first he obtained some small grants which he used to do small-scale studies, then a bigger grant from a municipal authority which needed a sociolinguistic study, then he studied for an M.A. during a period in which he was unemployed and finally (after all these things probably started to stick out in his C.V.) he obtained a doctoral grant from the Catalan government.

In any case, at the time he was not fully aware that by writing the project in multiple versions he was also gradually developing his idea in concrete ways (often with the risk of ending up being committed to a preliminary idea that was not fully mature). He was also learning (by doing) what we might call the "research proposal" genre(s) as well as constructing his own position, his "identity" within the academic community in a broad and loose sense. So, despite the fact that some academics treat thesis projects as just part of the paperwork, Joan believes thesis plans should be treated with care and awe. He invested time presenting his project at conferences and in departmental seminars so that other people could find flaws or ways of improving them. Good methodology courses often allow people to develop their methodological thinking applied to their own project, and these can be very helpful. The first chapter Joan wrote of his thesis was the methodology chapter, which, in the end, he decided to drop altogether, because it had been useful for him to think about it but it was largely irrelevant for the readers. And during this process the project kept changing. Although it arguably stayed within terms that were consistent from its inception up to its realization, the terms used to define its elements were corrected, reformulated, reordered, reconsidered and rephrased many times.

The research plan had to work not only as a plan that had to be feasible and acceptable to his funders and teachers. It also had to work for most of the audiences it had at the time and would eventually have in the future, such as language activists, politicians or journalists. And Joan also took particularly seriously the issue of how his project had to be explained to his informants, which included also trying out several drafts in seminars and with friends about how the project could be described both orally and in writing.

In a way, the project narrative for participants anticipated how the results were to return to society in terms and intentions that were transparent and comprehensible to general audiences; and even at this stage he would find reasons to go back to the main objective and rework it. One issue that was central and potentially sensitive to participants was not to phrase the project as if there was something fundamentally wrong about speaking in Spanish. Catalan sociolinguistic literature often lent itself to this interpretation, even if it was not necessarily intended. Moreover, participants' experience of language learning was largely one of subjection to the evaluative and judgemental eye of the language teacher and, indirectly, of the linguist. So although in the end the actual phrasing of the research questions varied according to the audience to which it was presented, Joan had to work hard to make the different formulations consistent and valid for all audiences.

With hindsight, Joan now sees his first research plan (in its many formats) as a statement that defined his identity as a researcher. After all, those who read applications were often more interested in the project than in remembering his name. The project was essentially the first story he would tell to people whom he met in class, in departmental corridors and in the first conferences he attended. Particularly when you go abroad to do postgraduate studies, and you meet new colleagues, friends and maybe new romances in class or at the university, the chances are that your project becomes your banner, the figurehead people first see in you after your height, your gender, your accent and the colour of your skin.

For Joan, the research proposal genre was, like job interviews, the typical communicative event about which you can get tons of authoritative advice but in which, in the moment of truth, you are in fact on your own, particularly because it is your story and nobody can tell it for you. He also learned that research proposals (must) contain as much rhetoric as any other form of social communication, and its reception is subject to the same politics of everyday life that are found in all social milieus. Whether research plans are intended to get funding, to obtain consent from participants or to participate in academic activities, for Joan writing research plans has invariably involved continuous redrafting and rewriting, just as one does when writing articles or books.

Designing Research Through a Tourism Nexus

With my preliminary experiences of researching Sámi tourism and questions of commodification of authenticity for global tourism markets, the next step I envisioned was to work on a research design around them. To me, research design works as a practice of scientific imagination: a plan of possibilities, choices and obstacles. My experience has been that I need to develop my research design before I can put it onto paper (or a screen). Of course, the two are closely interrelated and feed each other, but for the purpose of trying to explicate the various steps in a qualitative research process, I am going to focus on the first: my experience of developing a feasible research design before writing it in the format of a research proposal.

I touched earlier on the political aspects of researching Sámi authenticity, especially in contexts where the political discourse of rights controversially encounters economic profit, as in tourism. Designing research in this context requires, at a minimum, a recognition of the wide range of interests and investments in tourism at play, as well as an explication of your own interest here: why, how and to whom does studying tourism in this context matter?

Further, to me, research design needs to simultaneously do at least two seemingly contradictory things. First, it needs to have a clear structure that helps delineate the terrain I am investigating in order to achieve the goals of my particular project. This includes a map of the terrain (the part of the rhizome I will focus on); a set of interconnected nexus (key sites) to allow both sticking to the plan without getting lost in the forest, but also some openness to discovery and some means for evaluating my choices along the way (the reflexive, recursive aspect of qualitative work); back-up plans with alternative routes when things go wrong or do not work out as designed (and this will happen) and a vision of the goals (to remind me what I am trying to achieve with this design).

To check my preliminary findings (and hunches) on the commodification of Sámi and other kinds of authenticities, and to find my key sites, I cast my net wide to explore experiencing, eating, seeing, hearing and feeling authenticity that could be branded as indigenous, northern, Lappish or Arctic in a tourism context. Based on the preliminary mapping from my own work on this and similar topics, the most promising sites for studying commodification of authenticity seemed to me to be spaces, practices and products where authenticity was produced (made available, packaged and marketed) for tourists to consume (to buy, to experience, to see). These were to be found, for example, in souvenir and handicraft shops, in museums and hotels, in the products themselves and in tourism programs. As the various social media forums (hotels.com, TripAdvisor, websites of service provides, discussion forums) are an important part of the tourism business, as well as of the tourist experience (e.g., to share your pictures, to post your reviews), I wanted to include relevant social media sites in the design, i.e., sites where producers and consumers marketed, commented on and talked about these products, services and programs. Including social media also nicely complemented my ongoing work with more institutional media spaces and the questions of authenticity there. An unexpected rhizomatic connection!

I soon realized that some of the authenticity products might be produced and consumed in institutional spaces, like in the Sámi handcraft association store, some in highly competitive private markets, like the Sámi tourism business, or both. Also the temporal and spatial dimensions might vary: some of the services and products might have a long history, some may only last one season. Some may always happen in the same location, others may travel with the tourists. I deliberately did not decide in advance where this nexus might lead me, but I was prepared to think in some specific ways about what routes might exist and need exploring. However, to know what is unique to this place and what it shared with others under similar conditions, a multi-sited research design was needed.

Once I had identified the potential key sites (authenticity nexus), I imagined how to trace the circulation around and through them: what kind of data to collect and how to get access to them. This was also a reality check moment: there were still many possible sites to focus on (many shops, hotels, tourism programs) and only a limited amount of resources (time, funds, skills, bodies). I needed to make grounded choices (select the trees), and scale down without losing sight of the bigger picture (the forest, the argument). Given my overarching questions about the politics of Sámi identity, I wanted to focus on sites in which the producers of the products and experiences were locally understood as belonging to the Sámi community. I was particularly interested in the ways in which they constructed authenticity (or not) in their business and how they positioned themselves with respect to indigenous status. Similarly, I wanted to know if this mattered to the tourists, and if so, how. Due to my previous and current work in the region, I had a good idea which products and producers would be ideal candidates, so the next step was to find out their willingness to take part in the research. Before asking this, I needed to figure out first what kind of data I would need and how I planned to document it. All this information is needed for informed consent, of course, both in an ethical and a practical sense, since my potential participants wanted to know in advance what kind of access I would need in terms of time (how much, when) and documentation (pictures, recordings, interviews).

However, in all research design it is good to include a contingency plan for the (very likely) moment when things do not go as planned: the business is closed down, the tourist group does not arrive, the research permission is cancelled, your recorder is not working, the informant was not that informative. In many research plans this is discussed under the topic of "risk management."

As we mentioned in the body of the text, ethics is part of all stages of research, and is usually most explicit during the research design phase. In my case, working in a small site and briefly encountering tourists who are on the move complicates the basic principle of research ethics concerning informed consent, privacy and confidentiality. In the context of a Sámi village, for example, anonymising your informants may not always be possible, as insiders will be able to infer identities based on such information as a person's language skills, their unique business (there just are not that many people who run inns or sleigh rides) or their life history. Also many participants might well choose to be named, perhaps because they are proud of what they are doing, or because the concept of anonymity makes no sense to them. In practice, how much identifying information is covert or overt, shared or not is a question of mutual agreement and respect: with each informant we need to discuss the ways in which they wanted to be identified in the research, the ways in which they might be identified and what kind of information they thus might want to share for research purposes. Tourism adds another complication because of its ephemeral nature: tourists come and go in flows and patterns that are usually beyond the control or even the knowledge of the researchers. Informed consent might be difficult to obtain from a fast-moving group of tourists, nor would they likely have time or patience to hear me talk about my research.

3 Third Key Moment
Generating your Data

3.1 Fieldwork: Producing Data

In the previous chapter, we laid out our plans to pursue a research question by setting our current knowledge and beliefs against empirical evidence. That evidence, of course, has to be chosen, sought out and organized for analysis. It is inextricably linked to particular times, places and interlocutors. Here we discuss data collection as a situated process of producing data and, ultimately, knowledge, approaching social practices as they unfold. It occurs in the social world, not in a laboratory or an otherwise manipulated environment, nor by introspection. This process is called *fieldwork*.

The term derives from older ideas in anthropology about making a distinction between our ordinary lives and the new ways of doing things we discover in some spatially distant area called "the field." Today we no longer think in those terms, since the work we do is actually often at home, and the exoticization and othering produced by the distinction have connotations of power that we do not wish to reproduce. Nonetheless, we retain the term here for two reasons. The first is that it helps define a distinction in our stance towards what it means for everyone to engage in everyday life as opposed to what it means for a researcher to attend to the world ethnographically. It is also a particular kind of labour; it is indeed "work."

The field can be a site or a location, e.g., a town, a village, an institution, or a website. It can also be a combination of various sites in a case where you follow trajectories of particular individuals, objects or practices across time and space. It can be the activities of a group of people, wherever that may lead. Fieldwork thus always involves both a spatial and a temporal dimension. Traditionally, ethnographic fieldwork has been understood as a long-term, often uninterrupted, involvement with the people, community or practices being studied. But alternatively fieldwork may contain a series of separate periods of data gathering. Today, new technological practices and virtual environments have complexified boundaries around traditional notions of what constitutes "site" and "time." Thus, for example, a Facebook exchange can last several days or weeks and participants need not be co-present. This leads to discussions about the relationship between different data sets collected from different sites and at different times. Fundamentally, the idea of the "field" has become more complex and less bounded. Nonetheless, we need to make our own boundaries for our projects, or risk never finishing them.

In the previous chapters we emphasized that empirical evidence was essential to what we understood as a critical intellectual project of examining how language processes participate in the organization of social life and, hence, how people may have unequal access to resources. We now need to dig somewhat deeper into our understanding of **what this empirical evidence is**, bearing in mind our *constructivist* position in relation to knowledge: knowledge does not derive directly from evidence or experience, but is mediated by how we choose to formulate it and represent it in specific contexts of communication.

We start from **two main assumptions**. The **first** is that **data is not "out there" waiting to be sampled**. Instead, it is the product of a consensus on what particular experiences or materials can be used for analysis to support an argument. Potentially anything can become data in a research project: a multilingual receipt from a Sámi artisan shop, a Sámi language menu in a newly opened restaurant or photos taken from a guided tour in a reindeer farm. Data can consist of interviews with tourists, fieldnotes from observing guided tours, as well as the tours' social media marketing material. Data can also include the photos taken by tourists and discussions with service providers and local economic development consultants. It may include statistics of the number of tourists in the area or archival material of tourism development in the area. It can be a conversation between teacher and student, a graduation speech, a diagnostic interview between doctor and patient. It can be census reports on numbers of "immigrants" in a census district, or a YouTube clip about a local musician. This means that there is no "real" data or somehow "authentic" data out there, but in all cases collecting data involves human impact and includes (in fact, requires) particular ways of knowing. We as researchers take an active part in constructing, or *generating* it: deciding what counts as data, deciding how to analyze it, and deciding how to present it.

This brings us to the **second** assumption: all social phenomena, all data consist of **situated social practice**. We participate in constructing the data within a web of relationships, with each other, with other living things, with the environment or the resources we use and value. The social activities we are interested in occur in relationship to the threads that lead them there or lead them to the next thing. They have histories and geographies.

This is the frame within which we will discuss your **strategy** (that is, concretely what you will do) to obtain the evidence that you need in order to address your research question, both to be able to describe what is going on, and to explain it. Of course, constructing data requires that you gain **access** to the activities you are interested in, and that you have ways of building or building on **relationships** with the people you encounter there. Both of these are important things to think about, both at the research design stage and in the moment of constructing them.

Of course, you will already have made some *judgement calls* in your research design, when you decided what is relevant and feasible to do. However, no matter how detailed and rigorous your research design was, and how confident you feel about what you need to do, inevitably you will encounter some surprises; in that sense, you need to be prepared to continue to make judgement calls along the way. If your plan was well designed, it will help you considerably in these choices. However, the plan will not make them for you. This is why we referred to it as a set of guidelines or principles to carry out your project.

For instance, when negotiating access, you are likely to start by establishing contacts and find that some people are easier to relate with than others, that some spaces and activities are more accessible than others and that maybe some things happen unexpectedly (for better or worse).

For example, in order for Monica to start fieldwork in the factory, it was necessary to find a place where it made sense for a woman to work, given that the vast majority of the work was conducted by men. She ended up working in the quality control lab, which allowed her to see most of the factory, except the highest management offices across the street. She also had to accept that she would do no more than pass through the factory floor, so noisy that the men all wore earplugs, and so dangerous that the insurance company would not allow outsiders to spend any length of time there.

When Sari was mapping out what the tourists typically did in a small Sámi village (and before she knew it would be the crucial nexus to focus on) she hung around in various restaurants, souvenir shops and museums. In high season it was easy enough to blend in the groups of tourists, but in the quiet season Sari found herself among very few other tourists; after hours and days of "hanging around" in the same (small) places, she also started to "stick out." After a while, she started to talk with the shop owners and workers, building up a network relevant for her research later.

Joan was very happy about the initial contact phase with the youth groups that he joined. The groups presented the features that he had been looking for and their members were very friendly and willing to help. However, making things work required much more. He wanted to go out with them as often as possible, but it was not obvious to everyone what this entailed. One group was more formally constituted than the other, where people did not often go out together but split in smaller groupings of two to three people. Each small "unit" gathered to carry out specific projects: interested in buying off-the-beaten-track hardcore records? Meet older friends for a celebration? Joining a meeting of anti-conscription organizations? Hanging around in a rock band rehearsal? Joining a women-only outing? Joan had to develop some investment and involvement in each project. Some things he dared to do and some he didn't. Some situations and some people were easier to follow and record than others.

There may be many precise moments when you may have to make judgement calls. These might include: deciding which of two simultaneous events to follow; deciding whether to record a specific situation or not; deciding where to stand or with whom to have a chat; deciding how to ask for participants' consent both from an employee and her boss; deciding how to react when asked to do something by a participant; deciding how often to turn up to an event or in a space; deciding how open and friendly to be with participants you find joyful, attractive, powerful or rude; deciding whom to include in a group discussion; deciding whether an interview question should be dropped or reformulated; deciding the right venue for interviews or focus groups; deciding whether it is worth taking pictures or interrupting interactions at a particular event or deciding whether you have interviewed enough people.

In Monica's first school ethnography, at first the only teacher willing to let her come to his class was the teacher of the oldest children (he was also the only male; both gave him high status, she later came to understand). After a few weeks of coming to school three days a week, and hanging around the playground and the staff room, other teachers started to invite her to their classrooms. Soon all of them did. She then had to decide whether to accept all invitations, or only some; and how to divide up her time. She decided that it would be good to accept all, partly to have good relations with everyone, but also because that would allow her to see to what extent age and teacher style might have anything to do with language practices in the school.

Sari's preliminary idea was to do ethnography of the tourists visiting the Sámi village, but she soon realized that the busy tourists, who stopped in the village only for a short while and were always eager to continue their journey, were not warming up to her attempt to interview them, to ask them to show what they had bought or to show the pictures they had taken. She then contemplated focusing on the travel agencies, but abandoned this idea as soon as she realized that they were operating outside of Sámiland. Instead she decided to focus on the nexus that are more permanent in this quickly changing terrain: the tourism service providers.

Joan found out that hanging out with the people he researched required enacting relationships that ordinarily develop very differently out of the affinities that people find by attending the same school or living in the same neighbourhood. He could not just hover around silently, but had to take part in the talk and in the activities the others were engaged in. As he had to produce this affinity somehow artificially, he was initially very attentive to conversation topics, and to which individuals tended to control what the group discussed. He started by intervening minimally and in a non-committal way to simply not stand out. One particularly delicate point was relating to women. In one of the groups women and men's spaces of interaction were very delimited. Joan was allowed to behave a little oddly in comparison with other men, but he could not overdo it. As a man himself, he was not practiced in the way these women talked. So he trained himself to write down or mentally list conversation topics to sustain the intense flow of talk. He could not take part in conversations "as a woman," but he managed to act in a way that was not disruptive, to the point of being welcome at women-only outings. Eventually, this changed his own communication habits with family and friends outside the field, too. In any case, his access to each individual was different, asymmetrical. He could not get to know everyone in the same way.

When things do not work exactly according to plan, you may understandably have misgivings about yourself and others. You may feel that the planning you did was wrong, or that you are not honouring your commitment to your supervisor(s), your study program or your funding agency (as spelled out in your research design). Remember that this is a normal, frequent and in fact healthy sign; you are really exploring new ground. So allow yourself to step back, revisit the initial rationale and the key principles that informed your research plan, and renegotiate some aspects of the project with participants, colleagues and supervisors. In principle, there should be a way of achieving the same goals by reworking some aspects of the means, but sometimes you need to rethink some aspects of your design, and perhaps even of your research question. This is why questions have to be open, and why it is always necessary to be ready to decide that you may have been wrong about something.

In the next sections we will address each of the main strategies for constructing data in turn. We will discuss what it means to observe activity, elicit accounts and find material traces, and how to record them for analysis. Here, *strategies* refer to the kinds of activities you will engage in in order to, first, **identify** relevant data; second, figure out how to position yourself to **inform** yourself about it (usually called collecting data); and third, **document** it for analysis. We discuss the three activities that are typically involved in ethnographic work:

- **Observing**: Finding out what people do. What languages do they speak? How? With whom do they interact? While engaging in what activities? These are just some of the **doing** questions one can ask.

- **Eliciting**: Finding out what **accounts** people provide, that is, what people **say** about things: what they tell you or others about what they think languages are good for or what aesthetic properties they have; why they think their child isn't talking at the age of five; how they feel about starting to learn a new language.

- **Collecting material traces**: Finding out what material **traces** there are of activities and accounts, that is, what the traces are of people doing and saying things. These may be texts (minutes of meetings, newspaper articles, websites, legal documents, medical charts) or other forms (drawings, maps, artworks, music, artefacts).

The three typical ways we outline above are usually called *observation, interviewing and gathering documents*. It is this whole range of activities that are commonly called *field-work*. We discuss each in turn; we will then discuss documenting the data you construct.

3.2 Observing: Finding Out What People Do

3.2.1 What Is the Point of Observing?

As a research method, observation was developed in a period when scientists thought they could grasp the true nature of the physical and social world by standing outside it and observing it. As we have said, this is not an epistemological standpoint we share. Nonetheless, we continue to see value in setting aside preconceived notions in order to discover what else might be going on out there in the world that we normally fail to see because we are looking elsewhere, or stubbornly using our habitual frames of reference to try to understand everything. Through observation we are able to see new things, or see familiar things anew, and understand the world in new ways, in other words, to learn—which is what research is all about.

Observation is the signature method of ethnography. Sometimes scholars distinguish between *participant observation* and *non-participant observation*. This distinction assumes that there is a difference between observing while being engaged in activities with the people who interest you, as opposed to being on the sidelines (like a "fly on the wall"). In our perspective the distinction is not so clear-cut, since we are always engaged in some activity, and even flies on the wall have a viewpoint. We suggest, instead, that you think about your relationship to ongoing activities and participants, and about how you manage the obligations and entailments that stem from your multiple positions in relation to both participants and activities. It certainly makes a difference to understanding people, spaces, time and activities if you yourself are socialized into participating in them. However, at the same time, if you are too close to things, you risk falling into the taken-for-granted assumptions we all use in order to function in life, and missing out on what makes things tick.

Put differently, observation is about making familiar things strange, and making strange things familiar. It is about seeing the patterns in social activities that show us how social life is organized, whether or not we, or the people we are working with, are conscious of them. Ethnographic observation helps us notice things about actors, communication, space, time and the material world that we might not notice otherwise, and so it clears the decks for a fresh analysis of what is going on, and of what matters in a particular context.

3.2.2 What Should you Observe?

There are two sets of answers to this question, and you need to keep both in mind. Think of them as a two-by-two matrix as illustrated below. One axis makes a distinction between focusing on a synchronic description of what is going on at a given moment (i.e., "here and now"), versus following how interactions produce consequences over time in terms of people's access to resources or other relevant implications. This corresponds with the analytic distinction we set up in the next chapter (Moment 4) between the first step of analysis (mapping what is going on now) and the second (tracing its consequences for people). The other axis deals with "open" observations of everything you can see and hear, versus observations directed by your research questions ("focused"). It allows you to test your hypotheses (focused observation on the things your research design set up as the data you will gather) against what is actually going on, and things you might not have anticipated. You should make sure to cover the ground of all four cells. We will discuss Table 3.1 by column, from left to right.

(1) *Open/Now*. In response to the question "What should I observe?" this cell suggests that you observe everything in general, i.e., the *actors*, the *objects*, the unfolding of *time*,

Table 3.1 Matrix of Axes for Observation

	Now	Consequences
Open	1	3
Focused	2	4

the use of *space*. You need to ask who is doing what, with what (or whom), how long things take, where things are located or how they move through space. You need to do this as though you had never seen these things or actions or people before. This way you can be sure to inventory everything that might possibly be relevant to your research question(s), even if their relevance may not seem obvious to you in the moment.

(2) *Focused/Now*. In response to the question "What should I observe?" this cell suggests that you focus on things relevant to your research question. For us, that would have been things like: who speaks Catalan or Castilian, French or English, Sámi or Finnish? When do they do so? To say what? When what else is going on? Or it would have been things like who gets to play what role in the production of beer in a brewery, or of news at a media outlet, or of what might count as enjoyment on an evening out with friends.

If you only stay in the first cell, you risk getting stuck at the level of description and losing sight of your research questions. If you focus only on the second cell, you risk missing things relevant to your research questions that you may not perceive immediately. Instead, when you notice things that you don't understand, you can ask how they are connected to the processes you are interested in. When you think that you have a good description of the process, you can check to see if it accounts for everything you are seeing or hearing. This recursive, iterative process helps you formulate hypotheses and test them against what you see and hear. Now let's turn to the right-hand column.

(3) *Open/Consequences*. Here the aim is to identify sequences, or processes, to get a handle on connections amongst phenomena, and through them to identify what kinds of explanatory data might be available to you. For example, you notice a group of students in the corner of a playground and realize that they are all girls. You watch them for a while. A boy comes over to them speaking Spanish; he leaves after a short time. One of the girls goes around to another part of the playground and the girls from the first group call her back in Catalan. Is there a connection? If a girl goes away from a group, is there social pressure to remain? Does that pressure make it difficult for a girl to speak, or even learn, Spanish? If so, what are the relevant dimensions of the episode that you might want to start focusing on, such as gender?

(4) *Focused/Consequences*. Here the aim is to dig deeper, and project forward, allowing you to decide what might be the next step to focus on. For example you conclude from your observations in the previous cell that you need to focus on gender, language and space. Do the boys always maintain Spanish no matter where they are? Do the girls do the same for Catalan? What happens if they do not?

Another way to think about these four cells is to use them to identify and **understand patterns**, in the form of very basic correlations and sequences. You want to establish how actor-action-place-time go together, and what are the recurrences. You also need to see how these patterns connect up to the circulation of resources, how people make sense of them, and what value they give them. As we discuss further below, this is a process of constantly making and testing hypotheses, and adjusting observation strategies accordingly.

Identifying such patterns or relevant sequences is not easy. However, there are clues or telling signals that you can pay attention to. These generally come in the form of some kind of **violation** of the pattern to which people respond. For instance, a newcomer (maybe even you) gets corrected for doing something wrong; the correction tells you what the convention was that you broke. For example, Monica was once invited to accompany a researcher to an elementary school in New Zealand. To make the students comfortable with her, she did what she usually does in Canada: she sat on a desk. The researcher grabbed her arm and dragged her off, explaining later that it is considered worse than rude to put your derrière on a surface used for work or eating.

Another way to discover patterns presents itself when they get **disrupted** and people have to adjust. When regular outdoor events, such as recreation breaks at school, get moved inside by snow or rain, different people control the use of time and space. Or perhaps people realize that their decision has consequences they don't really like. For example in a francophone minority organization it had long been the custom that only francophones could participate in activities. One year, the members of the executive board decided it would be nice to have a party, an event to which family members would normally be invited. But then someone realized that the president was married to an anglophone who spoke no French, and the usual rule would exclude him. This caused a long discussion about the heretofore implicit convention, and whether under contemporary conditions, when more and more francophones were founding families with non-francophones, the rule might have to be revisited, and means other than French-only spaces found for the maintenance of French.

It is the reaction of participants, of course, which tells you some norm has been violated, so look for the laughter, the apologies, the yelling, the cold silences, the escorting out of the intruder, the commentary on what just transpired. You can try to work out from that violation what the norm was, what its value and meaning were and for whom (maybe the elders are shocked but the youngsters aren't), how the social order and the moral order are connected (What is shocking, enraging, annoying, pleasing, gratifying? What is it called: respect, immorality, rudeness, politeness?). And then look for how people work at restoring social order, at re-establishing the routine, the pattern you had spent so much time deducing from correlations of actor-action-place-time.

3.2.3 Why, When and How Should you Record These Observations?

Let's start with a few words about various ways of recording observational data. (Concrete tips and examples can be found in the Shop Floor section.) The major methods of recording are *fieldnotes* and *audio* and *video recording*, but you can also take *photographs* or *make maps* and *drawings*. Sometimes, recording requires two steps: turning jotted notes into an intelligible narrative, or transcribing audio- or video-recorded data. Also, many researchers directly involve participants in the making of these records, for example through keeping a diary or writing a blog. Here we will limit ourselves to discussing the more traditional method in which the researcher is centrally responsible for her own records.

No matter what method is used to record observational data (audio recording, video recording, making fieldnotes, photographing, collecting materials) they all involve selection, based on your judgement calls: whom to record? What to write down? Which angle to use when photographing? This is what we referred to earlier as data being constructed or generated rather than "existing" out there, waiting to be collected. There may be things going on out there, indeed, but you are responsible for the selection and the angle from which they are picked up.

Recording observations has two goals. The first is to help **establish patterns**. By taking notes at least every day that you are collecting data, you can take down the descriptions of what occurs and what co-occurs with what. At first, of course, you have little idea what any of it means (many people find this disconcerting and disorienting; think of it as being in discovery mode). You are uncertain about what might or might not turn out to be relevant. But by establishing a record over time you can see what does and does not reoccur, and under what circumstances; you can see what consequences might unfold over a time period longer than a day; and you can check your memory. Did this person ever show up before? Is this the same student who got kicked out of Science class last month? Is the article they are discussing the one I saw that person writing last summer? Do students start talking all at once every time the teacher organizes the class into small groups? How does the teacher respond?

The act of recording observations is also an act of **proto-analysis**, which is the second goal. You select what to attend to; you try to make sense out of how things seem to fit together. You fully engage with the experience through the act of turning impressions into data. Eventually you can develop *hypotheses* and test them against observations from the next day, week, or season, or against other forms of data. Because of the recursive nature of the process, records also allow us to go back to events after the fact when we want to test new hypotheses that emerge as we go along.

A practical choice that you need to make is whether to record information (in any form) while observing things as they happen or afterwards. The **advantage** of doing so in the heat of the action, so to speak, is that you are less likely to forget things. There are two major **other considerations** though. The first is that you risk not noticing things that are happening while you are concentrating on recording other things. The second is that you might erect a barrier between you and the people around you. It is difficult to participate and write at the same time, and if you are using a notebook or a laptop, the object may act as a physical wall separating you from the others, and could identify you as an observer. That might be a good thing, but you should at least consider its potential consequences. For research teams, it may be a solution to have one researcher taking notes and another participating in what is going on.

Certainly, it is important to think about what it means to people that you write (longhand or on a computer), draw (maps, pictures) or otherwise record what they say and do, in a language they might or might not speak or read, using modes of representation and technologies of communication they might be more or less familiar with than you (cameras, computers, digital voice recorders). One possibility is that you offer to let people read your notes, look at your drawings or photos, listen to the recordings you make (but don't force them to do so, obviously). Their interactions with your modes of data collection will not only help you form a relationship of trust, they may also help you understand what the process means to them.

After Joan had spent a few weeks with his participants, he was worried that they seemed to feel a certain sense of unease. He judged that this was caused by the fact that people had a very vague idea about his project (some more vague than others), so that they were wondering what exactly Joan was attending to about what they did and for what purpose. So Joan decided to develop his notes into a first draft of analysis, a general description or characterization of the groups of five to six pages, and gave it to the participants to read. The text was very welcome and it prompted discussion and commentary that was in turn very productive for the project.

In schools, students often express an initial curiosity about recorders, and want to use them. Younger students usually want to know how they work, and hear their voices played back; older ones like to make jokes or mock something or someone, often each other, or you. This initial round helps demystify the process, recalibrates the question of who is watching whom, and brings to light how students understand recorders and recording, and the nature of your activity.

Fieldnotes are a central, yet somewhat invisible, practice of collecting ethnographic data: we seldom see what people's fieldnotes look like, or hear accounts of how and why they were done the way they were, or hear about the process of turning these notes into telling accounts (the ones we get to see in the publications) of the topic examined. Perhaps this is because fieldnotes can be seen as a kind of backstage scribbling and they may seem too personal, messy and unfinished to be shown to any audience. At times ethical practices of anonymization may also be the reason why the fieldnotes cannot be shared; we promised to make sure that others will not be able to identify our participants, but we need to record identifying material in our notes, for our own purposes. At the same time, making fieldnotes, like any other research practice, is a skill that can be learned.

Fieldnotes can take a diverse array of forms of notes, writings and other materials upon which researchers base their observations. They come in different shapes and sizes, from very detailed writing to jotting down keywords and taking pictures of the key moment or actors in the activity. They are sometimes done at the same time as the activity, or afterwards based on your recall. Often fieldnotes made on the spot are complemented with more detailed accounts from the researcher, written after the event, related to the observed activity or people. They can be a kind of running log written at the end of each day, with fully fleshed-out details. Alternatively, fieldnotes can be organized into sets of separate sequences relevant to the topic examined, or they can be almost fully composed narratives with elaborations and interpretations.

We, too, vary in the ways in which we write our fieldnotes. For example:

Joan never was a very effective on-the-spot note taker, whether in class, in professional meetings or in fieldwork. So in his study he preferred to spend time after the event to turn his experience into a relatively structured narrative of what had occurred. In the process, as he tried to come out with coherent accounts, new ideas and hypotheses came to his mind, and he became more aware of what additional information would be good to test them and what strategies he could develop in the field to pursue questions.

Monica usually writes up her notes every evening or the day after observing, preferring to be directly involved in what is going on, but not wanting to let too much time erase her recall. There are exceptions to this; sometimes she wants to remember exactly what someone said, and has to write it down immediately or risk forgetting or distorting. Sometimes she wants to keep track of where participants are sitting or standing, and uses a quick drawing to note positions. Sometimes life intervenes and she has to wait two or three days before finding time to write up her notes. And sometimes she is in a place where not having a laptop or a phone or a notebook is odd.

Sari has often made quick notes on the spot, resulting in almost unintelligible jottings. Later in the day, or after an event she has written longer accounts. She also uses photographs as a way of documenting what was happening in an activity: what were the spatial arrangements, who was doing what, what came first and what next, who got involved, who remained on the sidelines. Together with the fieldnotes, this data helped her to identify key moments, activities, roles and participants.

To varying degrees, fieldnotes typically include:

- factual information (time, place, participants, sequences of events, length of the event, etc.);
- observations from our different senses (what we see, hear, feel, smell and even taste);
- notes on what was said, and on what happened;
- details relevant to the phenomena we examine (language choices, music preferences, food and drink prepared or consumed);
- questions and notes to ourselves, for example to find out more details about a specific event or person, or reflections for future observations.

Monica's fieldnotes from her school ethnographies tend, for example, to mark the ways in which time is organized (such as when classes begin and end, what is used to mark that boundary, how students and teachers shift their behaviour at those moments). She often draws the spatial organization of the school, classrooms and other sites as they become relevant (the playground, the soccer field, the parking lot, the cafeteria, the "smokers' area," the corridors) and how people situate themselves in and through those spaces. She notes verbatim things people say that seem relevant to her question and that she may hear in passing (the use of languages other than French, say, or comments people make about other people's behaviour). The bulk of her notes, though, are about the activities she observes, from formal classes to school assemblies, to lunch, sports events, concerts or anything else that happens in school.

Sari's fieldnotes from the tourism fieldwork tend to be an array of quick jottings of observations, what people say, the events and their effect on senses (what can be seen, heard, smelled, tasted, felt). She tries to write down the sequence of the events, descriptions of activities and the ways these activities are framed by the hosts or guides, and how the tourists react. She tries to pay attention also to what happens in the background: how the workers prepare activities or experiences, how everyday life continues, or how the tourists decide to do something else than what they were supposed to do (and become what Sari calls "jaywalking tourists"). Sari has a tendency to also accumulate pieces of the material environment that the tourists are surrounded with: brochures, entrance tickets, souvenirs, postcards. In addition to fieldnotes, we often rely on **mechanical recordings**, using audio and video recorders. In our digital age, we often tend to orient first to getting machines to record things for us. There is a lot to be said for what can be captured by using recording equipment that lasts longer than our notoriously fickle memory, which can allow us to revisit events long after they are over, and which can capture information at a level of detail far beyond our usual sensory capacity. We have all had the humbling experience of having been absolutely sure that it was the older man who spoke, when in fact the recording clearly shows that it was the woman beside him, or that she said she would be happy to change the rules, when in fact she hesitated so much in speaking about it that it would be fairer to say she was ambivalent. Or that we heard "lead" when actually she said "leave." Video recordings also afford many details that we cannot normally and reliably capture with notes and drawings, such as constant changes of position or of physical alignment between people, stares, or gestures accompanying statements. At the same time, let us express some caveats about using recording equipment.

Caveat 1

Audio and video recordings and photographs are not views from nowhere. We choose when and where to set them up, so they'll capture what is in their range and from a specific vantage point. Further, our ideas about what is relevant to record need to be understood as proto-hypotheses about what activities or which people are relevant. Indeed, such recordings need to be accompanied by fieldnotes which explain under what conditions a recording was made, and why we chose to make that particular recording, as aids to being able to interpret the data a recording captures. Having said that, some researchers advocate putting a microphone on a particular participant and just letting it run, in the absence of the researcher. We can think of this perhaps as trawling. This can certainly yield some interesting data, though it might be hard to interpret and it may raise ethical questions (for instance, people who have not consented may get recorded).

Caveat 2

Recordings do not speak in and of themselves. Just as we start really engaging with data when we write notes, or draw maps, we are only able to make sense of audio and video recordings by engaging with them. This requires multiple viewings or listenings, and some form of transcription. Transcription itself is far from a neutral act either, especially when we transform the spoken word or the non-verbal gesture into the written word. We need therefore to at least try to come to grips with the choices we are making.

Caveat 3

Recording often makes people more self-conscious of their behaviour, more attentive to social exposure or to other risks. This makes sense when you consider that good recordings always provide more detail and are taken as much more credible than anything you can say or write. Further, in the current age of surveillance, using equipment to record, as opposed to using a notebook, or even waiting until later to write up notes at home or in a café, is not a neutral act. Many people have good reasons to feel nervous about recordings, and you should think about what might happen in case your notes and recordings were to be subpoenaed.

The means that you use to record observations require spending enough time to get a sense of what is more or less intrusive, that is, comfortable for the people you are working with; establishing enough of a relationship so you can ask them how they feel about what you are doing and getting a sense of what works best for your goals. (Here is another moment where judgement calls are likely to be necessary.)

It is impossible to say how detailed your fieldnotes should be, how long, or when you should stop making them. It is impossible to provide a recipe for when you should supplement them with photographs, audio or video recordings or rely mainly on such recordings. Here are some general guidelines to bear in mind: You should stop when: (1) people ask or tell you to; (2) you can see that people are orienting to closure through the organization of temporal and spatial dimensions of the activity and (3) you keep seeing the same thing over and over again, and you are learning nothing new (the point that, in Moment 2, we called "saturation"). Of course, the first principle trumps the other two. And you should always let people know in advance that they should tell you when they want you to temporarily hit the (real or metaphorical) pause button, or when to press stop permanently. The Shop Floor section gives you some concrete examples of fieldnotes from our own work.

3.3 Eliciting: Finding Out What People Say

Why not just ask them? Finding out what people think (or how they represent it) can help you find out about people, events or other phenomena you would otherwise never have known to be relevant (or which would have taken you much longer to discover on your own). It can help you explain why certain things happen or why people do certain things (although perhaps not directly). It can help you understand better what matters to people and why. It can help you grasp how they understand the world and how they formulate this understanding in specific ways. Indeed, many of the hypotheses and "consequences" that you want to follow up can only be addressed with the help of participants' accounts.

3.3.1 Interviews as Accounts

Elicitation is a term generally used to refer to data collecting methods in which the researcher tries to draw out explicit accounts from participants. There are different kinds of elicitation methods or prompts that can be used, including photos, drawings and material objects. For example, Sari has asked tourists to share their photos as a prompt to hear their narratives related to what they considered the most interesting sights and things to do while in the village (it turned out, however, that the tourists were willing to talk about their experiences, but not really to share their photos). In other research related to multilingualism in a Sámi community, Sari asked people to draw language portraits, with different colours indicating different languages, to map daily activities, and to take pictures of people, events and places relevant to their Sámi language. In language biographical interviews, Sari asked participants to bring an artefact that was significant to their Sámi language repertoire, starting the interview with a discussion of that object (they turned out to include such items as books, handicrafts made by a grandparent and inherited jewelry).

For his focus group discussions, Joan printed cards in different colours with short questions or topics such as "can a boy and a girl just be friends?" This way, rather than voicing the questions aloud and imposing his agenda very ostensibly in the conversation, he allowed people to circulate the cards and discuss and joke about the possible questions that might eventually be brought to the common floor. But usually we carry out elicitation without such prompts or forms of non-verbal representation. Let us call all these forms of elicitation *interviews*.

Interviewing is a data collection method used across several disciplines and for multiple purposes (consider, e.g., marketing interviews, customer satisfaction interviews, etc.). It is intended to **elicit** something from participants. In qualitative research, interviews usually refer to in-depth, semi-structured or loosely structured forms of interviewing. Sometimes the term *ethnographic interview* is used when researchers combine close observations and interviews with key participants. Interviews that emphasize people's own accounts of their life histories and trajectories are often termed *narrative interviews*. Often interviews are organized around something that serves as an initial topic, as Sari showed: a photo, a story, a meaningful object about which people have stories to tell.

While interviews may vary in terms of their framing, formality and length, the key logic and rationale for us to collect interview data is to try to ask questions that elicit experiences and understandings of the people we are interviewing (cf. Mason, 2002). In this sense, ethnographic interviewing elicits people's narratives, accounts and articulations, their discursive construction of themselves and others, of the events and their conditions and consequences. Interviews can also be used to collect explanatory data (say about the conditions under which something happened, or the position of a participant with respect to the resources involved), and undertake the work of tracing the circulation of people, resources and discourses (see Moment 4).

The first thing that we must recognize when engaging with interviews is that we can never find out what people "really" think. The idea that thoughts are unique individual possessions lying somewhere in people's minds is a cultural idea, and not one that everyone shares. We ourselves tend to believe that what we understand as thoughts are formed in social interaction. We believe that one person can think many, often contradictory things at different moments or situations, and even at the same time. As a result, we believe that getting access to someone's thoughts and their perceptions of their experiences really means being present when they provide a *narrative*, or some kind of verbally explicit *account* of something that they put together for our benefit, sometimes right then and there, sometimes drawing on narratives they have already formulated and used in some ways under other circumstances. Further, if the content of those narratives comes out of social interaction, then it will matter a great deal under what conditions they emerged. It is important therefore to look not only at the narratives themselves, but also at the conditions in which they are provided, for whom, and over the course of what kind of activity.

It is also often important to first spend time observing under what conditions accounts emerge, who provides them and who the audience may be. Accounts are conventional forms of communication that emerge in everyday life, and it may be of interest to sample some of them, including to see how they vary according to context or addressee. These accounts may well give you plenty of data on their own. If you still want to ask for other accounts, then by then you will have a better idea of how to do so: who might be open to your approach, where the encounter might best take place, who else ought to be present, what other activities might coincide (sharing food, perhaps, or listening to music) with it.

No matter the type of qualitative interview adopted, the key issue for us when interviewing people is that it is a situated and co-constructed activity: it is a "real" communication event in sense that it is influenced by all participants (the researcher included). Interviews rely on people's capacity and willingness to verbalize, interact, remember and share experiences and understandings of the topic examined. Researchers have to be willing to listen to stories without pre-existing conceptualisations of what the outcome of the interview should or should not be.

3.3.2 Interviews as Socially Situated Events

As we said earlier, asking (and responding) is not as simple an activity as one might think. Just like everything else, it is a situated activity. "Asking" is a culturally variable practice (both in form and meaning), so it is best to learn as much as we can about the shapes it takes and what it means to the people we are working with. In some communities, it is rude to ask direct questions. As journalists know well, people in powerful positions may feel threatened just by the fact of being open to interrogation. Even when left unanswered, some questions may be damaging. It may also be important to find out if some kinds of people (often elders) are the appropriate people to approach, at least at first. It may be inappropriate to be alone with members of a different gender category. And probably in every community, people will have ideas about when a conversation can take place, where and in the presence of whom. It is therefore always useful to explore what other ways of eliciting accounts might be available and meaningful in the context in which you work.

Let us share a few examples of the difficulties involved in eliciting accounts from our own work and that of others. In a now classic example, Briggs (1986) describes his mystification while trying to learn about ceramic production practices in New Mexico. All his direct questions (What is that? Why are you doing that? How do you make that?) were met with silence. Forced to stop asking questions, he started paying attention to accounts as they appeared in the community he was living in. He discovered that no one there ever asked a direct question. Most of the time, information on the kinds of practices he was interested in was embedded in shared activity. Sometimes indirect statements could be used to construct a frame in which a narrative could be offered. But one individual could never force another to provide a direct account. In this case, "learning how to ask" meant learning to stop using direct questions, and start attending to context-bound verbal accounts.

For Sari, interviewing small schoolchildren about their linguistic repertoires and practices did not go anywhere; the kids mainly responded to everything with a brief "I dunno." She therefore worked with the teachers to find another way to elicit accounts. They designed drawing and photography activities around language practices and identities. These joint activities (an example of collaborative ethnography) provided Sari both a possibility to observe the kids but also to talk with them about their languages and practices and experiences around them. In this case, "learning how to ask" meant learning to stop using direct questions and instead taking part in familiar forms of classroom activity. After his ethnography of Barcelona youth, Joan undertook a project to sample a much larger number of life history interviews of adolescents from different areas of Catalonia. For practical reasons, he decided to contact the interviewees via the school network. Although participation was in theory voluntary, he found that many interviews were much less productive than expected. Particularly the young men of the profiles he had researched earlier did not trust him because they did not know him at all, and they associated him with the school authority who had in practice recruited them for the interview. It was really hard to get anything beyond monosyllabic answers.

The silences Sari and Joan encountered need to be explained. They can be a symptom of the unequal relations of power between those of us familiar and comfortable with a verbally explicit style associated with education and the state (and its power), and those who are marginalized by these institutions. Sociolinguistic research by its very nature is logocentric; we tend to fetishize language, even in situations where too much writing and talking can be counterproductive. The French linguist Robert Lafont found this out in the 1970s (Lafont, 1979) when he and his team were trying to mobilize speakers of Occitan, a minority language, to fight for their rights. What they failed to account for was that, as university-based researchers, they were understood as having better Occitan than anyone else, and so the people they wanted to speak to were intimidated. Monica found this out when working with parents unfamiliar and uncomfortable with the verbal forms of schooling, which are also the verbal forms of the interview; or with adolescent boys, very polite, but also for whom masculinity precludes a great deal of talk, especially with a woman.

Silence can also be an act of resistance. Doctors ask us to reveal intimate things about ourselves, lawyers want us to provide accounts which can have major consequences for our lives; border guards interrogate us. For indigenous people, ethnographic research has often been exploitative and harmful. Many people have had brutal encounters with the askers of questions. Some people may explicitly refuse to talk to you; it is important to be attentive to what that means no matter what your position (as more or less powerful, more or less familiar) and relationship with the people you are working with.

Finding out what people think, then, requires first and foremost that you understand the **interview as a social activity**, which, like all social activities, is traversed by relations of power and a variety of available meanings. You can therefore approach the issue of how to ask in two ways, both of which take this frame into account.

One important way is to attend to what actually goes in the interaction between you and the person, or people, whose accounts interest you. Clearly, **silences** matter. So too do **explicit comments** about the encounter, the account, your relationship or the context. For example, in Monica's experience, people often make comments about not knowing whether they can answer her questions or provide the right information. This indicates that they understand the interview not to be in their control, and to be oriented toward the establishment of some kind of truth, or correct account, which the interviewer will be in the position of judging. People often also make negative judgements of their French skills (as Lafont found), or alternatively, they correct Monica's French. These are all modes of negotiating relations of power, at the same time as they are strategies for establishing what the encounter is supposed to mean. In Joan's experience, it is common to get a torrent of commentary of this kind the moment he switches off the recorder. Once interviewees have done the job of putting their views "on record," they feel they can turn to the more personal relationship with the researcher by providing off-the-record thoughts that may be crucially relevant to what is being researched.

In addition to understanding the interview as a social activity broadly, you can attend to the *discursive framing devices* which orient both to the content and the context of any account: hedges, hesitations, pauses, reformulations, pronominal choice—the whole arsenal of stance-taking mechanisms is relevant to understanding what people mean when they say something. This is most important at the analysis stage (see Moment 4), but you can attend to such phenomena "on line" as it were, while the conversation is unfolding. The same is true of attention to how an interview is structured as an interaction: who **controls** the **turns at talk**, and how the **sequence of turns** works, how topics are introduced and developed and in whose terms. For instance, one crucial aspect of any analysis of an account has to do with topic initiative: did the participant bring up a given topic herself, or was it mentioned because you asked? In interviews we typically want to obtain the forms of representation and of reasoning that participants normally employ. So if we rush interviewees to comment on a topic, we may also impose our own forms of framing and expressing that topic. To prevent this, we try to design and conduct interviews in a way that prompts and questions are as ideologically "polyvalent" as possible, and that interviewers may freely shift from one topic to another, without needing prompts. However, no two interviews are ever the same, which means that you will have to keep intervening and making decisions "in real time" as to what to bring up and how to do it.

3.3.3 Interviews and Decisions

Typically, the people we want to interview are key participants in the activities we have been examining or key actors associated with the topic in question. So, for example,

Monica interviewed representatives of francophone community organizations and institutions when she wanted to find out who was in a position to define what "minority francophone" might mean in public discourse. These were people who headed the organizations recognized by the government as representing "the francophone community," and hence eligible to apply for funding. They were the ones the media went to for commentary on issues related to the politics of bilingualism, or francophone rights. Joan tried to interview all the members of the youth cliques he studied, which was a manageable number. However, some members declined to participate. Later on, he found that those who had declined were precisely the ones who were peripheral to the forms of gender display that he eventually came to describe. Sad as it was to miss these interviews, this was an important datum in itself. His hypothesis was that these persons were subject to constant sanctions for their (mild) deviations and were wary of exposure. Sari interviewed people who worked for tourism business in a village that was marketed as a tourism destination: tour guides working in the key sites, marketing staff in those sites, and Sámi business owners and seasonal tourism workers in the village.

A question that is repeatedly asked by our students, colleagues, reviewers and funding agencies is how many interviewees are needed? Once in the field, once you have met the actual participants, or once you have started interviewing some of them, you may have to revisit your plans and make further judgement calls based on your objectives and anticipations. At first you might not know who the key participants are, or you might not get direct access to them. Educators are often extremely busy, or you might not know which students are the "popular" ones, or whether you should approach the medical or administrative director of a hospital first. In these cases, you might need to do background interviews with, for example, spokespersons of associations or institutions, or workplace directors or bosses, or simply any person who might be willing to talk with you about the research topic and, in this way, gradually navigate the terrain and relationships of trust and access. Otherwise, you might start with group interviews in order to gain a sense of people's meanings and understandings, and then perhaps proceed to more focused interviews with all or some participants. In still other cases, you might hold group interviews after individual interviews in order to get a better sense of what is shared and what is not with all interviewees and to invite their reflections on your own interpretations. Or the other way around, as Joan's story at the end of the chapter shows.

Sometimes these conversations are recorded, other times we rely on our fieldnotes. This choice depends on multiple factors including, for instance, the ethics and consent of informants (see also Moment 2). It may be that the research topic is so sensitive for the informants that they do not wish to be recorded, especially in a context where there has been abuse of public records and personal information. Sometimes recording an interview makes the informant aware of the "weight" of her words, and hesitant to discuss a certain topic or to be considered an "expert." In such cases, requesting to record an interview could be a deal breaker for the participant. It might also be that the researcher does not want to record the conversation for the reasons listed above, or simply because it feels unnecessary (although we do feel that recording allows for much richer possibilities for discursive analysis, and do facilitate data retrieval). In any case, we want to insist that both ways of doing ethnographic research interviews—with or without recordings—are equally valid, and the choice depends on the specific needs that we have in that context and the possibilities or obstacles that we encounter.

In our attempt to understand informants' experiences and understandings of the research topic, it is often helpful to ask them to give examples that illustrate the topic from their point of view. Respondents may be tempted to give "generic" answers, e.g., what they "usually" do, or what unspecified "people" do, "as a general rule." This may be a perfectly legitimate defensive strategy: if you do not say what you do or think, you do not risk any sanction or need to justify yourself. But then you may end up with interviews in which the material produced is very vague. So instead of asking very general or abstract questions, it is usually fruitful to ask for interviewees' specific accounts, experiences or memories relevant to the topic examined. This relates to the ontological commitment of the whole business of doing ethnographic research: as we are interested in how big social processes operate situationally in people's lives, the depth and complexity of these processes, we need to ask about specific, situational rather than general questions.

For example, it is usually a bad idea to ask people "what is your identity?" Instead, one might ask a question like: "The mission of the school, as stated on your website, is to provide a means for French to flourish. Can you tell me about that?" When discussing informants' language repertoires, Sari often asked about how people remember their language use at key points of their lives rather than asking about their language skills or competences. So she would ask for example if they remember what languages they used and heard around them when they were a child. And what happened when they went to school, entered working life or started a family. Joan always includes in his interviews questions about key experiences connected to language: he asks participants to retell something that happened to them and made them change their understanding about language issues, or to start using languages differently. He also presses for people to recall occasions in which they have been censored or praised for using language in a particular way.

In ethnographic interviews, you try to come up with prompts and questions that maximize the interviewee's ability to produce situated, contextual knowledge about the processes and experiences relevant to your research questions. One part of this is careful planning based on what you already know about your site. Another part is flexibility: throughout the interview, the interviewers need to "think on their feet" or even think aloud, and listen carefully, picking up verbal and non-verbal cues from the social situation and the dynamics of the interaction. Similarly to any other interactions, interviews seldom go exactly as planned, although it is rare that they also deviate completely from the plan. So in preparing data collection, it is good to be prepared for changes and aim to find a balance between the expected and unexpected, more flexible and more fixed structure. Just like writing fieldnotes, interviewing, too, is a research skill that can be practiced and developed. In his first research involving interviews, Joan decided to do a "pilot interview," a first interview with a person of a similar profile but not from the specific target groups. When he listened to the recording, he found out that he spoke two thirds of the time, which seriously restricted the options for the interviewee to voice her own mind.

Finally, interviews are also often productive activities that may have material and ideological implications. They may well create a space for reflection and dialogue that participants had not experienced before in relation to the issues that you raise. Thus, they may reflect in new ways about the subject and perhaps make new connections. In this way (like in conventional talk therapy) the interview experience itself may be transformative for the individuals or for the groups involved. This raises new political and ethical questions. Some of them have been aptly addressed in the literature on "action research," i.e., research that includes some form of direct political transformation in its goals. In that sense, interviewing is not a bracketed experience, but one that participates fully in the rich texture of participants' experiences and knowledge production, as it does in ours. This is why in some circumstances it may make sense, for instance, to interview people more than once to capture how their views evolve.

3.4 Material Traces: Other Voices

While much of what we do is ephemeral everyday activity that leaves little in the way of a trace, there are nonetheless many things that do leave material traces. This is also a relevant source of data. Social actors frequently inscribe their participation and get inscribed in social institutions through texts: for example, medical, educational and criminal records historicize subjects. Institutions themselves operate on the basis of legal, financial and communicative records that often need to be kept for accountability and transparency. Some institutions actually focus on accumulating and preserving texts. And, of course, the mediated world around us provides an abundance of multimodal texts from the Internet and social media, which have provided new means of textual and audiovisual production, consumption and retrievability. Some materials can be generated through research processes, e.g., diaries, biographies, photos, drawings, documentaries, etc. More and more people construct their own narratives through social media, posting on YouTube, Vimeo, Snapchat, Instagram, Facebook, Twitter and so on (at least those were the popular platforms when we wrote this in 2017).

Many of these are language-related texts, and we will mainly discuss these. They may include things like budgets, advertisements, job descriptions, annual reports, memos, school records, correspondence, informational brochures, websites, Facebook accounts, media coverage, recruitment or orientation packets, contracts, records of court proceedings, posters, minutes of meetings, menus and many other items. But others take a variety of other forms (maps, drawings, tools, clothing), and you should be attentive to all of them. For example, in a high school, you can learn a lot about what the relevant social categories are by looking at how students dress and listen to their music. As in good detective movies, any small detail may be important.

So depending on your research design (research questions) and the ways of collecting the data, you might end up with *textual data*, e.g., documents, media texts, legal and historical documents. For example, Sari makes use of reviews of the key tourist destinations and sights in Sámiland provided in social media (such as the site TripAdvisor), as it opens an interesting window onto how the value of a tourism experience is constructed. In his latest projects, Joan has found that institutions provide a wealth of information on their websites that he earlier had to gather through interviewing. This has made him remake the process of interview design, using the websites not just as "data to be analyzed" but also as material through which to engage in dialogue with participants.

You might also collect *visual data*: pictures or video recordings taken by you, provided by your informants or circulating publicly through social media. This data may well be multimodal as is often the case with social media or interaction data. For example, Sari pays attention to how iconic Sámi indexes (dress, reindeer, symbols, colours) are re-used in tourism advertisements and websites. One of Monica's participants pointed out to her the appearance of stealth art on the telephone poles of a francophone town, which took two forms: colourful abstract art, and brief sayings (in both standard and vernacular French) photocopied in black and white on small flyers. Someone was clearly trying to say something to the citizens of the town.

Material data includes artefacts or items that you collect from the site (e.g., souvenirs, postcards, receipts) or that are showcased in your site (e.g., items on sale, art, handicrafts, food). When examining together with a colleague the souvenirs that the tourists bought when visiting a Sámi village, Sari bought the most popular ones (according to the salespeople) for a closer examination. During his fieldwork, one participant gave Joan a penknife as a present. In a time in which those knives were often used in street assaults, Joan wondered for a long time about the meaning of the present.

Aural data (e.g., multilingual announcements or the choice of music in different languages) or *spatial and temporal* arrangements can also turn out to be important data for your research: how classrooms are arranged, whether class is announced by the ring of a bell, how town boundaries are patrolled, at what time it is considered appropriate to show up for a drink with friends. Sari pays attention in the tourism sites to Sámi language use or Sámi music, as a way to see if aural resources are used to create a feeling of indigenous space. Joan paid a lot of attention to who was seen often close to whom and more or less separate from the main group, as a way to gauge who were the main producers of discourse on language and gender, and whose practices made them (materially) peripheral. Monica found that a school's decision to confine smokers to a space behind the school created a space where other (often illicit) activities could go on outside the scope of surveillance of school authorities.

Such materials are situated differently than spoken exchanges, but they are equally amenable to analyses of power relations, management of resources and diachronic processes. Documents and textual artefacts are invested with varied forms of symbolic power, in terms of who produces and uses them, and they can be revealing data for critical language research either on their own or as prompts to be discussed, for example, in interviews. Material traces provide you a check on, or elaboration of, elicitation and observation data; they may tell you something about institutional processes that help explain activities observed and accounts provided; they may help you understand what resources are important to your participants. At times, textual, visual and spatial materials may be the only data that you will have access to, for example in examining past events or when tracing a historical development of a current debate or practice.

In Sari's fieldwork in Sámiland, for instance, many of her informants referred to legal texts, like language laws (or the lack thereof), when talking about their language biographies. When Sari asked tourists why they decided to visit a particular village and to take part in a particular tourism activity, some informants told her about a particular text in a travel magazine that captured their attention and prompted their decision. People also produce lots of discourse material themselves: tourists may be active bloggers or reviewers of tourist destinations. The tourism service providers carefully craft the material they make public on business websites and social media accounts. They can also use signs (e.g., written in Sámi language), pictures (e.g., of reindeers), and artefacts (e.g., the Sámi flag or a shamanistic drum) to create an experience of an authentic Sámi place for tourists.

One of Joan's projects involved research on the teaching of Catalan to adult immigrant women; here one important piece of data was the textbook and other teaching materials used in classroom activities. First, these materials provided a wealth of implicit statements about how participants understood that languages were learned, what aspects of language were important to learn, who the learners were and even what forms of social relations were sanctioned (e.g., who performed domestic tasks). Second, the way these materials were provided (free of charge, or not) and the way they were actually used and circulated during the activities had also implications for all these issues, and left in turn additional traces in them (students scribbled things, teachers added corrections). Joan also took often pictures of the blackboard before it was cleaned off for new tasks.

Thus any texts, pictures and artefacts relating to the place, people and activities we study may become part of our data. Similar to interviews, texts can also be interpreted against the big research questions, by using, for example, discourse analysis (as we will see in Moment 4). And similar to interviews and observations, these materials, too, are produced in a specific context. As ethnographers and discourse analysts, we want to know as much as possible of the conditions of the production of this kind of data, too.

3.4.1 Strategies for Collecting Material Data

There are a number of strategies to consider when deciding what kind of material data you might collect for your research. Here we provide the most common ones. However, as happens with other modes of data collection, collecting, organizing and analyzing material data takes time and resources and should be delimited by a reasonably consistent plan. In the time of the internet, smartphones and scanners, it may well be that there are more potential materials out there than you can actually handle.

The first and generally most productive source of material data consists in what your informants have made relevant when you observed and interviewed them. For instance, the tourism services providers Sari interviewed and observed kept referring back to various tourism development projects that had provided support and marketing material for local entrepreneurs, in addition to holding training workshops where different marketing materials were produced. In order to find out more, Sari searched for documents about these projects: project descriptions, reports, training material, websites and marketing material. In this process, Sari also found media coverage about related events, as well as participants' social media comments about them. In the end, Sari took part in one of the project's training workshops to observe for herself what was happening there. This was a way for Sari to produce a discourse inventory of the key site she was examining. Monica and her team examined the material used for training call centre representatives in order to find out what kinds of scripts were preferred and why. What kind of persona were the call centre representatives supposed to project, to what kind of client? How did this persona fit into the company's goals? How were the scripts articulated with the way work was organized? What effect might this have on how workers were evaluated? During his fieldwork, Joan was especially attentive to any form of cultural consumption to which research participants oriented. In Barcelona, bars usually have on hand print media (magazines, newspapers) for the clients to read. Joan's participants in one group never touched the newspapers, while they sometimes picked up sports tabloids, and they sometimes bought music magazines. Checking the types of texts present in these publications, and how participants selected what to read, was also relevant information.

It is also very often advisable to avail oneself of data that can relate to the historical development of the phenomena that you are studying. You might need to go back to archival data (e.g., land records, municipal council meeting records, media archives) to find the historical roots of the current debate or conditions. For example, what kind of documents would shed light on how the particular village started to be branded as an authentic tourist destination? This kind of data would allow tracing back the genealogy of the discourse of the village as an authentic tourism destination. What kind of documents would help understand the rise of the call centre as a means to replace fishing and manufacturing in the New Brunswick economy? You might need to check secondary data to gain, for example, background information about the amount of investments in the region, and increases or decreases in the number of inhabitants, workers or visitors. Joan, for instance, checked census data on language and other demographic factors to choose the neighbourhoods in which to do fieldwork, and used these data to build a sense of the local context in which participants lived.

When going through these documents you might want to keep an eye out for **moments of "cracks."** These could manifest in the data as disagreements, contestations or multiple (conflicting) views, and reveal both the stakes and the stakeholders. When you have a lot of material to browse, it is often a good idea to take this as a selection procedure: to look for trouble, so to speak. In each case, the development of conflict may flag questions about who count as legitimate participants when making decisions, about what they value and why, and what potential consequences are planned or feared. Rather than systematically scanning a specific source, it may then be more productive to investigate this conflict further, i.e., to undertake a small textual ethnography of this debate and relevant discourses that allows you to understand what is at stake and for whom. In terms of data collection, this would mean going back to archival data as well as current media, legal and policy documents. It might also lead you to observe council meetings, for example, where these issues are debated and decided, and to interview people involved in making these documents or implementing the decisions. This kind of data collection is yet another example of the rhizomatic approach: you start with one nexus to follow a yellow thread, which you found to be tangled with a green thread, leading you to yet another nexus.

Usually you end up with pieces of all kinds of data, textual as well as visual and material, and are not quite sure what to do with them all. We will talk about analyzing data in the next chapter, but at this point it is good to remember that everything we collect might end up becoming research data (or not) and, for that reason, it is important to keep track of its trajectory and identification: where, when and how did you find or collect it?; who has produced it?; and what are potential copyright issues?

In sum, you have a wide range of possibilities for generating data. You may have to make some choices about what is feasible, and whether you prefer to generate multiple forms of data around a smaller field, or use one form over a wider field (often this is interviews, because they are easier to schedule, and take less time). In all cases, you will need to think about generating data that allows you to both describe and explain, and about the claims that you can make on the basis of the data you generate.

3.5 Summary

In this chapter, we have discussed the third key moment in critical language research: identifying and collecting data. We argue that the data is not "out there" but is constructed through human activity that we, as researchers, are part of. Doing research involves making constant choices and requires us to be reflexive about them. We understand this as a process involving a series of "judgement calls," with consequences for how and what kind of data we collect.

In ethnographic research, the actual data collection is often called *fieldwork*. We argue that it is underpinned by three key interconnected aspects: access to the field, relationships to the people in the field and constructing the data. The three key ways of collecting ethnographic and discourse data are *observing*, *interviewing* and *collecting materials*. In each, the aim is to elicit situated accounts, articulations and artefacts that are helpful in producing situated, contextual knowledge relevant to your research questions.

To do this, you need to find an organic balance between flexible and fixed plans for data collection. This key moment also involves thinking of the whole life cycle of your data, including data management and archiving. In critical language research these are not simply technical matters, but highly political and critical questions, related to ethical commitments in your research and to your own social position as knowledge producer.

In this chapter we have:

- Discussed the nature of fieldwork as the central mode of producing descriptive and explanatory data in critical ethnographic sociolinguistics.
- Emphasized that fieldwork requires making important judgement calls during the whole process.

- Presented observation, elicitation and examining material traces as the three main modes of fieldwork.
- Examined the ontological basis of the knowledge each mode can produce, that is, as experience, as accounts and as traces of situated social practices.
- Discussed how to negotiate the affordances and limitations, both practical and epistemological, of each mode of data collection.
- Discussed the ethics and politics of different forms of fieldwork.
- Presented methods of recording data: especially fieldnotes, and audio and video recordings.

Keywords: fieldwork, data collection, judgement call, ethics, politics of knowledge, interviews, observation, documents, fieldnotes, recording.

Interviewing in Context

Joan's experience of interviewing in his Barcelona ethnography provides a good example of how data gathering activities influence each other. He still looks back at those interviews as the best in his career. Most participants came with a keen interest and were willing to make their views heard, some of them polemic, respectfully but assertively. In later projects, he has found people generally more guarded and less open.

With hindsight, Joan believes that the interviews benefited from the way he had done observation, participation and focus groups earlier. He had spent a few months hanging out with two youth cliques as they met in the evenings and late at night. He had invested the first weeks building rapport with the participants and making sure that his presence was not disruptive or especially noticed. To do so, he had to learn to perform the type of talk that took place in collective conversations in a bar terrace, but he also had to get to know each participant individually and find issues and lines of conversation that he could develop with each of them. The issue was not so much to become invisible but rather the opposite, to acquire the type of visibility that is expected of each group participant. Even if they knew that Joan was doing a study, in practice they could only feel comfortable if they knew how to talk to him in a way that made sense in that particular context. In this first period he chose not to take notes or do recordings or comment on anything that would distract him or the others from what the groups felt were the legitimate activities and forms of participation in that context. He did keep a diary that he wrote from the privacy of his home and which he also used to list conversation topics and material that he could use to build up the rapport. Joan started recording spontaneous conversations once he felt that this was settled and he himself could attend to the ongoing talk like all the others.

By chance, Joan decided to start a second period of fieldwork by distributing copies of a short report of his observations that included a preliminary description and characterization of each group. The prime motivation of the act was to display openness in relation to the research process and provide opportunities to respond to his interpretations. The gesture had, however, wider consequences than the one intended. The participants were piqued particularly by his observations about gender relations; and although they did not engage with the issue immediately, they debated it at great length on the occasion of the focus group discussions he organized later. Interestingly enough, they never actually responded to Joan's description, but got into a lively debate amongst themselves about aspects of gender relations that they felt affected how they related to each other and to others. Similar lines of reflection were also pursued in relation to language, social inequality and other political issues.

It was at this point that Joan started asking each participant individually to have a private conversation (an interview). Interviewees then mostly used the occasion to continue all these conversations, conversations that Joan had perhaps partially triggered but which somehow connected with issues that they cared about and sometimes discussed themselves. For some the interviews were also a good occasion to get their views heard because they had not had as much time to reflect and talk in the focus group, and probably because their views were still evolving and they needed to further elaborate on them. The result was a wealth of very rich and nuanced accounts about experiences and moral reflections that proved very productive analytically.

Thus the success of the first interviews had very much resulted from the long intervention of Joan in the dynamics of the two groups and which had eventually led them to incorporate in their debates aspects of the research questions adapted to their own specific agendas. Joan's later experiences of interviewing did not have this wealth of experience and relationships behind them: interviewees did not know him so well; many of them had not thought much about those issues either. However, the first fieldwork need not be idealized either: a few group members had declined to participate in the interviews. And when he started analyzing the data, Joan suddenly realized that all the refusals had come from people who occupied ambivalent positions in relation to the dominant gender dynamics of the groups. The no-shows, so to speak, were directly relevant to the research object and had to be addressed analytically.

Thus, the data yielded by each form of data gathering was intrinsically dependent of the relationship that he had built with the participants, and each form of data gathering fed into each other in specific and partly unpredictable ways.

Following Threads in the Field

In my experience identifying and collecting data go hand in hand. When I am able to identify people that I need I then know that I would like to interview them. And after interviewing, new suggestions for relevant data usually come up: a suggestion to interview guides, for example, or to look at the municipal tourism development plan. That is then what I would do next—follow the traces emerging for the data. This relates to the processual nature of qualitative research: when we are in the field we learn and understand the people, place and phenomenon we are studying better, and this leads us to the next nexus in our research rhizome. Sometimes it leads to reflection and to changing some of our research questions and focus. This is what recursivity means to me in practice: it refers to the cyclical nature of qualitative research, dynamic research design, and emergent data and questions.

In the project on peripheral multilingualism, my plan was to spend the first two years of the four-year project collecting a multi-layered but interrelated data set from the key sites by interviewing people taking part in tourism activities (locals, tourists, customers, tourist service providers) and by collecting ethnographic data (on-site observation and participation, using videos and photographs). I also wanted to collect discourse data that included promotional and informative materials, policy texts, web texts, online conversations, advertisements, tourist guides, media texts and relevant linguistic landscapes. My thinking was that interviews would provide me people's accounts and stories about tourism, while ethnographic fieldwork would allow me to observe the practices in action. Data from media, marketing or other such sources would help me find out how authenticity was discursively constructed in public spaces. Across all the data, I would be paying attention to circulating expressions of authenticity and the ways in which they were enacted and worked on. The plan was also to collect statistical information about the number of tourists and economic plans, in order to understand the value of authenticity in this particular market.

I identified eight key sites from the tourism trajectory, planning to interview people who worked in these sites (they were small, so interviewing key people meant perhaps one to three interviews per site), and observing host-tourist interaction and tourist activity on as many occasions as possible. I needed to observe the key interactions and activities enough to see a range of ways in which authenticity was produced and consumed, keeping an eye out for recurring patterns and disruptions. I estimated that this would require three to five observations of activities that I knew would typically last one to two hours. From my preliminary fieldwork, I also knew that tourists would be hard to interview, but I was hoping to be able to talk with them, even if only briefly. To counter this, I included in my social media data comments and reviews made by tourists related to selected sites over the two years of data collection. At this point I did not know how much data this would amount to, though I knew that each site typically contained some tourist comments.

Finally, all this data collection had to be embedded in a relationship of collaboration with the people that I was researching, with opportunities for dialogue (often discussed as knowledge mobilization or knowledge transfer by funding agencies). I tried to operationalize this commitment by building in activities such as discussions, meeting, talks, working on various documents at various times throughout the life span of the project (policy documents, funding applications, guidelines).

I was aware at the time already that this approach would yield lots of data. To balance this, I was counting on the relatively small size of the place and my ability to return to the key sites over and over again. I was also working with a team of researchers. But I needed to parcel out activities over the total of four years of funding for the whole project in ways that allowed for making connections between all the different sites and subprojects, engaging with participants and preparing publications and next steps. I set a time limit of two years for primary data collection and analysis, the third year for complementary data collection and further analysis, and the final year for making connections with relations, with participants and publications embedded throughout.

So in practice, while examining tourism development in Sámiland, I collected data by interviewing, observing and making fieldnotes, and collecting key documents, e.g., from media, municipal economic development and statistics. My interviews varied from very informal discussions into carefully planned narrative research interviews where my aim was to try to collect people's narratives of the changes in the region and the community. My observations included making fieldnotes, taking lots of pictures and sometimes also video and audio recordings. The textual data was collected by saving the key documents to a hard drive.

4 Fourth Key Moment
Analyzing Your Data

4.1 What Is Analysis? What Does It Feel Like to Do It?

In the previous chapter, we discussed how to identify and organize your data so that you can describe what is going on, explain it and figure out what difference it makes and to whom. In the Moment we are addressing here, you now have to work with your data, and actually figure out what is happening, why and with what consequences. Most importantly, you need to figure out what story the data tell.

Data analysis is the way that researchers build new knowledge on the basis of their data, and so it is a key step in your transformation from being a knowledge consumer to a knowledge producer. This is the longest chapter in this book, and it has been the most complex for us to write as well, because the act of creating something new is not easily broken down into a series of clear technical steps. Moreover, the act of creating or saying something new is not really something that can be planned in predictable ways. Instead, we show you the ways of doing analysis that we have found useful.

At this point, the trees are plentiful, but the forest seems hard to discern. Often people feel that their data is far too thin to be worth anything, or on the contrary, it seems overwhelmingly endless. Others may be overconfident, not realizing that it is in fact necessary to lose your bearings in order to see things you might otherwise have too easily collapsed into the old, familiar frames of reference. These are both normal reactions. This chapter aims to help you navigate between these extremes, with strategies for slowly making out the forest as you go along.

These strategies can be described as four sets of activities. We think of them as *mapping*, *tracing*, *connecting* and *claiming*. These four analytical activities allow you to figure out what kinds of people do what kinds of things, why, and with what consequences in terms of their ability to gain access to valued resources, or to influencing the conditions that give those resources value. They lead you to the argument you want to make: that something is happening, for specific reasons you identify, and it has observable consequences. Because these activities are as rhizomatic and recursive as any other part of the research process, you have to decide to enter at some node or another, and see where that takes you. The analytical processes that drove your research design and data collection will have led you to some preliminary hypotheses. Use them to decide where to begin mapping, what to trace, and which connections to look for. Putting together what you find in that way allows you to not only make claims, but also to assess their scope.

Each of these steps relies on mustering both ethnographic and linguistic evidence. Your research is not only about language; indeed, your sources of evidence are also mostly constituted by linguistic materials in and of themselves. This is a signature strength of a sociolinguistic or discourse analytic approach: it allows us to see exactly what kinds of processes are involved, to materially examine exchanges and follow their consequences, and to identify which linguistic resources are involved in the makings of inclusions and exclusions, the makings of value, and so the makings of difference and inequality. We therefore spend some time in this chapter laying out some of the ways you can mobilize the materiality of linguistic form and practice in your analytic procedures.

As linguists, we are fully aware that we cannot summarize and map out fully in a few pages the affordances of an ethnographic analysis that is sensitive to language. It would carry us beyond the scope of this book to do justice to the potential of very diverse fields like pragmatics, discourse analysis, conversational analysis, or variation analysis. Moreover, we are not really willing to present linguistic phenomena as separate from other features of social action or social actors. But we do believe it necessary to identify what we see as the three main dimensions of communicative practice through which language is especially useful as a lens for identifying material that is socially relevant: *form*, *sequence* and *metacommentary*.

So, first, there is the matter of distribution of linguistic *form* in speaker's practice; here we attend to how any bit of language, short or long, can be used to make the contrasts on which categorization rests. These can be used to mark off groups (those people speak Catalan, these ones speak Castilian; those ones affricate palatal stops before high front vowels, these ones do not). Speakers can build on these distinctions to use those associations to construct other meanings, symbolically positioning themselves in the speaking position of one or the other group, calling into play what those groups and their relationships might represent (more or less power and prestige, femininity and masculinity, urban or rural lives and so on).

Linguistic form, as conventionally understood, is often amenable to description and categorization, and hence relevant in the first stage of analysis (see *mapping* below). However, there are subtler elements in talk that are often much more important to a social analysis, such as the fact that people speak in different *voices*. People are complex social agents who enact different personae (adopt different *voices*), which in turn point towards specific personal, social and ideological *stances* (people are not always 100% behind what they say, they do not always speak with their own words). The linguistic contrasts used to index them can also be used to make other kinds of differences, such as organizing information (distinguishing, perhaps, old from new information, or what I believe from what others say), organizing interaction (distributing roles or turns at talk), or the nature of an activity (has the meeting begun now?), including of a communicative activity (or what are conventionally called *genres*: is this a lesson? a speech? a chat?).

We will see below that voices can be both mapped and also be treated as *traces* of wider processes.

Finally, linguistic forms and voices can be assembled to identify what we call *discourses*, understood as historically embedded, relatively enduring and systematic ways of signifying events, practices, and relations through semiotic resources. Identifying discourses requires connecting forms, identities, activities and spaces. They contribute to our understanding of what is taken as the "truth" or "knowledge" in a given situation as well as of the construction of identities and subjectivities of the people we work with (and our own).

Sequencing is also a productive dimension of linguistic analysis. Here we can see how the use of linguistic forms one after the other can structure relationships and discourses over time periods both brief and extended. We can see not only who deploys what, but also how that plays out in terms of who controls participation, whose ideas get taken up, what resources are exchanged. Attending to communicative practice over time allows us access to the short- or long-term (often perverse and unintended) *consequences* of what people do and how they do it, within the constraints they encounter, as well as how processes divide, merge, converge or otherwise do or do not intersect. In the next section, we examine some examples of how the logics of face-to-face interaction bring about specific social configurations.

Third, we have access to *metacommentary*. As people talk, whether to us or to each other, they often signal in a variety of ways what they think about what people are saying or doing (including themselves). This may be explicit ("I'll sound stupid saying this, but . . . " or "I love your accent"), or implicit: people might sigh, hesitate, reformulate, laugh or comment indirectly. Even as social research itself may arguably be characterized as metacommentary on the communicative constitution of social relations, it is worth bearing in mind that social actors (research participants, colleagues, stakeholders) are capable of analyses and counter-analyses themselves that constitute both our data set and the field upon which we project and defend our claims.

Now let's turn to each of the elements of analysis, and examine more closely what each might consist of. Given that each research project has its own specific focus and questions, you will need to translate our terms into your own experience and plans; our examples may not match exactly, but the comparison can shed some light on what your project uniquely contributes to the literature.

4.2 Mapping (and Categorizing)

Mapping refers to the activity of organizing your data (or elements in your data) in a systematic way, informed by the rationale of your work. In simple terms, mapping involves addressing the question of **what there is**. So, going back to our forest and trees metaphor, this analytical activity involves mapping out what there is in your forest, or in your whole data set. Depending on what you are researching, you might map everything (making an inventory), or you might do a pilot mapping and see what the forest looks like if you map different kinds of trees, or different kinds of animals living in that area, or sounds or clearings.

More precisely, mapping in critical language research is about figuring out first what relevant categories are at play, that is, what the meaningful boundaries around linguistic or other communicative forms, people, things, spaces, time and activities actually are: what kinds of resources are at stake, for what kinds of people (in what social positions), in what kinds of activities? What social practices do they engage in? How do they mobilize language to engage in activities? Crucially for critical language research, this activity also involves mapping out what resources have value, for whom, and under what conditions. Second, it involves situating them in relationship to each other, in time and space.

Mapping provides a good way to get familiar with the details of one's data and, at the same time, to gain a general overview of its scope, i.e., to see what terrain it covers. You want to both be able to take in the extent of what it covers (and by extension, get a good idea of what it does **not** cover), and see what it contains, so that you can later explore how its elements connect to each other.

The basic "zones" or "features" of the map are the *categories* that you see as most relevant, understandable and transparent. By categories, we mean the various logics or principles that you use to organize, group or sort out your data into an order or into smaller groups. To go back to the idea of a skein of multi-coloured wool: will you sort it by colour? By texture? By what you are going to make out of it? Deciding what logic you will use to sort your data is the first step in the analysis. If you are unsure, you can test your idea. Sort part of your data according to one logic (say, colour)—what happens? How about if you sort it according to its use value? What happens now? Which one is more helpful in finding an answer to your research question; or do you need to find yet another possibility?

Having said that, for the purposes of the kind of research we are mainly discussing here, it is important to pay attention to the relevant types of social actors, to the resources they exchange, to the activities in which boundaries are made and resources produced, circulated, consumed and valued, and, of course, to the communicative forms involved, e.g., languages, forms considered "dialects" or "jargon" or other linguistic or semiotic features, both in terms of how communication is involved in regulating boundaries and the participation of people in activities, but also as a potentially valued resource in and of itself. These are the building blocks of a critical ethnographic sociolinguistic and discourse analysis: how language is involved in the making of social difference and social inequality.

You need to discover these categories in two ways. The first is in what is observable to you: who deploys what linguistic forms and practices, how, when and where; how language relates to how people orient to each other, in space and time. The second is in how they talk about the making, unmaking or continuation of categories, that is, how they are rendered meaningful through discourse.

4.2.1 People

Your people categories should be defined on the basis of concepts or properties relevant to your research questions. For example, in the brewery, Monica mapped out which employees spoke French, which spoke English, which used both. She mapped out where they were to be found in the organizational structure (that is, what jobs they had), whether they were male or female, more or less how old they were, whether and how they moved around the building, who interacted with whom during what kinds of activities. You might want to map out, instead, who uses specific communicative practices, such as social media; who talks in class and who is silent; or perhaps what kinds of questions are found in what kinds of standardized tests. Joan started by identifying styles of speaking, and found that in one group, men used swearing, banter and sex-related language combined with a specific accent reminiscent of Southern Spanish; whereas women in this group and both men and women in another group spoke in other ways. He then used these linguistic contrasts to build different categories of gender display.

It is helpful in this process to also continually evaluate to what extent your research participants actually fit your assumptions, and make hypotheses about unexpected or unlooked-for profiles of people. For instance, Monica thought that her map showed that all the lower-ranking workers were francophone, until she came across one anglophone in that category, who worked alone supervising some storage tanks (unlike the francophones who worked in teams on the shop floor). Sari wanted to identify native speakers of indigenous Sámi languages, and found out that people were reluctant to claim such an identity for themselves. Instead, they referred to other people in the community as native speakers. They were, however, willing to share stories about how they encountered different languages in the course of their lives.

More than one people category may be relevant to one single person. And you will likely see some people moving across boundaries. So, for example, the new francophone arrivals in the school Monica studied navigated the social order in different ways depending on gender. Boys started participating in pick-up soccer games with their classmates on the playground, which they could do without speaking English. Through that participation, they learned English, and became part of the "bilingual" category. Girls had no such pathways available to them, and built francophone social networks across class groups. Joan found that one of the groups was strictly monolingual. No one used any language other than Spanish. However, he later found out that some of its members presented themselves as bilingual in other contexts with other young people or with work colleagues. Sari worked with many people who counted as "Finns," "Sámi" and "Northerners," sometimes in different contexts, sometimes simultaneously.

However, it is worth recalling here that your people categories are fundamentally social categories that people enact (or are seen as enacting), rather than the actual material bodies that do the performance. The ability to identify such nuances in the enactment or animation of specific social categories is one of the affordances of close linguistic analysis. Joan found that he could understand the meaning of Catalan and Castilian for his participants by mapping out the types of characters that people mimicked when they code-switched into Catalan or Spanish: formal authoritative persons, popular characters, non-masculine voices, or faulty speakers. Monica has found consistently that people make a distinction between kinds of French, opposing "Québécois" (even when spoken by people who have never set foot in that province), indexed by low pitch, specific phonological features (such as affricated palatal consonants before high front vowels) as well as prosodic ones, and use of specific morphological, syntactic and lexical variants, to "français de France," and sometimes, "normal French." Sometimes these are consistent preferences: in the high school the former was used consistently by the "smokers," who tended to congregate behind the school, skip class and be assigned to lower academic streams. Sometimes the same person can use more than one: one student, usually known as a "normal French" speaker with bilingual practices, could morph into a speaker of both Québécois and français de France on stage at general assemblies or in class. Here metacommentary can help the mapping and its interpretation: you hear the use of labels, or discussions of who uses what and what it sounds like; Luc might be jeered when he spoke français de France with friends, and applauded when he did so on stage.

People categories are sensitive material and should be handled with care when presenting results. We shall discuss this aspect further in the section on ethics, but for now we simply wish to point out that your audiences will pay special attention to whatever people categories you use and will expect empirically supported and finely tuned definitions, and for good reasons. People categories are the ones that "travel" most easily outside academic discourses and into public debates and governmental procedures that may be consequential for specific social groups. For example, Monica once wrote a paper with a colleague in which they used the labels "franco-dominant" and "anglo-dominant" to refer to students who were seen to use one language or the other most often, that is, they referred only to frequency of practice (Mougeon and Heller, 1986). Very quickly, these labels were taken over by the education system to refer to perceived individual linguistic competence, and used as the basis for the development of programs and curricula aimed at increasing the competence in French of "anglo-dominant" students. Joan has recently been using the term "new speakers" to focus on how people cross linguistic boundaries and hence may participate in language communities different than their "native" ones. However, he has tried to avoid precise definitions of who exactly qualifies as "new speaker" for the fear that they might be misused in political debates or administrative procedures, for example, in order to distribute resources differentially in schools, or perhaps exclude people from immigrant, refugee or citizen status. Sari found out that some of her research categories, such as "super-Sámi" and "neo-Sámi," are used by the community members, often with humour, to describe a person's language and cultural practices and trajectory.

4.2.2 Resources

These are the things, whether material or not, that have value and are exchanged; they are implicated in the making of the boundaries that divide one category from another by virtue of where their circulation is facilitated or blocked. Mapping linguistic resources can include documenting the occurrence of: (1) different linguistic or paralinguistic features (e.g., a given "accent"); (2) different languages, linguistic varieties or registers and (3) different discourses or genres. This can also refer to a relatively systematic presentation of, or a stance respecting, a topic that circulates across particular communication events, for example, discourses of language endangerment, of language proficiency or of the value of multilingualism or of English. We need in particular to attend to the value of linguistic resources and the effects of deploying them. For example, the "smokers" described above not only spoke "Québécois," they also tended to form their bonds and boundaries by sharing material things connected to their bodies (cigarettes, make-up, earphones) or money (they were constantly asking for a few dollars). We can see these practices as modes of building trust (the interest or necessity of which we then of course have to explain via tracing and connecting). You couldn't enter into that exchange network if you didn't speak French the way they did, but at the same time just speaking it was not enough on its own to earn trust. In Sámiland, category membership as a Sámi is formally decided on the basis of a number of criteria; it is not necessary to speak Sámi to be recognized as one (since many people were assimilated by force), and conversely it is possible to be rejected even if you speak Sámi. Recognition gives one access to a number of formal political and economic resources (such as voting in the Sámi Parliament and reindeer herding), as well as the less formal legitimacy that adds value to, say, your tourism business. Here the question arises of what role speaking Sámi (and which variant of Sámi, recognized by deployment of which forms) does play in category membership and both formal and informal distribution of access to the resources Sámi control.

4.2.3 Activities

Where do you find those resources and those categories of people? What activities do they engage in? You might have observed these, or perhaps people have been telling you stories about the things they do, or you may have a collection of documents whose content signals activities in which they are used (report cards, tourist information, telephone books, catalogues). For example, Sari collected data related to tourism activities. The first round of mapping this data involved grouping the activities around those that involved Sámi cultural practices or elements in them, and those that used other elements, such as nature, climate, or Arctic flora and fauna. She also mapped out what kinds of people participated (e.g., where they were from, whether they travelled alone, as couples, as families, groups of friends or organized group tours), and what kinds of resources circulated there (e.g., performances of reindeer herding, sledding, "typical" food, jewelry, souvenirs). She also saw tourist buses stop in front of only one of the several souvenir shops in town, leading her to think about how this particular souvenir stop was constituted as an activity. Joan was interested in what it meant to be a "Catalan bilingual." He started by mapping out the moments in people's lives when they first began to use a different language to participate in social relations and activities. These turned out to cluster at specific points: when entering kindergarten or primary school, when starting secondary school, when entering university, when they started work, with specific sexual partners or with their offspring. Monica found that in the brewery, French and English were kept apart, except in the weekly meetings of the engineering department and in interactions between a bilingual secretary and either her anglophone boss, or members of staff asking her for translations of English into French. In the high school, English was kept out of humanities and social science classes, but admitted in science labs, albeit with intense flagging, metacommentary and translation.

4.2.4 Space, Time and Material Objects

Activities unfold in space and time, and people use them to signal when things start and when they end, as well as who can participate and what can circulate there. And in addition to what people do and the ways they speak, there may be a wealth of materialities that are relevant to your questions, particularly how these materialities get inscribed in social practices: dress, objects, tools, food, etc. Together with her team, Sari made an inventory of the souvenirs available for the tourists, and categorized them according to the images or representations of Sáminess and of the North they used. The life of youth cliques in Barcelona revolved centrally around specific spaces (bars, discos in designated areas of the town), times (late at night, the later you went to bed the more successful the night was supposed to have been) and objects (the design of spaces and props in bars, the possession of specific clothing or narcotics). For example, some men carried hashish, allowing them to organize control of the ritual of smoking it and to gain prestige by sharing it generously (it was expensive). In order to participate in the activity, some women took it on themselves to help prepare the joints even though they did not smoke it themselves.

There is an important aspect to mapping that should inform our approach to the whole data set, which is the principle that there should be a place for everybody or every phenomenon that is relevant. Although there may be good reasons (mostly practical) at some points to reduce or delimit the data set, these decisions should follow the logic of sampling and derive from the research questions. Otherwise, the "map" should include both the phenomena that are easy to categorize and those that are difficult, both the expected and the unexpected ones, both the "straight" specimen and the "deviant" one, both the rules and the exceptions. Indeed, anomalies (such as the anglophone worker in the brewery basement) are extremely important analytically, because they test the adequacy of your categories. If you can find an explanation for why they are anomalous within your map, they may strengthen the plausibility of your analysis. If you cannot, they require you to go back and figure out what was wrong with your categorization that prevented you from accounting for them, and to work out a categorization that accounts for them as well as the others.

A practical tip: Sometimes mapping can be quite laborious work, and if you try to attend to absolutely everything you see and hear and read, this stage could go on forever. Remember to use your hypotheses to guide you to what is relevant and what is not. At the same time, this is also a moment where you might discover that there is a much more important thread for you to follow, or a different formulation of your research question that makes more sense given what is actually going on. For example, one of Monica's students was interested in what difference it made to Portuguese women working in a Toronto factory to have access to English classes in the workplace (Goldstein, 1997).

In mapping out language choice, she discovered that, contrary to the intent of the government-funded program, the workers, who came regularly to class every week, never actually used English when they were working. At first she despaired that her thesis had just vanished into thin air; then she realized that, on the contrary, this apparent paradox was the really interesting thing to examine.

Generally, mapping is how you get started figuring out what to look at more closely. It shows you that you need to ask questions about why a weekly engineering department meeting is different from other activities, what is so special about that bilingual secretary, why men and women youth groups in Barcelona act differently, or why Sámi does or does not show up in tourism activities. To start answering those questions, you need to start *tracing* where the people, resources, activities come from and go to, across space and time, and how the deployment of language facilitates or hinders those circulations.

4.3 Tracing

Tracing is an analytical activity used to find out more about the specific categories and resources that you are focusing on. At the "mapping" stage, we put together types of activities, types of people, types of resources and we worked out plausible descriptions of them: "smokers," "Sámi," "tough guys"; in and out of class, out on the town, reindeer hunting; academic success, job promotion, community prestige. *Tracing* focuses on the processes involved in how people and resources circulate over space and time, and how activities persist or change. We pick specific categories of people, practices or phenomena and we follow them: we examine where they appear, when, how often and in what conditions or with what implications. Going back to our forest and trees metaphor, let's say that your (informed) decision is to focus on butterflies in your forest. You would first need to map all the kinds of butterflies that there are in the forest, and then try to find out as much as you can about these butterflies: for example, how long they have been in this forest, what and how much they eat, how they move around different areas, or whether they live in other forests too.

More specifically, in critical language research *tracing* refers to following the circulation of these categories: How do resources get produced, circulated, consumed? How do people come to the activities where that happens and where do they go next? Where do people and things come from and go to? How do activities start, unfold and end? In language biographical interviews, many informants used the category of Super-Sámi to refer to certain type of (old school) Sámi activists who have been visibly and actively involved in promoting Sámi rights and language. Who were these people? How had they gotten involved in activism? Were there people around they had worked with but who are no longer on the scene? How had the bilingual secretary learned both French and English, and why did her boss not speak French despite a forty-year career in the brewery? Did the gender differences in the youth groups play out in other arenas of participants' lives, e.g., in their families, in their jobs?

Tracing is about the elaboration of *trajectories* or patterns of *circulation* of activities, people and resources. It involves tracing their histories: where do they come from? How did they end up here? This step sets up a relationship between the descriptive and the explanatory data, since you will discover which threads tend to end up where and when, that is, under what conditions they can move in time and space, and where.

The notion of *trajectory* reminds us that any element of social practice has a **history**, that it draws from past events and past experiences of the participants and contains elements that constrain options for future developments or consequences. The biographies of participants may be the most obvious examples, particularly when our questions have to do with the reproduction of social difference and their consequences: languages, social class, race, gender or sexuality are not elements that participants can create anew on the spot, and their position in relation to these axes of differentiation is something that gets negotiated along the lifespan—even at times in the interactional moment. But these (and other, often more local) categories are connected to processes of producing and circulating resources, and hence to the interests of social actors. This is why biographical information, commonly collected through in-depth interviewing (though also at times through visual means such as drawings or photographs), is often sought after in ethnographic studies. However, it is not only people that have histories, but also activities, resources and discourses, in the sense that social actors commonly draw on ways of saying, roles and forms of constructing objects that must be somehow familiar to participants even if they adapt them or transform them in unexpected ways in a particular situation.

Tracing need not always literally involve following the evidence across different contexts (which is not always possible); it also involves treating the material effectively as a *trace*, as pointing to an elsewhere. The different speakers that appear in talk, the "voices" people express, can show you the way to trace the circulation of specific people and resources across different life contexts. Thus, for Joan, the fact that people mimicked characters associated with one language or another in Catalan indirectly revealed the types of situations in which participants had come into contact with this language: on TV, at school, at work. So these linguistic "special effects" provided clues to people's biographies, and Joan could further explore these clues through accounts found in interviews and focus groups. In these accounts, it became clear that people changed their patterns of language use in other areas of their lives. He could then trace what kinds of people changed their patterns and when.

People, activities and resources are also spatially distributed. We pick up on ways of doing things that we see in one space, and import them into another. We ourselves circulate among a variety of social spaces. The notion of **circulation** expresses the idea of movement associated with space and time (in both a sociocultural and a physical sense) and it directs our gaze to the ways in which people, specific practices, discourses and artefacts are either kept static or put into motion.

Although it may appear very simple in principle to note down which people, practices and discourses seem to be able to appear and where, or seem to "move" more easily or not, the implications can be profound. Some people may be able to access only what goes on at particular places and times of the day. Some people may feel that they can say some things only in specific locales and/or in the presence of specific people. Some statements or ways of talking may be seen as appropriate for many contexts and some for very few. Thus describing common patterns of circulation of activities, people and resources is a first important step to understanding how processes of inclusion and exclusion are performed, how specific ideologies gain legitimacy and how all these may be consequential for people's access to material and symbolic resources.

One could do the same with linguistic features that index different things in different conditions, and have different values. So for example, Monica found that French-educated African immigrants to Canada arriving in Toronto were shocked by several things: the fact that students at school spoke English so often, that their French sounded so different from the French they were used to, the fact that French class in school had different kinds of activities than the ones they were used to and the fact that most people in Toronto expected blacks to be English-speakers. In order to understand any of this, it was necessary to understand how the forms, bodies and practices in question circulated from one context to another, with different interpretive frames and with different meanings and values.

Tracing, then, helps you discover where and how things happen, in what sequences or cycles, and under which conditions, so you can take a closer look at why that might be the case. It helps you see how social categories form, and whether they are stable and unified, or shifting and blurry. It helps you see what linguistic resources are valuable for whom, and where and how people deploy them in navigating the varied circumstances of their lives. It also helps you see what is meaningful to people. In that sense, tracing is about laying the groundwork for identifying *discourses*, which bring together different but interrelated sets of social practices, social relations and views. For example, Sari looked for statements related to Sámi language. She then examined how these statements were organized and expressed, including, for example, whether and how Sámi is constructed as valuable or important, for what reasons, for whom, what it does or does not mean to speak it or write it and what kinds of activities are associated with it, on what kinds of fields: do people talk mainly about linguistic variability? Multilingualism? Do they connect Sámi with fields like education? Politics? Tourism? Finally she traced how different discourses on Sámi languages circulated in social networks and across discursive spaces, for instance in the media, in education, in public statements, in speeches, or in private conversation.

A practical tip: be aware of the danger that tracing can become just another round of mapping. While it might well be that you need to do another round of data mapping, when you undertake tracing, you are supposed to go "deeper" into your data by finding the evidence about how the features of your map came to be where they are. In most cases, you will not have absolutely all the dots of a trajectory or circulation and you may have to construct it out of partial or incomplete material (as with Joan's voices, Monica's new francophones, or Sari's "elusive" native speakers). In rare cases, you might want to go back to fill in some gaps, but you can usually work well with what you have; all data sets have limitations, there are always threads you cannot follow and threads that you will have to plausibly reconstruct to the best of your abilities and your data.

Through tracing, you are setting up a relationship between descriptive and explanatory data. Now you have to figure out the connection between the two: what does one have to do with the other? In other words, you are moving from description to explanation, in getting prepared for making an argument based on your data, instead of just describing it.

4.4 Connecting

Connecting is the means we use to provide an informed explanation for what we have mapped and traced in the two previous interrelated steps of the analytical processes. It formulates relationships among the categories, trajectories and circulations identified and defined earlier, in order to discover the conditions and consequences of circulation across spaces, and thereby explain what happens to people and resources under what kind of conditions and with what consequences, what kinds of transformations may happen and why. This is the foundation on which you build up your argument.

It requires making hypotheses as to the relationships among the categories and processes you identified earlier, leading you to build a bigger picture. It can involve making connections across your data (the different kinds of butterflies in your forest seem to each specialize in specific kinds of trees), or to the previous research (how your butterflies are similar to or different from the butterflies in the last forest you studied) or to other things going on in or around your forest (some of butterflies in your forest lose their favourite trees to logging, or to climate change; others are not affected). It allows us to see what makes specific categories and trajectories possible, viable and reproducible, that is, how our categories and trajectories connect with concomitant conditions and processes. It is not the statistical probability that something will happen that matters here; rather, we look for substantive, meaningful connections and consequences.

Connecting turns your focus to the details of the observable processes where things actually happen. This is where ethnography's ability to provide substantive explanations meets the ability of sociolinguistics and discourse analysis to show in fine-grained detail exactly how people combine the multiple forms of communicative resources available to them (including the ones they make up) to make boundaries, make value and produce observable consequences. In that sense, we want to argue that this is where ethnography earns its stripes: as a powerful mode of explanation.

For example, once Sari was able to identify clusters of expressions around the topic of Sámi language, she could both trace their circulation and make connections within the discursive forms and with other discursive expressions. She could, in the first instance, look in detail both at the choices of linguistic material at work and at the workings of the argument or narrative. She could identify the category labels used and link them to comments, say, about how someone was an important and valuable member of the community, or how it was a mystery as to why someone's application for status was rejected or accepted, or how it was understandable that someone didn't speak Sámi because she had been sent south to school when education wasn't regionally available or how important it was to fight for Sámi-language education locally. Monica could link the use of code-switching and features of vernacular French in interviews with working-class women in service positions in a bilingual town to their admiration for a European colleague's "wonderful French," as well as to their hesitations around claiming strong positions on such questions as what languages they spoke to their children and to their narratives about being discouraged from using French by anglophone husbands or paediatricians. She could then place these accounts in relation to those of middle-class women in Ottawa, where the federal civil service is a major employer and prizes French-English bilingualism; in these accounts there are no hesitations, there are no admirings of the interviewer's French, but there are narratives of militant struggles for the use of French in daily life, all the features of standard French, and flags around isolated English terms or reported speech (such as, for example, a supermarket cashier's response in English to a question in French).

Thus discourses too must be set into context, so you see what conditions help explain their occurrence; they can be set into sequences, so you see what the consequences are; and they can be set in relation to their characteristics and to each other: do they co-occur? Are they oppositional? Complementary? Perhaps most importantly, in doing this you can see how discourses of language intersect with discourses of gender, of race, of religion or of class.

At the same time, connecting also shows you how identity categories are historical and social, discursively constructed and enacted in situated interaction, and therefore, too, subject to change. Connecting allows you to see why people do what they do, in the ways they do it: why A and B always co-occur, but A and C never do; or why they co-occur here and not there; or why C and D always occur one after the other. This is the moment where we see the exchangeability of symbolic and material resources, their evaluation, and what that means for individuals and the categories they orient to. The next step will be to make the connections to the resources (un)available to people to explain what their interest (however completely unconscious and possibly unintentional) might be in practising inclusions and exclusions. What resources do certain kinds of people mobilize with the consequence of gaining access to an activity where other resources circulate? What happens to them? What happens to those who try and fail? So for example, Monica found that the anglophone manager was the last of a series of management employees the company had recruited as trainees from Scotland in the mid-20th century. The others had either retired, or moved to other parts of (English-speaking) Canada to open new branch plants. The new young francophone manager was the first to be recruited out of technical, post-secondary training—which hadn't even existed in francophone Canada until about eight years before he was hired. He was hired and promoted over the more senior anglophone manager at the time the language of work policy was being implemented. Code-switching in their meetings allowed them to save face in what might otherwise have been a tense situation. Working-class males in Barcelona had little access to the kinds of white-collar jobs dominated by Catalan speakers. Their jobs required a certain kind of tough masculinity associated with the work done by Spanish-speaking immigrants from southern Spain. For them, speaking Catalan meant giving up that masculinity and the solidarity that comes with it. Women, however, tended to have service jobs in which their bilingualism was an asset; in addition, of course, as women they were less in conflict with the connotations of femininity associated with Catalan.

The connections you make are relations. You make hypotheses out of simple adjacencies (things that tend to appear together), coincidences (things that often appear at the same time in the same places), sequences (things that tend to follow each other in time or space) and the interrelations among them. The same applies to the trajectories and circulations, as you constantly query why some behaviours or developments are possible, or more durable, and why some are apparently not. At the same time, it is important to also account for sudden changes, anomalies, cracks and absences when you compare your findings in the data or when you put your findings in relation to previous studies. Just as mapping anomalies allows you to test whether your maps and accounts of circulations hold, examining the relationship between the typical and atypical when you make connections will allow you to get at what really makes a difference in explaining why people do what they do, or what happens as a result of their activities. Sari found that the one place where Sámi identities were mocked was in television performances by a female Sámi comedy duo. These women were recognized as Sámi, and thus were positioned as mockers of self, not other; that is, their position allowed them distance from the dangerous position of being seen to reproduce the majority devaluing of Sáminess in mockery from southern Finns. Through humour, the duo was able to foreground the tensions around the ways in which "Sámi" category boundaries are fixed or unclear, as well as around the combination of stigma and romanticism with which Finns and tourists treat it.

Connections point to explanations to answer the question: why? Explanations are the bedrock of our claims. More broadly, they allow us to return to our research question and answer not just what, under what conditions, with what consequences for whom, and why, but more broadly, it allows us to answer the question: so what?

4.5 Claiming

The final step of your analysis will be *making a claim*. Here you have to judge what mapping, tracing and connecting allow you to say in relation to your research questions, that is, about how and why language matters—in other words, what is at stake, and for whom. Sari might claim that that using Sámi languages for economic purposes in tourism (e.g., in branding or marketing) has created new values for these languages as indexes of something unique, different and local. This is a form of commodification, which requires branders and marketers to orient themselves in a new way to indigenous languages now that tourism has become one of the world's major industries. Joan claimed that his data showed the complex ways in which the social and gender inequalities that structure employment were projected onto different forms of appropriation of linguistic resources that one could notice even in informal contexts not subject to institutional regulation. Language policies encouraging the use of Catalan would need to take such complexities into account. Monica claimed that the "language law" did not cause French to become the language of work in the brewery; rather a host of political economic factors (such as the expansion of the Canadian market, better educational opportunities for francophones, increased reliance on technical training over apprenticeship) helped explain the increased presence of credentialed francophone managers who needed to be seen to be performing French as a way to consolidate their new privileges, but who were able to mobilize forms of *sub rosa* English to avoid overt conflict and maintain access to the knowledge of anglophones.

At this stage, it is particularly important to think about the ontological *status* of your data, and about the *scope* it covers. Regarding *status*, you need to remember to think about what you can say, for example, on the basis of having seen something, on the basis of someone having told you about it, or on the basis of your close analysis of the relationship between the form and content of their account. For example, many researchers worry because they have learned about certain "facts" in interviews, hence as reports that can potentially be challenged. The solution to this quandary is to be clear about why you think something did or did not happen. Regarding *scope*, you need to ask whether your data allow you to make claims only about the participants, activities and resources in your study, or about the wider categories and processes they were chosen to represent. What is the range of things your claims ought to cover? What can you really say about what? As we said earlier, you'll need to remember the difference between what people do and their accounts, and look carefully at both consequences and commentary before attributing meaning to anything. By the same token, you need to ask whether your case is representative, and if so, of what; or telling, and if so, why. Crucially, these two questions depend as much on your data as on how your data figures in the wider context of the research in your field. Is there conflicting evidence in other studies? Again, of what kind?

Let's work through one detailed example. Below you will find a transcription of an interaction that occurred in the mid-1990s in a small city in Catalonia. Joan spent several months visiting a Catalan language and literacy class offered to immigrant women by a charitable organization for which people volunteered to work as tutors (Pujolar, 2007). The extract in Table 4.1 is from a pedagogical activity in the form of a definition game in which the player, in this case the student Maia (a Senegalese woman), must describe an object drawn on a card so that her fellow students can guess what object it was, but without ever naming the object.

Although the learning activity was supposedly devised to create space for students to practise language, it is the tutors (Cris, Carme, Alejandro) who did most of the talking. In this section (and in most of that class) the other student "players" stayed quiet. How to explain this? In the actual recording, one piece of evidence is the rapid pacing of the sequencing of turns, with little lag time between them. So possible hypotheses are: (1) the student was unable to produce Catalan, and so remained silent; (2) the tutors thought she was unable to produce Catalan, and so jumped in and performed for her; (3) Maia was unused to such games; or (4) simply needed more time or (5) was worried about self-image in front of the tutors or fellow students. In any case, the tutors decided to fill the silence, unwittingly cutting Maia off from a chance at a turn at talk (and the other students to participate in the game). Another piece of internal evidence is the sequence from line 18 onwards. Here Maia said in Castilian that she didn't know how to talk, and then that she didn't know how to talk "like you." The tutors interpreted this to mean that Maia did not know the Catalan word (or perhaps much Catalan at all), and offered Maia the possibility of using Castilian, though she then said in Catalan that she

Table 4.1 Excerpt of Catalan Classroom Activity With an Immigrant Woman (2002)

Original	English translation
1 Cris: ara maia tu.	*Now you're on, Maia.*
2 Carme: ho has d'explicar eh? # no **3** diguis qu' és.	*You've got to explain it, OK? Don't say what it is.*
4 Cris: (no) pots ensenyar-ho.	*You can (not) show it.*
5 Carme: tu explica-ho ## a vere ## per **6** què =serveix?.	*You explain it. # Let's see. # What is it =for?*
7 [Maia riu]	*[Maia Laughs]*
[. . .]	
8 Carme: =ah ### per què serveix # vere.	*=Ah. ## What is it for? Let's see*
9 Maia: és una cos+/ [es posa a riure; Carme i **10** Alejandro riuen].	*It's someth- [She laughs; Carme and Alejandro laugh].*
11 Cris: on està # digues on està ## on es troba **12** això ##.	*Where it is. Say where it is. # Where do you find it?##*
13 Maia: @Spanish [=! l]<no sé como> **14** =hablar [riu].	*[loud voice and in Spanish] I don't know how to =talk [laughs].*
15 Carme: =ahaha [riu] # sí # a poc a po:c.	*=Ahaha [laugh]. Yes. Take your time.*
	[Carme, Cris and Tura keep insisting for 20 seconds; Maia repeats that she cannot do it; Carme and Alejandro tell her to do it in Spanish]
16 Maia: @Spanish [=! l]<no sé ha- no sé como **17** hablá (ba usté)>.	*[loud]I don't know how to talk (like you).*
18 Carme: bueno digue-ho aixís # digue-ho així **19** # eh # de la teva manera maia és igual # **20** encara que no ho diguis en =català. **21**	*Well, just say it this way. Say this way. Er Your way Maia; it doesn't matter; even if you don't say it in =Catalan.*
22 Alejandro: @Spanish =en castellano.	*=in Castilian [the local denomination of Spanish].*
23 Carme: tu digue-ho en castellà és igual.	*Do say it in Castilian.*
24 Maia: @Spanish no sabe @Catalan **25** [$al]<castellan>	*[in Spanish] Don't know [In Catalan] Castilian.*
26 Carme: no saps # sí home (xx) # mira si ho **27** estàs diguent # no =sabe	*Don't know? Come on (xx). Look, you are saying it. Don't =know.*
[. . .]	
28 Alejandro: @Spanish cómo hases =para	*[Spanish] How do you do =to*
29 Maia: @Spanish =para duchar.	*[Spanish] =to have a shower*
30 Carme: eh? a això # però digue-ho sense dir **31** dutxa # però bueno # com ho explicaries ## **32** com ho explicaries # eh? ## o sigui hem dit **33** una cosa hem dit una cosa qu'era per està **34** estirat i l'altra # dret ## no? # o sigui això **35** només ho pots fer dret ##. **36**	*You see? That's it. But say it without pronouncing the word "shower." Anyway. How would you explain it, eh[?]. # That is, we have said one thing one thing was to lie down and the other # standing, # right? So you can only do this when standing.*

Note: The default language of the interaction is Catalan; see transcription conventions of type 3 in the Shop Floor.

didn't know the Castilian word either (line 24). Here we have some evidence that one of the frames the tutors were using was indeed the idea that the core problem Maia had was lack of Catalan.

This episode can be used to link interactional features with the history of language instruction for immigrants in Spain and elsewhere, and with local ideologies of language and nation in which the idea of teaching "immigrant women" "Catalan" made sense. It can help us understand how the analysis of one instance of linguistic form and practice (in this case, especially of conversational structure and language choice between Castilian and Catalan) may reveal ideologies and social relations of wider significance.

What to make of this? With an isolated example, we can only point to the relationship between control of turns at talk and positioning of people as speakers or non-speakers of what seemed to be a relevant axis of differentiation, Castilian versus Catalan (although Maia, as all Senegalese people, spoke other languages). But we can link this interaction to others in the same course, with Maia and with the other students, to see if similar things occurred—and it turns out they did. One consequence was the development of a discourse among tutors that this profile of students made poor learners.

The interpretation had to take into account the nature of the activity and the trajectories that explain why it come to be, why it existed in this form, and how the participants, both learners and tutors, came to be co-present (the tutors, for instance, were Catholic voluntaries with no traning as teachers). This leads us to the intersection between early 21st-century patterns of migration to Spain and nationalist discourses in Catalonia, as well as to neoliberal states offloading of services to such populations as immigrants. Among other things, it leads us to a prevalent discourse in Catalonia that it is harder for immigrants to learn Catalan than Spanish, which was consistent with the idea that immigrants could not incorporate the forms of communication associated with belonging to the local community. It thus became difficult for the tutors to examine alternative strategies and explanations (after all, maybe it was the tutors who had chosen the wrong activity?).

One additional affordance of this form of analysis is that it makes us keenly aware of how vulnerable social interpretations are: the participants in this occasion could have come out with potentially many different explanations and evaluations of what had been going on (from (1) to (5) above, maybe even more). Attention to the minute details of the sequence may allow us to understand how specific interpretations come about, how grounded they really are, and why and how they can be contested.

Claims then are also, in their way, hypotheses. They are hypotheses about what ought to be happening in similar conditions, or about what might happen next, to different kinds of people, to resources, to activities. They help not only to understand what is happening and what it means to people "here," but also to imagine and anticipate how the processes will evolve, and what the likely consequences will be for to people both "here" and "there," that is, in similar kinds of contexts. They extend the thread of the specific study again across time and space beyond it.

They also loop you back into conversation with other stakeholders. People who share an interest can respond to the claims you make. You might discover new stakeholders and new conversations this way. They might show you things you hadn't noticed, and they might lead you in new directions. Certainly they allow for the only form of action about language issues that matters, which is action in interaction with the others in the field. This means that your claims have to be understood as connected to the ethical and political dimensions of doing this kind of work, in this way.

Other stakeholders, of course, include other researchers of various kinds, indeed anyone who has produced knowledge on this topic. You have to situate your own specific contribution (what your data uniquely tell you) in conversation with what is understood to be already known. Sometimes you can draw on other forms of knowledge in the scaffolding of your argument: evidence from other studies or from other reliable sources (quantitative and qualitative), concepts from existing works in our discipline or in others, logical reasoning or evidence from introspection or imagined scenarios. Feedback from others helps us sharpen your ability to formulate arguments in ways that make sense in our fields.

Of course, as has been the case with every other part of the process, the four activities of *mapping*, *tracing*, *connecting* and *claiming* never fall out neatly as a sequence. Not only do the four activities feed into each other, they also leak into the moments before and after. Thus, you get interested in (mapping) specific categories because you suspect that they constitute traces of processes that you may reconstruct by connecting how they emerge at different times and in different spaces. The analysis often draws your attention to things you hadn't been thinking about before, and so you go back to mapping or tracing before moving forward again to connecting. Maybe you weren't attending to drugs and alcohol preferences as a relevant mode of categorization, and in order to fully understand what you are seeing in the data about youth groups, you must both get a better handle on the exact nature of the drugs and alcohol people consume or refuse to consume, whether this is understood to index other preferences, and an idea of what other categories or practices such consumption is distinguished from (smoking cigarettes? Younger drug consumers?).

We are often tempted at this stage to start reading again, in a search for existing accounts for what we think we are seeing, or even for helpful theoretical frames. While we won't forbid you to keep reading, we do want to warn you that often this is a way to stay within the comfort zone of knowledge consumer rather than producer, and to protect ourselves from the uncertainty that this moment necessarily involves. By the same token, don't assume that the analysis is obvious; it does take painstaking work to patiently test your hypotheses against your data.

4.6 Analysis as Ethical and Political Conversation

Analysis is not only as rhizomatic and recursive as the rest of the research process, it is just as *dialogical* as all the other previous stages, in the sense that it is founded on a **conversation with significant stakeholders.** In the same way that our object, goals and plans had to be negotiated with colleagues, institutions or research participants, analysis is basically a conversation with those who have done **work similar or related to ours in the past, and with all the other stakeholders involved**. Because we have defined our work as being about language issues that matter, we have assumed that they matter to many more people than us.

In some ways, the process of mapping, tracing, connecting and claiming involves entering into conversation with people. We form hypotheses, and ask the data whether they are warranted or not (people often talk about this as "interrogating the data"). But of course the "data" involve real people, with real feelings and opinions, and real stakes in the game, real interests to pursue and protect. Although social scientific analysis has similarities with the procedures of interpretation that we conduct in everyday life, it also has special demands in terms of accountability, explicitness and relevance related to our role and responsibility as knowledge producers.

You must organize and formulate our analysis in ways that are relevant and intelligible to our interlocutors, and with due attention to the empirical and conceptual bases of your argument, so that our colleagues, students, research participants and anyone else with an interest in your work (civil servants, government officials, community activists, institutional administrators and so on) can in principle trace our reasoning back to our data and judge it on its own merits. It is this explicitness and this traceability that determines the specific ways in which data analysis is conducted and presented in social research (and also how data is recorded and stored). Although it is imaginable to perform data analysis in total isolation until the moment of evaluation, we do not recommend it. On the contrary, what we recommend is constant dialogue with different types of audiences about what issues may be important, which points were well expressed and which arguments need to be more convincing.

The ethical commitment in data analysis means not only consideration for fair and accurate use of the data, e.g., within the limits of the informed consent, but also discussion of it in ways that take into account what the analysis you are undertaking means to the other participants in the conversation that is your field. It may mean seeking out, or fielding requests for, actual conversations about it. In the end, of course, the analysis is your responsibility alone; you have to be the one to argue that this data warrants this description, and this explanation.

People may not always be happy with the knowledge you produce of course. In Moment 5 we will discuss further what it means to provide different kinds of accounts for different kinds of interlocutors, with different, and maybe even conflicting interests. Here let us just end with the reminder that your analysis has to hold up, even if people disagree about what to make of it.

Most typically, researchers worry about offending, upsetting, disturbing or distressing their research participants, particularly after they may well have shown great generosity and patience during the fieldwork. Let us take a common research context: a school. Your description may affect the teachers, the administrative staff, the educational authorities, the students or their families. You may find that teachers or students engage in explicit or implicit discrimination in terms of gender, race or disability, sometimes when they act with the best of intentions and care. You may even be convinced that we all would act like them were we in their place. Thus the researcher may well be tempted to avoid specific issues, or carefully doctor the phrasing of the description and argument, and then feel guilty that she or he is distorting or misrepresenting the findings. Again, this tension is not so much about the interpretation of the data, but about the way in which interpretation, and the whole research process, is inscribed in human relations and has implications beyond it.

Whatever conclusion you (decide to) reach, people ought to be able to agree that things are the way you have described them. They might prefer alternative explanations, but yours ought to be backed up by your data. They may care less, or more, or differently, about the consequences for themselves or others, but that is not a matter for the analysis itself. We have discussed the principle of reflexivity in the previous chapters as involving the obligation to consider how the social position, origins, trajectory and interests of the researcher constitute the orientation of the research. In relation to data analysis, reflexivity involves thinking not just in terms of what representation of your argument best depicts the data; but also what options are going to be best suited to the forms in which your arguments will be circulated and consumed. This is the subject of the next chapter.

4.7 Pulling It Together

Mapping, tracing, connecting and claiming are interpretive processes. We might think of the first three as ordered from less to more complexity, although in many ways mapping is about establishing your description, tracing is about finding relevant explanatory data and connecting is about using the latter to explain the former. The fourth, claiming, is the argument that you make on the basis of the first three; it is where all this analysis is supposed to lead you.

So mapping, despite being an eminently conceptual exercise, retains a connection with easily recognizable elements of our data set and resides in what we usually call "description" (what people are doing and saying, how those practices are temporally and spatially arranged—that is, what happens when and where—what resources are circulating). Description could be said to cover the representations of your data based on sensory perceptions that you would assume other people would share. Mapping involves the first abstraction out of this material consisting in setting up categories and establishing positions and adjacencies.

As we move to tracing, the descriptions that we propose imply more active intervention by the researcher in defining something that is not so obvious for everyone to see and hence must be duly defined, described or justified. It involves making hypotheses about where phenomena come from, or seem to be heading to, or present specific ways of changing and transforming.

Connecting captures the work you do to find explanations, by linking your findings so far to a "bigger picture," whether that picture is drawn from previous research, existing theories or ongoing social processes. Moving along this continuum of levels of analysis should also make you aware of how active and creative interpretation is, how socially and discursively constructed your conclusions are and how inexact it is to claim that they "simply stem from the data."

Claiming is about linking your specific research findings to the broad issues to which you originally linked your research when you were designing it. This is where you see what it is you can say not just about the people, places and moments you learned from, but what you can argue the implications are. In other words, this is where you build up and put forward your argument within the discipline and within the constellation of stakeholders concerned with what you study. Your evidence does not speak for itself; it is you, as a researcher and knowledge producer, who is responsible for making the claims based on your results. So at this stage you need to figure out and formulate what your argument is, how you back it up, and how you will express it in a way that makes sense to your interlocutors.

Data analysis does potentially involve substantial solitary work. However, it is helpful to both think of it as a conversation with others, and to actually undertake it dialogically. Even when a project is formally over, continued dialogue, whether in the form of fieldwork, teaching, presentations or publications, or for that matter during chats during seminar coffee breaks or interviews with the media, will keep the analysis going over many years.

The endgame is that (1) you have to produce an account that helps understand and explain the questions that you addressed, (2) your account sheds light on similar processes and (3) your interlocutors must be able to see how you came to your conclusions. Research as knowledge production is a socially constituted process, which implies that our research must also be "reflexive," i.e., accountable to the specific social conditions that constitute our own point of view and which also impinge on the conditions of circulation and reception of specific ideas.

4.8 Summary

Here is what this chapter has covered:

- Analysis involves procedures of interpretation not essentially different from ordinary ones but that need to be accountable and systematic.
- Analysis requires researchers to develop new arguments of their own for the academic community and for other stakeholders.
- We envisage four types of thought process in data analysis: mapping, tracing, connecting and claiming.
- Mapping involves identifying the key categories in your data to arrive at a situated description of the issues you are examining.
- Tracing requires identifying how key categories move in time and space across your data.
- Connecting means to link the phenomena identified with the bigger picture in order to provide an explanation.
- Making claims is the final stage to formulating your contribution to the field from your data as a result of analysis.

- You should understand your data as being not just about language, but as containing linguistic evidence that deepens other forms of ethnographic data: linguistic form, sequencing and metacommentary are key elements.

- Be prepared to go back and forth between the different analytical procedures.

- Remember that your analysis is a process situated in a web of social relations that you have to attend to in its ethical and political implications.

Keywords: sociolinguistic analysis, discourse analysis, ethnographic analysis, visual analysis, mapping, tracing, connecting, claiming.

Joan's First Coding

Joan analyzed his first sizable data set when he transcribed and "coded" six in-depth interviews for his Master's thesis (Patterns of Language Choice in Equal Encounters among Bilingual University Students in Catalonia. M.A. Thesis, Lancaster University, 1991). He first transcribed all six interviews with a computer that did not have a hard disk, and with word processing hardware that was not able to render Catalan or Spanish typographic accents. The word processor had some search functions for lexical items, but Joan decided that this was too clumsy a tool, because people do not always talk about their experiences of language choice with specific words (however, had he found certain words recurring, the search function could have been helpful, in the end). He decided instead to print out the six interviews on the continuous paper of the old dot-matrix printers and then covered his whole dorm room—bed, carpet, furniture—with the paper threads. Then he took out one pencil, one blue and red pen, and three marker pens of different colours, and started underlining the text of the printouts of the transcription according to six specific issues: being Catalan, the monolingual norm, the accommodation norm, the bilingual norm, changes of language choice and linguistic repertoire. These six aspects were directly relevant to the questions of how people decided to speak Catalan or Spanish (the different norms of language choice found in the literature) and how this connected with the way people understood Catalan identity. So every time someone said something about the need to speak one single language in a conversation, Joan marked it in yellow. And the other five issues he marked with different colours. When he started analyzing his data, he could turn around on his chair and see at once all the stretches in which someone mentioned each topic and then write down his report on how all the interviewees felt about this issue. In actual fact, Joan analyzed and wrote his M.A. thesis at the same time, which means that interpretation and text redrafting went hand in hand. He started by describing each norm of language choice in the terms in which the participants explained it, and also each person's ideas about Catalan identity. He was "mapping" language practices and linguistic ideologies at this stage (although he was not fully aware of it in these terms). One relevant datum was how languages figured in people's biographies (family language, school language), a basic form of tracing that allowed Joan later to build connections between people's trajectories and their linguistic practices and ideologies. Overall, he claimed that people developed different strategies to manage their linguistic repertoire in different conditions, and that the view that language choice derived automatically from ascription to Catalan identity was not accurate. Some of the participants, mostly Spanish speakers, constructed language choice as just a personal and practical matter and not as a collective one.

Linguistic Landscapes in Sámiland/Lapland

As a part of the Northern Multilingualism project, our research team wanted to know more about linguistic landscapes of seven central villages in the northernmost tip of the Sámiland/Lapland area across Norway, Sweden, Finland and Russia. As our first step, we agreed upon mapping out which languages are used in the public signs in these villages, and how they were physically laid out within the signs. I focused on one Sámi village in Finnish Sámiland. I mapped all public signs in that village and all languages in them. I mapped out the typical order of languages in the signs, looking for variation depending on who had produced the signs. This required me to follow the trajectories of these signs to find out who made them, who asked for them, who paid for them, what was their function, how long these signs had been there and what particular location they were found in. After this tracing, I was able to identify a pattern: in the signs produced by the state of Finland or regional authorities, the order was Finnish and Northern Sámi, sometimes followed by Inari Sámi and Skolt Sámi. The signs produced by the Sámi authorities had the opposite order, the Sámi languages first and then Finnish. I connected this alternation of language order in public signs to which authority, the Finnish or the Sámi, made them, making a claim about how inserting the semiotic presence of the state authority on the infrastructure of the landscape constituted itself a claim on defining the space either as part of the state of Finland or of Sámiland, the land of indigenous peoples. Based on these findings and the plausible explanation of the variation and order of languages in public space, I made a further claim that public signage is part of how power centres claim authority over the space, with an end result in this case of producing a space of multilingual conflict over social order and regimes of truth.

5

Fifth Key Moment
Making Your Story

5.1 Writing the Story the Research Tells

Writing up research reports is one more activity associated with research that is fraught with delicate personal challenges, unexpected difficulties and uncertainties. Many people commonly believe that writing is only about putting down what you have **discovered** after all the preparations, fieldwork and analysis. But this is misleading, basically because writing (particularly in the social sciences and the humanities) **is a substantial part of the process of thinking itself**. It is one of the key ways in which we engage in the process of producing knowledge. As such, it is not really just a "phase," a specific activity, of your research plan. It is the process through which you "find out" or "make" connections, interpret data, construct arguments, make claims and respond to colleagues or stakeholders.

One key aspect of the writing process is that it has an audience (or rather, it can have many audiences). This follows logically from our repeated insistence that research is fundamentally about participating in conversations. The potential multiplicity of audiences (colleagues, policy makers, practitioners) creates the need to produce different types of texts, sometimes in different languages, to adapt to the specific goals and expressive styles of each community. However, what is most important to understand about the audience is that it is implicitly omnipresent in the text, in the choice of wording, in the selection of the information to convey and in the way it is organized. Academic texts **guide** the readers along the process of following your argument.

For novice researchers in particular, writing involves the unsettling discovery that it requires some skills that are complex and very specific. Although writing is a common activity in our literate societies, and we may have practised it intensively throughout our education, and in online or other everyday environments, this does not mean that it is as simple and transparent as is often assumed. There is a really long way between texting our friends and completing a twenty-page argument that (extremely busy) university students and professors find worth reading. At the same time, writing is not the unscalable mountain it sometimes appears to be. It is another way of saying what you have to say, to people interested in listening.

For researchers, writing a thesis or a journal article is the equivalent of taking an exam in many ways. First and foremost, your written texts will constitute the main source from which your colleagues will evaluate you and your work. And second, (and as a consequence of the first) it is common to experience insecurity, anxiety and frustration during the process. On the flipside, writing can also be a truly exciting and rewarding experience, as you follow the flow of your ideas and apply your creativity to build new ideas and connections. In this chapter, we focus more on helping with the difficulties and the anguish of writing than on sharing its more thrilling aspects. As with anyone venturing into uncharted territory, anxiety and exhilaration usually come in tandem. As is also the case with oral presentations, there is no cure for the difficulties and anxieties people go through, and although they will diminish with time and experience, they are also a healthy, permanent part of the process. Even the most senior scholars routinely need the help of their trusted colleagues to read their drafts and help improve them.

Tensions about writing have not been made easier by the recent drive of the academic world towards forms of accountability adapted from the corporate sector. Our published texts are often now considered to be our main professional *output*, so that they do not simply determine the regard our colleagues have for us but also our working conditions and job opportunities. However, writing up research is not amenable to the traditional definitions of working conditions based on hours of work or scheduled activities (such as teaching or meetings). As Frekko (2016) pointedly expresses it, one key challenge of research writing is simply making it happen, that is, inserting within our daily work routines an activity that usually has long-term deadlines (so it is often not as urgent as other tasks), requires deep concentration (no distractions from visits or emails) and must repeatedly be left unfinished or pending. Writing an article or a chapter requires many hours, and we cannot normally cut ourselves off from the rest of our personal or professional commitments until it is done. In the Shop Floor chapter of the book, you will find some common practical tips about how to go about these issues.

In sum, writing is a challenge that involves our fundamental ability to **analyze** data and produce original ideas, our ability to **organize** our work and daily tasks, and our ability to **communicate** with others in an accessible, orderly and persuasive manner. Researchers are commonly faced with the need to produce texts of many different types. Here we are going to focus on two canonical research reporting genres: the thesis and the journal research article. We have chosen these two because they present together the basic range of requirements and structural features that can be found in practically all academic texts, so that criteria and procedures can be easily transferred from these two to others. Finally, in the last section of this chapter we shall also focus on non-academic forms of communication intended for more varied audiences (media articles, interviews, documentaries, social media posts, public talks, expert reports).

5.2 Researchers as Knowledge Producers

To address the procedures and experiences of academic writing it is essential to agree on what it is that we are doing, why (or with what aims) and how we stand as persons within this process. As with other research activities, when we write, we bring in ideas about science, research and communication from multiple walks of life and intellectual traditions. In this book, we have repeatedly affirmed our constructivist conception of knowledge production and this is the standpoint from which we address writing. This standpoint has implications for (1) how we understand that thinking and writing take place and how they interconnect, and (2) it has implications for understanding **the position from which we speak,** including (3) how we treat the audience in the text.

5.2.1 Writing Is Thinking

In common parlance, and also in some experimental natural science contexts, writing and speaking are seen as representations, i.e., as simply describing what we saw or experienced somehow. Thus, you run an experiment or a text and you get results that have specific implications. So when you write, you just report this. In the social sciences and the humanities (and often in the natural sciences too) there is actually much more to it. Once you have gathered and analyzed your data, what you have done and seen is just the beginning, just (part of) the material that you will use to do your own construction of knowledge. From this viewpoint, writing is an active process of creation of a new understanding about the social world (at least a specific aspect of it) that you must convince your audience is pertinent and useful here and now, and better, or more relevant, than what they knew so far.

The "convincing" is the key notion here, as it directs you beyond the data and into the web of social relations in which your texts must circulate and into the conversation of which they are a part. Academic writing crucially combines the descriptive mode with the rhetorical mode, and just as with any utterance produced in a social interaction, the text must contain an account or a story that the audience finds worth engaging with. More than that, it must make an argument, a claim. Although the concept of "rhetoric" has a polemical history, and some people consider it as the opposite of "objective," "scientific" or "rational," we see it as constitutive of human communication, including scientific communication. This does not mean that we recommend that researchers prioritize style, the use of cute metaphors or the display of linguistic ingenuity. Quite the opposite: the issues go far deeper, because rhetoric has to do with finding the best way to organize your text and phrase your arguments in a way that will be deemed acceptable ("hearable," "legible," "receivable") and memorable within the specific community in which they will be read.

So although you may have some thoughts provisionally formulated in our minds, you will find that writing them up does not often follow automatically: you must shape them into workable phrases chunked into paragraphs and, in the process, you become aware of novel aspects in your ideas and new connections between them. This is essentially what we mean when we say that **writing is thinking**. In our experience, a substantial part of the thinking process comes while and through writing. This is also the reason why we do not see writing as a specific, separate "stage" in the research process. After all, we do writing/thinking when we formulate the research questions or write down the research plan, devise fieldwork material or make fieldnotes. During the initial analysis stage, you may have written down a lot: memos and ideas, notes to yourself, drafts of arguments, mind maps, summaries of readings. Writing/thinking happens throughout the research process.

In this chapter we address the more concrete and focused aspects of writing/thinking, namely the production of texts meant for a readership, a specific venue of publication (a thesis, a journal, a chapter for an edited book), a limited number of pages (yes, even for theses!) and, crucially, one specific argument to make (amongst the many issues that your data and your research point to). Through the process of writing such texts, you will go through new thinking and new effort, no matter how much work you have done before. You will typically start writing a text with an idea in your mind (or a diagram jotted down on paper), but you will still have to deal with many obstacles during the process. Some of these may well have implications for your research questions, the data available or the way it has been archived and tagged. As a result, the recursivity found in all stages of research will also be evident here.

Let us adopt the basic example of the traveller who must cross a river. The traveller has a long-term goal, a destination, but she has had to adapt her path to the terrain. Now she has to cross a river, the river crossing being the specific article or chapter that must be written. The traveller has sought an area that appears shallow enough, and walks into the water (starts writing the text). However, during the crossing, she finds difficulties: at some points the water is too deep, or the ground too slippery or some stepping stones are too far apart. This is not unexpected; every single detail could not be anticipated from the shore. So she must find her way through by drawing on her resources, finding or building new supports or getting assistance. She will eventually cross the river (in most cases), but maybe not exactly in the way she had expected or from the first starting point chosen. Once she is on the opposite bank, she will have learned significantly from the act of crossing itself. Moreover, during the process, she will have to deal with details that are essential to setting up a path that can be trodden by others, which is what academic writing is essentially about. Thus, the kind of thinking that takes place while writing is just as important as any of the procedures that we have been discussing so far.

5.2.2 Who Am I?

Writing up research is fraught with contrasting emotions. Novice researchers in particular often find writing academic texts remarkably hard and feel insecure about how to approach it. However, overconfidence is also common and causes complications of its own. There is something very personal indeed in the process of writing, something which transcends the simple fact that, as human beings, we enjoy success and suffer with failure in everything we do. A critical aspect of this is the fact that we ourselves are a substantial part of the text, and that the texts also make what we are in important ways. Deep down, the key question is rarely one of just procedural or practical skills. The core issue is mostly social: the writer is taking up a new role, she is speaking from a position which she had previously rarely or never adopted. She is moving from a comfortable position as a student or apprentice (a passive knowledge user, or a knowledge consumer) to a researcher or an academic (an active knowledge producer). There is therefore an issue of socialization here, the also common experience of adopting and rehearsing a new identity.

Managing feedback is another soft spot. Even if writers may be initially happy about their first drafts, a common experience of frustration is to receive them back from supervisors, fellow students or journal reviewers covered with objections, comments and notes, most of them identifying difficulties with the meaning of specific concepts or with the development of the argument. To these difficulties, researchers writing in a language that is not their first language, typically English, must struggle to get around their insecurities about grammar, spelling or vocabulary. The experience may be discouraging, in the sense that people may feel inadequate, incompetent, not up to the job, or just very pressed with time. Joan's experience is a case in point. After obtaining a degree in English philology in Barcelona, and an M.A. in language studies at Lancaster University (UK), he started a Ph.D. His supervisor regularly returned his paper drafts with multiple observations on his argument and his use of English grammar. At one point, he even took a collection of these drafts and spent time listing and classifying all his writing difficulties. He was glad when, well into his second year, his supervisor distractedly commented, "Well, your English is beginning to take off." Similarly, when Sari started to do her Ph.D. first at the University of Amsterdam and then later at Lancaster she got lots of comments on her English writing (especially grammar) but also related to lack of a clear or convincing argument. It took a while (and several courses in English Academic Writing) for Sari to realize that her voice as an English writer needed to be quite different from how she has learned to write in a Finnish context. In English, she felt she needed to be bolder, more argumentative in a more explicit and rapid style of argumentation than would be conventional in Finnish-speaking milieux. Monica found that writing in French in Canada was often a collective project, with colleagues, assistants, support staff and family all weighing in (grammar books and dictionaries at their side) on the "right" way to express something, or the "right" format for a specific kind of text. While destabilizing at first, it helped her come to recognize that linguistic and discursive norms are, indeed, socially constructed!

When you enter a new clique of friends, get to know the family of your new partner, or get acquainted with new colleagues in a new job, you initially need to get familiar with the rules of the game and acquire a sense of how to speak in the new contexts. The same is true of writing up research. In many social contexts, this adaptation process is done gradually: we start out pretty silent, we gradually get more talkative. However, when writing the first research article or a thesis, we find that we must basically write in a manner equivalent to speaking loudly and bluntly straight away (and, moreover, often in a foreign language, typically English). We must say something new and assume responsibility for our work and our claims.

Additionally, it is also relatively disturbing to express oneself in a noticeably new genre, especially one with such evident connections to knowledge as power. Even if we are fairly familiar with the vocabulary, the conventions of text organization and the style(s) of expression found in our field, it is quite a different matter for us to actually speak or write like that. A genre is not just a harmless collection of textual and lexico-grammatical resources at your disposal; it also imposes specific forms of performance, self-presentation and relationships with the audience. Becoming an academic writer is tantamount to creating a new "me," and we may have difficulties in recognizing ourselves as the persons who speak/write in that way and with those words.

So the basic problem is: **who am I** as a knowledge producer? Who am I to speak like this, to use these grand words? Am I using them correctly? Who am I to criticize the authorities in our field, or to argue that previous research has not properly addressed a question? And, crucially, who am I to put forward this interpretation in front of people with much more experience and power? Additionally, we may be concerned about the responsibilities entailed by the research, and what its consequences may be for different people.

Although feelings of insecurity predominate in this situation, it is also common for some students to react in the opposite way and display overconfidence. Overconfidence is often a more delicate problem than the opposite, in the sense that it lowers the need to be cautious, lessens the readiness to listen and consider the views of others, and generally lowers one's guard with regard to the vulnerabilities of one's arguments (which are always there!) and one's use of concepts. This amounts to solving the problem by simply denying it and, at best, one ends up doing the adapting in the reverse order. Thus while most students will slowly learn when to speak and how to push their claims, and will gradually stop hiding their views by overloading the text with citations, the overconfident ones may have to learn the hard way when to shut up, that their views are debatable, and that they are not the first to come up with some of the ideas they express. Following the river-crossing metaphor, overconfident students just swim straight across the river and climb the opposite shore while pretending that they are not wet at all.

Whatever the specific solutions each person finds for her own endeavours, the bottom line is freedom of expression to voice any arguments that are reasonably supported by the evidence. However, one important convention is that your own specific contribution to knowledge must appear clearly delimited, and, particularly, well-distinguished from the contributions of others. You should neither hide your views behind citations of important figures, nor present all the points as if they were your idea. Your text will after all be one turn in a long conversation with others, both academics and informants. So just make sure that everyone is duly acknowledged and represented to begin with.

This principle, that your work is part of a conversation, informs in significant ways some of the common stylistic conventions of the fields that are described in the Shop Floor section: the use of the pronouns (I, we), the representation of sources and the need to qualify one's statements.

This section has discussed what writing is like from the subject position of the writer. But as we have said all along, knowledge production is a conversation, so you have to think about who your conversational partners are, as well as the conditions under which your conversation will take place.

5.2.3 Who Is My Audience?

Readers are the main relevant others that shape how we all formulate any utterance and, in this sense, academic texts are no exception. Although scientific texts often appear as if they are addressed to everybody and to nobody in particular, it is worth building a picture of whom we are speaking to and in what conditions our texts will be read. Some public speakers say that it is helpful to them to focus on someone in the audience as representing the kind of person they are trying to reach in the broader group. It is a way of reminding ourselves that our utterance is not just words but it has concrete recipients who are listening or reading as human beings. In our case, our audience is made up of many different types of people, although we generally assume that they share with us awareness and training about specific issues.

Conventionally, the audience of our academic texts is everyone that you can meet at a conference in your field or related fields. So attending conferences and getting to know people in them makes sense from this perspective (beside many others, of course). It is important to get to know them, talk to them, comment on their papers in public or in private, have lunch and coffee with them and learn about the different frames of mind they may have. Such conversations give you a better grasp on what ideas are commonly understood and taken for granted, what forms of reasoning are picked up more quickly and easily, what motivations they have or what issues trigger the most interest. Of course, you can complement this by also reading people's published texts, and perhaps their blogs, their social media presence or any of the other virtual means that present themselves. You will find that some colleagues are more formal or informal, more approachable or distant, more open or guarded, have more or less of a sense of humour, more sensitive to detail or more concerned about the big picture. In any case, it is of capital importance to get a sense of the actual people behind the texts, the theories, the ideas.

The main point here is that your texts will have to find a middle ground that is acceptable to all or most of them, in terms of how formal, how bold, how cautious or how meticulous you must come across as being. When you write your articles or your chapters, you will be basically talking to each one of **them** (even if you are not aware of this). This helps you to deal in a practical way with most problems and insecurities that you will encounter while writing: is another example necessary? Is this argument really convincing? Should this transcription provide additional details? Should I quote so-and-so here? All these issues can only be answered by combining your knowledge about the subject matter with your acquaintance with the people who constitute the communicative culture of the field, and with whom you should try to be familiar. One implication of this is that you may address readers differently in different languages because different languages typically involve different readerships. When Joan writes in Catalan, for instance, he can spare readers the many details of the Catalan sociolinguistic context. He has discovered, however, that this is a double-edged sword, in the sense that many Catalan readers may take for granted ideas and representations about the Catalan situation with which he does not agree. Nonetheless, the question of how much detail is necessary is addressed differently if he writes in English or in Catalan (or in Spanish or German). Monica finds that writing in French for a European publication requires much less attention to context, and more to fine-grained analysis, than writing in the same language for a North American publication. Writing for anthropologists in English always requires starting with a vignette, a practice which often seems odd to people trained in linguistics. Sari finds that writing about analysis of data from a Sámi context requires a lot of explanation and contextual information for an international audience to make the argument plausible for them.

In addition, you should think about the specific context of communication with which your text will appear, that is, in this case, the conditions in which people read academic material. From this perspective, bear in mind that people often read many texts quickly, even diagonally. This may be especially true for fellowship applications or funding proposals, which therefore need to hook the reader in rapidly, or risk losing them. What counts as a hook may vary, but it can be a telling case, or an indication of the big issue that you address.

More broadly, you need to think about the nature of the conditions of the market that you are in. There is increasing pressure to publish in English, although this can sometimes be accompanied by efforts to establish alternative markets for other linguistic areas, or by attempts at producing knowledge other than what is becoming hegemonic in a globalized, English-dominated world. You have choices to make along those lines, with concomitant decisions about what kinds of conventions make sense to you or are possible for you to aim for. Be attentive to the semiotics of authority, attitudes towards new knowledge or critique and forms of argument development that count as relevant in different linguistic traditions or disciplines. Decide whether the dominant modes work for you; if not, think about whether you have alternatives to propose and whether you can risk doing so. Just to give one example, Monica and a French (from France) colleague of hers living in Canada once submitted an article to a journal based in France. It was returned with the request to remove the whole methodology section on the grounds that a good article simply recounted the results. Monica and her co-author decided to argue that this was a neocolonial imposition of genres by the centre (France) on the periphery (Canada), and to present arguments for the intellectual reasons they thought it important to discuss their methods. The argument was actually largely accepted, and a compromise reached on what that section ought to include.

These conditions of "consumption" of academic texts impinge on the characteristics of textual genres that we are going to describe in Section 3 below. We have opted to address questions as they manifest themselves within the specific areas of publication in English presently considered "international," because most of us have to deal with that market one way or another at some point in our careers. However, this does not of course mean that the conditions we describe, or the suggestions we provide as a function of those conditions, are **universal**.

5.3 Genre Expectations

The ways in which academic knowledge is projected into texts have a long tradition around the world and have taken a wide variety of forms. In recent decades, the gradual consolidation of English as a global lingua franca has turned the conventions of the English-speaking world into the de facto standard of scientific presentation that is required for publication in the "top" scientific journals and book series (most of them in English and monolingual). This influence has also been felt strongly in the forms and procedures of academic organization: anonymous peer review, naming of roles (e.g., professor) or disciplines (e.g., area studies), evaluation at various levels or quality assessment exercises.

The authors of this book have been both subjects and agents of this process. Having begun our academic life in a time in which the field was more multilingual and in which publishing in French, Finnish, Catalan or Spanish was seen as normal, we have witnessed the crisis of French-English bilingualism in contexts such as AILA (the *Association internationale de linguistique appliquée*), in which half the audience would suddenly desert a conference room because a presentation was in French. We have also witnessed the establishment of professional and institutional evaluation procedures based on the quality of publications, as determined by agencies that develop a citation metric; these metrics inevitably provide the highest ratings to publications in English, because they reach the widest audience and because English-speaking academics read and cite few works in other languages. Numbers, literally, count in contemporary conditions of knowledge production. On the other hand, many academics share a sense that "smaller" languages, such as Finnish or Catalan, are valid and necessary languages for knowledge production. And, in any case, not publishing in languages other than English seriously hampers the possibilities of circulation of new knowledge and new ideas in many countries, such that the potential social benefits of our research are significantly diminished.

As critical sociolinguists we are not happy with the ways in which these developments often make linguistic and social inequalities more acute, and we are keenly aware that we ourselves have contributed to them in many ways—just as we do now, given that we are going to explain and recommend the current dominant procedures and criteria for academic writing that are the product and maybe the means of this English-language hegemony. Therefore, please bear in mind that we do not intend to **canonize** these conventions and our recommendations, and that we welcome innovations and transgressions particularly if these prove themselves to be viable in the production and dissemination of critical knowledge. We hope to make transparent enough what the rationale is for the current conventions so that they become open to contestation and improvement. Here we will focus on two established genres of academic writing: the *doctoral thesis* and the *journal article*.

One distinctive characteristic of a thesis is that it is not strictly just a report but also a display of expertise intended for evaluation. Theses are also relatively long texts in which it is expected that arguments are developed in full and in detail. In contrast, journal articles are expected to be more focused and specific, and thus require critical synthesizing skills. Other genres such as chapters in collective books, monographs, reports or even oral paper presentations generally combine characteristics from the two in different ways.

Table 5.1 Structure of Canonical Academic Texts

Item	Thesis	Article
1	Title and author details	Title and author details
2	Abstract	Abstract
3	(Acknowledgements)	
4	Table of Contents (Optional: figure and table index; transcription conventions).	Introduction: including . . . justification/argument summary or questions/ state of the art summary/theoretical framing/ method and fieldwork/structure of the following sections
5	Introduction	
6	Theory/Literature review	
7	Method and Fieldwork	
8	Data Presentation and Analysis	Data Presentation and Analysis
9	Discussion	Discussion
10	Conclusions	Conclusions
11	Endnotes	Endnotes and Acknowledgements
12	References	References
13	Appendices	(Appendices)

Table 5.1 provides an overview of the most common components of the two text types, which have a common structure. It is often possible to use different structures or variations of these, although we would then advise authors to explain to readers what you are doing and why, especially if you are being particularly innovative. Otherwise, as the practical saying goes, "as long as your thesis committee is okay with it . . .":

The first important aspect that needs to be borne in mind is that this structure provides a rough layout of how we expect the text to be read, but not of the sequence in which it is supposed to be written. Sections 1 to 5 are generally considered to be the last sections to be completed, although there is no harm in drafting them earlier. Sections 6 and 7 can usually be written fairly independently from the others, but should be at least drafted early on (in theses, they often come in the form of separate chapters, and of just two or three paragraphs in articles). Sections 8, 9 and 10 usually contain material that is more specific and unique to the research, and it is the ground upon which the argument stands or falls. There is, in any case, ample variation in the way people write. Joan, for instance, generally starts with a general plan in his head and follows the order of 5, 6, 7, 8, but ends up with a long text with many sidetracks. He then checks the whole structure, and starts eliminating large parts and synthesizing others, a step he may repeat several times, until he finally writes the conclusions and redrafts the introduction. Sari typically works simul-taneously on multiple nexus of the text: on the one hand, she keeps on working on the main argument throughout the writing process by writing the key paragraph starting with the opening "This article is about . . ." over and over again. This is because she needs to keep on working on the main argument she is making in this particular text, as opposed to aiming for an argument whose scope is too broad and general to be contained in a single article. For the gist of the article, on the other hand, she works at the same time with the theoretical framing (4) of the argument as well as the analysis of the data (8) in order to get the ideas and findings from both parts of the text (argument) to speak to each other. Once she is relatively happy with these sections, she starts to write the text in a chronological order from the beginning. Monica tends to start writing from the beginning, getting everything out onto the screen. Then she identifies what her core argument really is and restructures the text around it, eliminating sequences that she may find fascinating, but which do not help advance the argument. She then has to work at explaining how each piece of the argument prepares the next step, that is, on making explicit how you get from one place to the next in the argumentative sequence. This is one place where she tests her hypotheses, sometimes finding there that her data actually support a different argument from the one she thought she was making. Writing the conclusion is the last moment where this can happen, and often occasions a reworking of the introduction.

5.3.1 Title and Abstract (the Slogan and the Ad)

You should see these two elements as the ones most driven by concerns similar to those that apply in marketing. In practice, a title is the equivalent of a radically brief abstract akin to a publicity slogan. It serves the purpose of letting readers know what the text is about and whether they need to read it. From this viewpoint, the classical mnemonic of journalistic reports (what/who/where/when/how) can work well enough, although titles are so short that one must always make choices as to what angle must be given priority. You should also take into account the ways in which titles orient bibliographical searches and may be picked up by internet search engines (and for books, how they are marketed to libraries and bookshops).

You should make sure that you use terms that will be recognized by all the people whom you wish to reach, and that the terms used are essential keywords used throughout your text (e.g., it is unwise to include in the title specific terms just because they are momentarily fashionable in the field). The title should hint at the actual argument or innovative knowledge that you wish to put forward. To explore examples, we have chosen at random a recent edition of the *Journal of Sociolinguistics* (2016, issue 20:3), one of the leading journals in this field:

- Language policy, homelessness and neoliberal urbanization: The case of San Francisco's Union Square (Wee, 2016).
- Māori language revitalisation: A project in folk linguistics (Albury, 2016).
- Scalar politics, language ideologies, and the sociolinguistics of globalization among transnational Korean professionals in Hong Kong (Bailey et al. 2016).

Notice that all of them provide a sense of "locale," i.e., where the study and data collection took place: San Francisco, New Zealand (implicit in the term Māori for any sociolinguist) and Hong Kong. Otherwise the first will attract specialists in language policy together with academics interested in a critique of neoliberalism, and marginally in urban studies. In the second, "revitalization" calls upon a sizable section of the field. In the third, we find signals to people interested in the topics of "scale" and "transnationalism." Note that the actual arguments remain vague, the first and second suggesting the description or analysis of policy initiatives, the third ideas about language held by Korean professionals and their wider political significance. The first two contain a very typical caesura between a first phrase that is more general and a second that provides more concrete information (in principle). This is a very common stylistic device. It does not mean you have to use it, of course; there are good reasons, such as brevity, for using other formats.

"Abstracts" are meant to expand on titles. They are used by readers to decide whether they need to read the full text that follows or not. They may vary greatly in length from 200 to 4,000 words, but essentially they must contain at least each of the key items below, expressed in one or two sentences each:

- The research question.
- (Naming of) theory/main concepts.
- (Naming of) method and data collected.
- Summary of conclusion.

Readers will certainly not apprehend the argument in full; they are supposed to read the whole text if they want to do so. In some research traditions, abstracts may vary a lot in focus: some people argue at length why the topic is important but they do not explain the research; others invest a lot in describing their local context. In the English-language-dominated academy, justification and contextualization are accepted, but with restraint. You should always, though, point at your conclusions, that is, at the claims that you will be making, and not merely state that you will "discuss" a given issue or "analyze" something in one way or other without anticipating the outcome of it. In fact, it is typical in many intellectual traditions to conceal the final conclusion from the reader until the author feels that the time is ripe. To the reader accustomed to the conventions of the anglophone world, this is unexpected and may lead readers to believe that the text is unfocused, that it is "merely" exploratory, or that the author has not decided what her main points are.

5.3.2 Introduction (the Guided Tour)

Introductions show clearly how the processes of writing and of reading are very different things. Although readers are well advised to always **read** the introduction first, in our experience it is best to **write** them last. Drafting the introduction at the beginning can certainly help authors to build a preliminary plan for the text, but usually you will "discover" key elements of our argument as you spell them out. Introductions are like travel guides, so that they are best written when the author has visited the destination first.

The essential purpose of introductions is to inform readers about what they are going to find in the text, including the core take-away message (the claim). They therefore contain roughly the same components as abstracts, but since they are longer, you can be more precise and concrete. They also allow a more personal touch, so that the author can (moderately) spell out her motivations and hopes about what the research shows, as well as personal and professional circumstances impinging on it.

Introductions should leave no doubt or ambiguity about the contribution that the author intends to make to the academic and social conversations in which the work is inserted. They should therefore openly state how the argument illuminates how specific social relations are situatedly produced, what consequences this has for the distribution of resources, for the livelihoods of people and (if applicable) to the possibility of social transformation. It must also be explicit about theoretical and conceptual orientations (point to them, do not describe them or discuss them in detail here), or about the types and approximate amounts of data gathered, as well as any vicissitudes of the research process that need to be known to understand the decisions taken. The main justification for the choices made should also be provided, without major engagement in details about the strengths and weaknesses of different options.

Again, the introduction should anticipate as clearly as possible the results and the conclusions of the study, bearing in mind that the reader will not be in a position to judge whether the evidence and the argument hold until she or he has read through the whole text. Nonetheless, readers need to know where they are going to be led, allowing them to grasp how the text is organized and how important each specific part and argument is to the whole design.

A conventional final section of introductions is a description of the different parts of the text that follows, whether these are the chapters of the thesis or the sections of an article. This part normally takes up a single paragraph in articles; in theses it is useful to write a synthetic paragraph for each chapter.

To extend the metaphor of introduction-as-a-guided-tour, consider that the reader will expect to have your company throughout, not to "disappear" for long segments, and be very attentive at difficult spots. Expressions such as "hand-holding" or "signposting" are essential to the conventional rhetoric of contemporary academic texts. It is assumed that the author makes every effort to ensure that their reader knows where she stands and where the argument is heading at all times. This justifies many of the formal conventions described in the Shop Floor section.

5.3.3 Theory/Literature Review (the Conversation)

This part is conventionally expected in M.A. and Ph.D. theses as a separate chapter; but in articles and shorter texts it often gets just a few paragraphs in the introduction. In any case, the ultimate goal is the same: to locate your research in the context of the wider conversation(s) presently taking place in your research field and relevant to the issues you are researching. Because this is really its main goal, it is not uncommon for writers to find alternative ways of writing these parts.

The linguist Mikhail Bakhtin insisted throughout his books that what defines human action as "communicative" is the fact that everything that we say **responds** to what someone else has said. In ordinary speech, people interpret what we say as our reaction or response to something, even if we do not explicitly tell them what it is that we are confirming, denying or qualifying. The audience knows or imagines the context, the contents and sometimes even the people with whom we are implicitly talking. In an academic text, we must make sure that the audience is on the same page as we are. We must explicitly describe the conversation in which we wish to participate, and what we understand this conversation to be about (which is never exactly the same for everyone).

This is the part where an article and a thesis differ considerably. A theory/literature review for an article is not intended to display expertise, but simply to orient the reader. It also locates you and your research in a disciplinary terrain as the references, key terms and the stance you take on them tells the reader from which position you are writing your text. In the journal article, you can be as short as reasonably possible, as a few sentences and references may already be enough for a reader already familiar with your field. You may need to provide the definition of a concept to remind readers, or make sure that they are aware of how you interpret it. You may need to briefly remind them of the results of a selection of the latest research published. In an article, the main goal is to do this locating and reminding, not to develop or discuss the material written by others.

In Ph.D. and M.A. theses, this section is where you formally display that your knowledge of the field is adequate and sufficient for you to participate legitimately in the conversation. You are supposed to show that you understand what the relevant conversations are and who the relevant interlocutors are (notably other writers). You must provide definitions of your key terms and discussions around them (including critiques of them) that show your understanding of the main issues addressed. These sections may include different types of subject matter (theory, previous publications, even secondary data), sometimes combined. Different research traditions may even have diverging ideas as to what constitutes "theory," and thesis formats still vary considerably across networks and disciplines. The wealth of denominations for this section attests to that: theoretical framework, conceptual framework, state of the art, literature review, previous studies, previous research, etc. For us, they all boil down to the same aim, namely to place your work within the scholarly conversation (or conversations) in which you intend to participate and to which you intend to contribute.

These conceptual sections most usually take the shape of a "story" told in roughly chronological order. Starting from an "initial" moment in which your issue was framed or understood in a particular way, you report the debates and new contributions that have brought you to the present understanding of this type of phenomena. Or perhaps the story recounts how the phenomenon that you are researching has undergone different manifestations as shown by the subsequent contributions of different researchers. Intellectual trajectories are, after all, fundamentally dialogues and debates with a certain sequential logic. This is the equivalent of explaining what forest you are in, and where your tree is located.

One common difficulty with writing these sections is that it often makes sense to review different stories or lines of a different kind that are interconnected in complex ways. Even if your work does not cross disciplinary borders (much), you are likely to be concerned with (1) theoretical/conceptual trajectories, (2) the history of studies on your specific subject or object and even (3) the "context" or "history" of the people or sites that you are studying. While it is in principle feasible to explain all this sequentially, in practice it can be a bit messy. For example, in the (1) history of sociolinguistics there have been different ways of understanding what language is and how it is used, and this would be the theoretical/conceptual aspect of the thesis. However, in relation to (2) a given form of speech or language use (e.g., multilingualism) in a given context, there may be a history of studies and surveys conducted from different theoretical viewpoints that you also need to review. Finally, you may feel that you need readers (3) to know the history of the community of speakers where you do your study: origins, conflicts, economy, migrations, etc. Joan, in his thesis, included the aspects of (1) in a separate chapter on theory, (3) in the chapter on methodology and put (2) at the beginning of each chapter of analysis because it provided a good thread between other people's analyses and his own in relation to each topic. But he has read many theses in which (1) and (2) are dealt with together in "literature review" or "theory" chapters. Sari, in her articles about tourism in Sámiland, has often included the information about tourism in the region and key issues related to indigenous Sámi community in the introduction section, and then drafted a more conceptual section around key concepts (e.g., authenticity) using published work in tourism studies, anthropology and sociolinguistics. Monica often tells her students that she doesn't require a separate theory section in theses at all, but rather expects the thesis to show along the way explicitly how others' texts have influenced the arguments and the way they are made.

The three stories or threads may well experience constant interconnections; different existing studies draw from different linguistic theoretical traditions that may, in turn, follow historical and political vicissitudes. So should you tell the stories (1) one after the other, or (2) with repetitions that make the text long and tedious? Most often, no one except the writer can really make the final decision. There are no good and bad solutions here, but rather decisions that make it obvious that writing research is not just reporting, but has an important rhetorical component. The ability of the author to write, explain or tell stories (or to learn by doing it) is central to the whole exercise of constructing knowledge.

5.3.4 Method and Fieldwork (the What and the How)

The main aim of this section is to explain how the research process has taken place, in order to enable readers to judge the merits of your argument. Again, the logic of extent and detail works similarly to the earlier section: for journal articles, readers will want to know the minimum necessary; for Ph.D. theses, evaluators usually expect the author to justify her decisions and to show awareness of the principles behind the choice and characteristics of specific samples, sites, data collection strategies and analytical proce-dures. In short, Ph.D. and M.A. candidates must show that they know about research methodologies. So, drawing from the argument already developed in the research plan, they should justify their choices **in relation to their own study**, and focusing on the fol-lowing elements:

- Description of and rationale for the sites where the data was collected.

- Description of and rationale (or explanation) for the kinds people who have partici-pated as informants or research participants.

- Types of data gathered and used, and how they have been recorded (description of the observation activities, of the interviews, of the texts and so on) and rationale for each of these elements.

- Extent of the data collection performed and of the data base: time spent in the various activities, length of recorded material, number of interviews, focus groups, documents, etc and rationale for these.

- Data management and data analysis procedures: how the data has been transcribed or stored, coded or indexed, searched, counted, etc. and rationale for these.

- Other relevant details (and the rationale for them) such as (1) ethics and politics; (2) assistance obtained by colleagues, research associates, authorities, organizations, research participants; (3) difficulties encountered, accidents or circumstances that may have a bearing on any aspect of your research or (4) limitations or gaps that your data might have.

In a research article, you may be able to explain everything in a single paragraph or two, and may even skip some details if you can reasonably expect readers to take them for granted (e.g., people will generally assume that you have transcribed your interviews). It is nonetheless critical to make sure that you provide the information necessary for read-ers to grasp the scope of the claims that you are making, and the reasoning that drove the whole study. With more or less detail, you will also have to indicate how you ana-lyzed your data, and when relevant, locate your ways of analysis in the methodological conversation in your field. Again, in a thesis, you will need to reflect explicitly about the ways in which your choices of method, of sampling, of analysis allow you to support your claims but also how these choices inform the limits of these claims. In what ways could my analysis be relevant for other contexts? Or for similar kinds of phenomena?

In many instances, this section also includes the "context account," which we also mentioned earlier. Given that this part commonly presents a description of physical sites (institutions, villages, neighbourhoods, etc.), particular groups or kinds of activities, this may include general statistical data and a historical account about the site, the popula-tion or the activity in question. Again, at this level of decision-making, it is often up to each author to evaluate how the telling will best work: whether the contextual infor-mation will be best received in connection with the conceptual framework, with the methodological account, or maybe as a stand-alone section. However, it is important to bear in mind that these "contextual" descriptions are sensitive to the orientation of the research and to the social and political interests that have informed them, so that they should not be presented as innocent or just factual descriptions.

5.3.5 Data Presentation, Analysis and Discussion

This is clearly the core of the whole research process, arguably the "moment of truth." These two sections (8 and 9 in Table 5.1) must display your fully formed argument as it is built on the evidence that supports it, and expressed with all the detail necessary (though not exhaustively).

We are treating "data presentation and analysis" and "discussion" as equivalent because, textually speaking, they are not very different. In fact, the distinction between them is not universally accepted or expressed in the same way. They roughly correspond to the blurry earlier division between "description" and "explanation" discussed in Moment 4. So the "data presentation" is supposed to make room to present and explain evidence, although you are certainly advised to start leading the reader towards your conclusions. After this, the "discussion" need not stay so close to the data and should focus more on reasoning, weighing up alternative interpretations, linking your findings and views with those of other researchers, and eventually spelling out the full significance of your results for the discipline and, possibly, for society in general or specific interest groups.

At this juncture, novice writers may encounter forms of uncertainty related to (1) the amount of data that has to be presented to the reader so she understands and is convinced by the argument, (2) how to select the "right" pieces of data and (3) how to organize the different pieces of the argument. We have addressed some of these issues earlier in Moment 4, Section 4.1; but when it comes to formulating the expression of research results it is important to understand that the "amount" of data that you **need** in order to support an argument is not the same thing as the actual data that you need to **present** this argument for the reader. Thus, the concerns that you may have had when designing the project, doing the fieldwork, transcribing or coding do not apply automatically to writing. In any form of scientific communication, data is presented in a selective way and through varied forms of visualization: charts, tables, schemata, drawings, lists. In sociolinguistics, transcripts reproducing verbatim dialogues of research participants are typical. Which exact example you choose depends on the argument you are making at this point: it can be the most illuminating example of the issues in your data, or the most representative, or it can be the exception to the rule or it can be the most ambivalent and hardest one to analyze, thus pushing forward the limit of a concept or of an approach. The key here is to make a clear connection between the data, its analysis and the argument you are advancing at that particular point of the text.

The amount of data presented does not help in any way to make the arguments more solid. Readers simply need to see the data that best helps them understand your results. This means, for example, that they will be happy to see just **one** example of an event, expression or social practice that occurs very often. Readers probably need to know just how often it occurs and what it feels like, so to speak, "on stage." This would be presenting data with a "representative aim," i.e., the example stands for a class of equivalent or similar phenomena. Otherwise, some events or conversations may be important because they are unique (e.g., a disagreement), so that one single occurrence deserves attention because it illuminates a point. How much? How long? How detailed? How rare? How common? There are no answers that apply generally to all situations, except that they must be sufficient to illustrate your argument and to make it understood to your audience. Thus, if you have identified, say, half a dozen types of situation according to some classificatory criterion, it may make sense to show examples of each so that readers can judge how well your classification works. However, in some cases this may be best achieved by actually showing the cases that do not fit any of your classes. Similarly, some points may be best illustrated or argued by showing what is more common, and others what is rare or extreme.

Another common concern is whether description and explanation should be dealt with separately in different chapters, or together. Again, this decision can only be made once we have decided what the best way is to organize the different threads of the argument. Description and explanation can certainly share space in the same chapters, sections, even paragraphs, provided that we do not confuse readers as to what we base our statements on. Description, in this sense, rests more or less directly on what we perceive in the data. Explanation, in contrast, relies on rational or reasonable inferences that we draw from connecting elements of the description.

Just as we said earlier that the account of the conceptual frameworks, literature reviews, methods and contextual information could eventually be structured in many ways, more integrated, or more separate or more sequential, the blurred boundary between "data presentation" and "discussion" brings many researchers to legitimately present them together and organize their text according to other criteria such as topic, context, types of data, argumentative lines, or combinations of these. Again, the narrative preferences and abilities of each researcher will need to be mustered to strike the most harmonious chord between the structure of the account, the characteristics of each project, and the nature of the conversations that she is joining. In research articles particularly, there is no room for multiple sections and subsections, so that authors must often be selective and opt for the best and simplest solution. For theses in particular, it is important to make sure that the structure of the text will be received favourably by the potential evaluators (or, at least, decide how important it is to have the evaluators happy on that front). Joan, for instance, divided his presentation of the analysis according to the key features of the argument: separate chapters on (1) gender displays, (2) analysis of speech and (3) analysis of language choice followed by an "explanatory" chapter on (4) how these phenomena connected to each other. (1), (2) and (3) focused on presenting and interpreting data but also had important elements of discussion about each specific issue. (4), on the other hand, was mainly argument complemented with some data. Monica's thesis laid out (1) the political and economic context in which her thesis question was situated, before turning to (2) the site where she worked as a representative example of terrains of struggle over social inequality between anglophones and francophones in

Montreal. She then (3) presented the range of ways in which the process of francization/francophonization was occurring in different zones of contact. She then (4) explained (3) as a function of (1) and (2); and finally, (5) used what she saw as the local consequences of (3) to make broader claims about (1).

5.3.6 Conclusion (So What?)

The conclusion section is the mirror image of the introduction and, to express it roughly, it should really say the same (in fact, some people even acknowledge that they write both at the same time). The important difference, however, is that the reader gets to the conclusion after having seen all your theoretical discussion and analysis, so that you should now be able to state and defend your point more forcefully and clearly than at the beginning.

Conclusions should not simply restate the argument, although it can be useful to have it summarized, so as to remind the reader of the forest she has just walked through inspecting a bunch of its trees. They may also contain the broad claims that you now feel you can make, as well as descriptions of the new threads (or roads, or lines) that have now appeared before you in the rhizome and the future direction of the research they suggest. You might want to address what you think your research means for other kinds of interlocutors.

Thus the conclusion is a summary of the whole project with all the arguments spelled out as clearly as possible. It is based on the assumption that the reader will still have, more or less alive, in her mind all the supporting evidence that has just been provided. This text is also supposed to include reference to the "conversations," i.e., the previous studies or colleagues to which your study makes contributions, and complements or contradicts what had been held as valid until now.

5.3.7 Endnotes and Appendices

The authors of this book grew up in an area of the academic world in which footnotes and endnotes were not encouraged. Again, in some academic traditions, footnotes are often considered critical to scholarly contributions, either because they are seen as important to display erudition or because comprehensiveness is valued. However, the current social science trend is that, from a communicative point of view, if the substance of the argument is in the main text, then nothing that is important should be sidelined from the main line. And conversely, if something is not important enough, well, maybe it is not worth a footnote or and endnote either. So the total number of points eligible to be addressed in endnotes is by this definition zero.

However, academics, being people fond of nuance, often manage to find points that stand on an impossible middle ground between the "important but irrelevant" and the "relevant but unimportant," such as: (1) preventing objections to a point by bringing in more material that could potentially disrupt the argumentative flow inside the text, (2) substantiate a detail that may not be very important but could be of interest to some readers, (3) mention a source or acknowledge a contribution that cannot be quoted in a conventional way or (4) observe a side-implication that your argument suggests but which you cannot address adequately in this text. We generally agree that, barring the mandatory acknowledgement of sources of funding, and of colleagues and institutions that may have helped in any way, professional or personal, endnotes and fieldnotes should be avoided if at all possible.

Appendices are a different type of additional material. They are very rare in journal articles for the obvious reason that this type of text demands synthesis and puts the argument in the centre. In theses, however, there is the added goal of judging the whole research process from a pedagogic perspective and, in some traditions, a requirement to make the evidence available to the academic community. Thus, it is common to at least provide samples of all research instruments (questionnaires, focus group scripts, consent forms, coding maps) and in some contexts to even provide the full data set in the form of transcriptions, recordings, collections and archives duly indexed and organized. Here we recommend that doctoral candidates include whatever materials allow readers to best evaluate the procedures of data gathering and analysis, bearing in mind the distinction between the committee that will actually formally evaluate you, and readers interested in your work. Beyond this, it is a matter of finding out what is expected in each local academic tradition.

5.3.8 References

Beyond the principles that we discussed in the conceptual/review section above, references are components of academic texts that express the fundamental notion that knowledge is constituted or produced in conversation with others. We argued that writers must make sure that they acknowledge the source of the concepts, ideas and information that they have used as a basis for their study and to which their study contributes. Formally and conventionally, this acknowledgement is made through references, i.e., the citations of other academic works that we insert in the texts by way of author's surname and date of publication (generally, works cited must be publicly available, hence "published"). Sometimes this acknowledgement involves even verbatim quotes or short sections of the articles or books that we mention.

The actual formal and practical aspects of reference and quotation are addressed in the Shop Floor section. For novice researchers, however, insecurity is common as to how to decide which references are somehow "mandatory" and how many are expected. In the conceptual/review section we already observed that conceptual discussions often follow a chronological logic, which leads us to quote older works first.

The criteria about whose work needs to be explicitly acknowledged vary substantially in theses and articles, as well as in different regions or sections of the academic world. In some academic traditions, the reference section of the text was used to offer to readers a bibliography of works that had some connection with the topic at hand. In current academic publishing practice, references must be given only for works cited in the text, and citations in the text should be kept to the minimum necessary to follow the argument. Journal articles should be as economical as possible with the cited references, whereas in theses there is much quoting that needs to be done to simply display your command of the field.

There are three main reasons to quote someone: **first**, to duly acknowledge the source of an idea or information; **second**, to offer the reader the means to explore some point further or in more detail and **third**, to **guide** the reader. The principle of economy should be applied to all cases. For instance, you do not need to always quote the founding fathers of the discipline or works that are so well known in the field that nobody will really think that you intend to steal their ideas. Quoting a work universally known in the field may be useful from another perspective: it may simply direct readers to see your theoretical or methodological standpoint very quickly, so that it can save you the work of explaining it (but maybe just one such citation is enough in an article). You should also quote the most recent works directly connected with your study, to avoid giving the impression that you may have overlooked state-of-the-art research, and to best situate the conversation in which your claims participate in. Verbatim quotes of someone else's words must also be accompanied with a citation that includes the page where the segment is found. Generally speaking, you should quote everything that might eventually be missed by readers, to display that you are indeed in command of everything, and you should avoid quoting things that readers will assume that you know or are not directly relevant to your argument. But you may also economize, for instance, with authors who publish several texts on largely the same material or argument: just one item for each author may be enough.

Finally, there is a sizable minority of novice researchers that tend to misuse references and verbatim quotes in their early texts. That is, they tend to **hide** their views behind views of others, usually because they are insecure about stating clearly what they themselves think. It can also happen when researchers have been socialized in research traditions in which the author is conventionally **hidden** behind generic statements, or behind a generic "we" that is often ambiguous, sometimes referring to the author(s) and other times to the whole community of academics in the field. So instead of explaining and justifying their choice of method or a particular interpretation, these authors feel safer quoting someone else who says what they wanted to say. This practice is also called *argument from authority*, which is not necessarily flawed, but is generally ill-regarded (and especially in the English-speaking world). Moreover, texts that contain repeated instances of this tactic end up being confusing and difficult to read because readers fail to work out what the specific contribution of the author is.

The main point is that you can use references effectively to distinguish your own contribution to knowledge from the works that you build on and are in conversation with, and to delimit the boundaries of the conversations that you consider are relevant to participate in.

5.4 Knowledge Mobilization

One final aspect of academic work has to do with its dissemination outside the strictly academic world. While many scholars have long practised participating in multiple conversations (in anthropology, Margaret Mead is the most famous example; she used to write columns in women's magazines), for funding agencies and universities this is a relatively recent development, reflected in the various terms in circulation: *research impact*, *outreach*, *knowledge mobilization* and *knowledge exchange*. (We will use knowledge mobilization here.)

Theses and conventional academic publications are only in exceptional cases read by non-academics, which means that possible applications or benefits of our research are limited if no effort is made to publish our results in other contexts. This issue is of increasing concern to governments and funding agencies as they seek to evaluate the returns of their large investments in education and research. Moreover, governments are interested in working out which lines of research can be of more benefit to the public or to particular sections of industry. This is why governments and research funding agencies are increasingly demanding that academics consider the social or technological impact of their research beyond the immediate academic community when they design their projects, and that they plan concretely how to disseminate their findings beyond academic circles. Thus, while the dissemination or "popularization" of research was traditionally done by some academics who had this specific vocation in the past, this is now becoming a standard professional requirement. From a critical sociolinguistic perspective this is not an unwelcome development, given that critical social research has always aspired to effect social change.

In any case, we see two main aspects that need to be borne in mind when considering the question of knowledge mobilization for our research: (1) that we are talking of communicating with very different audiences and in very diverse contexts; (2) that we should be attentive to the position from which we speak as academics. Both aspects impinge powerfully on the vexed questions of how we must tell the story, from which viewpoint and in which style of expression.

The first aspect guides us to the question that there is not just "a general public" out there (that we could address by, say, writing in conventional newspapers or appearing on radio and television channels), but actually a myriad of interest groups whose activities and concerns may be closer or further to what we do. The concept of "stakeholders" has recently been used to point to the audiences that may have a "stake" in our work. It may point to any kind of professional group, government agency, private business, association, NGO, political constituency that may constitute a communicative community of some kind and in which we can either identify interlocutors or find venues to publish our material. Stakeholders can therefore be very diverse and they may offer very different types of outlets for communication, debate and dissemination.

The question of the position from which we speak is substantial, and has profound implications that we can only briefly discuss here: it applies to the role of the "expert" or the "intellectual" in society, and the conditions of sociopolitical validity of the knowledge that we produce. In short, who are we to speak and why should people listen to what we say? In Western academic traditions, scientists have traditionally been treated as authorities and their statements as representing publicly sanctioned truths that could be delivered as unidirectional speeches, sermons or lectures. Critical sociolinguistics is not fully comfortable with this "Enlightenment" conception of the intellectual in which a socially prescribed hierarchy somehow pre-establishes whose voice, whose viewpoint and whose representation is valid.

One alternative way to approach this is to work collaboratively, i.e., by extending the circle of people with whom we have conversation. Or we can orient more toward co-designing research and knowledge together with key stakeholders. For example, Sari has found it useful to initiate and organize various kinds of discussion and conversation events and opportunities with the tourism entrepreneurs who took part in the research for exchanging ideas, expertise and experiences. This has taken different formats: sometimes this has meant a discussion over a cup of coffee; another times a group conversation or seminar, e.g., on role of narratives in tourism development; taking part in training future guides for the region's tourism industry or inviting a new expert to bring in different perspectives to the topic. Other forms of knowledge exchange have included organizing a photo exhibition, parents' evenings, and teachers' in-service education events. Monica has turned to a website as a means to involve participants and engage in conversations with interested others. The website includes case studies embedded in an interactive map of Canadian francophone mobility for which participants provide narrative, photo essays, artwork, links to their music or any other form of expression they wish to share. It is possible for viewers to send in comments or their own narratives, engaging directly with the material on the site and the people (researchers and participants) involved at least in its initial iteration. It has a playlist of relevant songs, to which viewers can add suggestions. It can be used then for presentations to a variety of audiences, from other academics to policy makers to community leaders. Joan has recently turned to Wikipedia as the world's most consulted source of scientific knowledge by the public. Inserting new entries or contributing to existing entries makes some concepts and ideas easily reachable via the internet. Wikipedia also has the advantage to provide a good infrastructure to insert versions in multiple languages.

The principle of reflexivity adhered to in this book has key implications in this regard, as it involves the need to (1) problematize the position of the researcher together with that of the researched and (2) to treat methodologically all discourses and viewpoints as (in principle) debatable with regards to the contexts in which they emerge. This means that knowledge mobilization and outreach is basically conceived as a dialogue in which the voice and interests of non-academic participants must be allowed to be put on the table. In the contemporary world, more dialogical genres are gaining ground, as they allow participants to gradually adjust to each other's perspective, terminology and interests. Not that dialogue is in itself an innovation, it being the preferred format used by the classical Greek philosophers, notably as it appears in the writings of Plato himself.

Good journalists may also set up interviews that take the form of a dialogue that may be communicatively very successful. However, although many arguments can be made in favour of dialogue as a principle, it is not always possible, or expected, or enjoys enough of a tradition or provides the most economical form of knowledge transfer in all contexts.

The rhetorical nature of writing, discussed above, comes to our aid here in the sense that our narratives will invariably need to be reformulated as a means to perform this approximation or this dialogue. We need to think about elements that make our position credible and convincing, namely the evidence, the rigour and the argumentative consistency. At the end of the day, this amounts to saying that, yes, you should publicize your views in press articles, the radio, TV, blogs, videoblogs, social media outlets, professional newsletters or even works of fiction, and you will have to find the best register for each.

5.5 Summary

Here is what this chapter has covered:

- Writing research reports requires the development of complex skills and an intense personal investment.
- Writing academic texts requires novice researchers to display and expose themselves as knowledge producers: to act out a new identity.
- Writing is part and parcel of the process of data analysis.
- We start all texts with an argument in mind; but we must adapt it to the unforeseen turns and complications that we find in the data and/or in our reasoning.
- Academic texts are part of conversations with other colleagues whose ideas must be clearly represented and acknowledged.
- It is essential to have readers in mind when writing. Conventions of academic writing generally serve the primary purposes of (1) announcing the argument early and clearly, and (2) guiding the reader well through the descriptions and interpretations of the data.
- Academic texts must generally focus on clearly specified arguments and not provide any additional information or commentary not directly bearing on them.
- All the arguments must be sufficiently supported by the data and the reasoning that the text provides.
- Making research results accessible to people outside academia is necessary to ensure that society benefits for it.
- Disseminating research results to wider audiences requires adapting the way to communicate them in a responsible fashion to each context of communication.

Keywords: knowledge producer, genre, rhetoric, description, interpretation, argument, audience, conversation, academic writing, knowledge exchange.

Writing in English

Joan had to learn and adapt to the conventions of English-speaking academic writing when he started his postgraduate studies in the United Kingdom. It was probably easier for him than for most of his Catalan colleagues because his undergraduate degree was in English and he had always been attracted to English and American cultural production in literature, cinema, rock music or science. However, he came from an academic tradition in which a lot of procedural learning was implicit, and rarely formally addressed and exercised in class. For instance, one of the most important academic genres in the teaching of literature at the time was the "text commentary." Whenever someone asked how these had to be done, they were told to read the authoritative texts of literary history or stylistic analysis. As a result, students of his generation tended to somehow adopt or imitate the style of their preferred authors. There were some dangers in this. For instance, the sociolinguist Lluís V. Aracil (1982) was top on his list, but he wrote in a very personal style; and his texts were not research reports, but conceptual discussions with a lot of irony, sarcasm, implicit collusions and virtually no formal citations.

When Joan moved to Britain he found that local students, on the contrary, possessed a much more elaborate literacy training. Although British students often derided the writing conventions that they had learned, it was quite a discovery for Joan to access a language that one could use to discuss how to write texts and the rationale behind the conventions. He also had the opportunity to participate in courses and workshops on the matter, and to appreciate the fact that, in some contexts, having clear rules had palpable advantages.

After his Ph.D., Joan started working in Catalan universities, where he brought in the literacy culture that he had learned as a graduate student both into his teaching and into his work as reviewer in local journals. One telling experience is when he had to review articles written in Aracil's style and he had to conclude that (at least in these specific cases) the argument was not clear, the sources were missing and there was no new evidence. He feels that this is one of the ways in which he has been an active accomplice in the construction of anglophone hegemony over academic communication. Although he was willing to make allowances for different conventions of writing (and allowing that Aracil's original texts are still powerful texts), in these cases he felt that they made poor scholarship. For Joan, this is a good example of how hegemonies work because, in his experience, the adoption of English-speaking literacy culture was experienced as enabling because of its explicitness and accountability. More often than not, students who fail to follow these conventions in M.A. or Ph.D. theses also run into serious difficulties of clarity, cohesion and coherence. On the other hand, he also finds publication outlets in English sometimes too restrictive in their specific demands for data-based arguments as against more open conceptual discussions.

Writing as Exploration

Writing to me means finding out what I think about the issues that I am examining. In this sense, writing to me is a journey of discovery: what there is in my data and what is my argument. At this initial stage of my writing I formulate my research question into an argument that I test in my thinking/writing. I find that thinking of myself as being in a process of making an argument that I back up with evidence from my data, helps to shape the task of writing an article, for instance, into manageable steps.

I need to write a lot in order to get everything out of my head and to see and assess what parts make sense and which do not, at least for the argument that I am trying to make. Writing at this early stage refers to a variety of activities: it can mean free writing, just jotting down my thoughts in random order and simply writing and writing. Usually this materializes into a long, winding file that I call "dough," by which I mean that this text serves as a resource for the development of my thinking, but will still need lots of work. I am also a fan of using all kinds of visual tools to help me to find my key argument and the evidence I have for it. So I draw mind maps and I write lists. But my very favourite tool is Post-It stickers. I use different-coloured stickers for research questions, data, concepts and findings, and jot keywords on them. Then I organize them into groups and into a different order in order to test my argument and whether I have evidence for that. Different-coloured highlighters are also useful for this purpose.

Usually these activities help me to see at least two things: I have more data than I need (so I need to choose) and my argument is too broad and thus not clear enough, so I need to rework my argument as well. Once I am more or less happy with the gist of the argument, I start to write (again), but knowing that I will return to this exercise many times before my article is ready. One consequence of this kind of writing is that it generates lots and lots of text; this makes my colleagues and friends, who know my way of working and from whom I ask for feedback, sigh. That is why I am in a continuous process of trying to learn to edit my own text into a more manageable and more focused text. Hence, the several rounds of Post-It stickers and highlighting, too.

I do not write in a linear way, but rather in a rhizomatic way. This means that I go back and forth among different parts of the text, get lost in sidetracks, despair at dead ends and navigate across different possibilities of how to argue my case. Sometimes stretches of text come out in Finnish, some in English; some thoughts come out as a sentence, some in a form of dots or lines. But I need to keep writing in order to find my way out of the forest of theoretical concepts, social issues and the richness of the data.

In my writing rhizome I have several nexus: the argument, data and methods, context, theoretical framing, findings and discussion. I typically write something around each nexus before I try to put them together in a linear form. I often start with the data and methods nexus, then move on to theoretical framing and findings nexus, working on these two simultaneously. When I get stuck, I write the contextual nexus. And I leave the introduction and discussion nexus towards the end of the process.

In working towards a publishable text, I go several rounds in this rhizome, stopping in one nexus, moving back and forth among the nexus, until I think that the text starts to make some sense. I think that this kind of writing helps in finding connections in your argument. But it also runs the risk of repetition and circular argument. Again, a moment for visualization of the key argument and the way it is advanced in the text is needed.

I also need conversations with my colleagues. This, too, can take several forms. At the early stage of planning of the argument (and the article-to-be), I find it useful to discuss, brainstorm and test the idea (argument) when talking with colleagues over lunch or coffee, when I teach students discourse studies, and when presenting the early drafts of the argument in a seminar and in conference papers. At the minimum, I get to hear myself how the argument sounds like; but this also allows me to see if it makes sense to the others, and what parts of the arguments give rise to lots of questions, indicating to me that at least that part needs more work.

I seek comments for my writing throughout the process, but especially at the beginning (testing the argument, checking if the evidence is there), and then in the moment when I need to lock down what the actual (single) argument in this particular article is and how I am going to write the story around it (the structure, the logic of the article). I have some colleagues whom I consider my trusted critical friends; they know my work and my way of working, and they know what I am trying to say in my text more or less. These people are irreplaceable for my thinking and writing and their feedback is often quick, to the point and extremely helpful. The shared collegiality makes this also typically a very quick and smooth process. However, I also seek comments from people who might be a bit outside of my own field of expertise in order to initiate conversation beyond the most immediate academic work, and to test if the argument makes sense to others, too. I might also seek comments from key stakeholders, for example, when talking about the implications of my work. And for important grant proposals, I seek comments also from my family members, who are not working in the academy; many of their comments have helped me to see how I could make my case in a more accessible way, or how to better, more convincingly support my points.

My experience is that all writers struggle with the feeling of lack of time for writing, regardless of the conditions of your personal and working life. I think that this feeling is your fellow traveller throughout the writing process, and you will need to find a way to deal with it. What works for me is to write regularly (yes, almost every day, a bit like it is good to exercise on a regular basis, not only once a week or a few times in a month) and to write at the time of the day when my brain works well and I feel decisive. To me, this is early morning hours, before the rest of the world wakes up. So instead of checking my emails and doing all other tasks so that I could "then" focus on writing, I start my days with writing. Depending on the circumstances (the family issues, work, travelling, etc.), I might work fifteen minutes or a couple of hours; everything counts. After my morning writing session, I feel good; good about the research as it has advanced, good about the text as it has been advanced (however little) and good about myself as my mind is more content and clearer after jotting down some thoughts on paper or screen.

Another strategy to navigate time constraints as an academic with lots of other responsibilities (and as a person with her own life, too) is to seek writing partners and to organize writing retreats. A writing partner is a colleague who also wants to share experience of writing, get feedback on her texts and most importantly, wants to have deadlines and be able to meet them. So most typically, we are not co-authors of a same text but rather writers in a similar kind of path and rhythm. I need deadlines (in order to surface from my ever expanding writing rhizome); having a writing partner gives me a good motivation to respect them. Another way of helping in writing is to organize a writing retreat: a dedicated time and space for writing in a structured way, including time for writing and feedback. I have organized writing retreats varying from a half a day in a far corner of the university space with a coffee in our thermos, to a three-day retreat at a beautiful cottage with full board. I think that while nice surroundings make the experience special, what matters the most is that the people taking part in the retreat are committed to the task and deadlines, and generous in terms of providing feedback and support. These are not events for hanging around with your colleagues and friends (as needed as that is, too), but an intensive moment of collaborative thinking, writing and reading.

Writing is often discussed in terms of how hard and time-consuming it is. And yes, this is true. But I also think that it is rewarding, exciting and inspiring. I feel privileged that I have a job that allows me to think, read and write and to have meaningful conversation with other people interested in language issues that matter.

6 Shop Floor

6.1 Introduction: What Do We Mean by Shop Floor?

This section is where we have put all the practical tips that we have to offer for the four moments where such practicalities rise: Moment 2, designing your research, Moment 3, constructing your data, Moment 4, analyzing your data, and Moment 5, making your story.

The examples come from our own experiences, that of our students, and that of our colleagues. We hope you will find some tools you can use in here. You should not feel that you need to use all of them, or even any of them. It is a good idea to take part in various methods courses available to you and to read about other research methods and procedures explained in more extensive manuals. And you can combine what we suggest with the skills that you have acquired in your studies or elsewhere.

As has been the case throughout the book, we have been very selective and concentrated on addressing some of the most common research procedures of critical language research. We hope that you will be able to *transfer* our examples to your cases.

The Shop Floor is not a chapter like the previous chapters. We call it Shop Floor to convey the idea that knowledge is a product, and requires producing, using some concrete tools. High quality products require both a grand design, and some nitty-gritty work. You will find here a place where the messiness of the practical process of doing research gets laid out, tools strewn around, to be picked up when needed. The section is crafted as a resource site that you are welcome to visit whenever you want to get your hands dirty. So you are not supposed to read it through, from beginning to end, like the other chapters.

For each of the key four moments we have collected different kinds of resources, tips and examples that we hope will be helpful to you when working on a specific moment of your research. Below, you will find such things as examples of research proposals, ethical guidelines, data coding and writing tips. In some cases we have provided some reflection on the tools we discuss; in others we simply summarize concrete steps or models in a table or bullet point form. In some cases we provide examples from our own work. Whenever possible, we have given you summaries in bullet points, but we also discuss some of the areas where there are some issues you might want to think about when evaluating whether these particular tools are useful or not. Please feel free to dip in and shop around—whatever works for you.

6.2 Moment 2: Designing Your Research

There are two practical areas to think about at this stage. The first is what you need to know about preparing proposals for theses, or for formal research projects. As the demands for these two are very similar, we will focus on research funding applications. Thesis proposals are usually somewhat less elaborate versions of research proposals, so most of what applies to the first will apply to the second. The second is the process of ethical review, which incorporates many of the principles and practicalities of fieldwork.

6.2.1 Proposals

We can call "research proposals" a genre, although you may find very significant differences between various calls and institutional guidelines. No two funding agencies ask for the same format, not even for the same abstract length. Some research proposal forms ask for "objectives" (or "aims" or "goals"), "hypotheses" or "research questions" (or any combination of them, including all of them), "justification" (or "rationale," or "motivation"), a "state of the art" (or "theoretical framework), etc. (and more or less equivalent terms in other languages). Each institution has its own expectations to which one's agenda needs to be "translated."

Different agencies request different things, so of course you need to be careful in reading the instructions about what is expected. One key aspect of any such application is to have a good grasp of the expectations of those who are going to review and evaluate your proposal: Are they academics in your field? Can they come from any discipline in the social sciences or the humanities? Or even from other disciplines or outside academia? You need to adjust your argument and style of writing accordingly. Further, does your proposal lay out the types of projects, orientations and goals that are going to be prioritized? Make sure that you have the right audience in mind and that you write in a way that connects with it. Do not hesitate to contact funding agency program officers, who are usually glad to help you understand their instructions, as they frequently get applications in which applicants have forgotten essential aspects or misinterpret the instructions. Many universities also have staff dedicated to helping you acquire funding and thus to learn how to write successful research proposals. These people often have technical knowledge and experience that can be valuable to you.

Drawing on our experience in writing and evaluating research proposals, we think that there is a certain structure common in many such applications. We have opted again to use the metaphor of "forest and trees" to illustrate the building of your argument in your proposal. And a new metaphor, too—the hook.

Structure of a research proposal:

(1) The hook. Evaluators typically read many applications at once for any round of competition for funding. You need to grab their attention in the first sentences. A good hook identifies a general problem that any reader from any field of life would agree is worth investigating. It is a brief statement of the nature of your forest, if you like. Examples might be: indigenous peoples' struggles for self-determination, what happens to refugees, educational possibilities for minori-tized groups, how children learn to understand gender and sexuality or coping with structural economic change. (This is just a list of what happens to come to our minds as a way of showing you the order of generality a hook should have; it is not an indication of what we think is most worth investigating).

(2) A statement on why the hook is important, theoretically, socially, politically, eco-nomically, or, which of these conversations you intend to participate in. It is worth reading the documentation of the funding institution, because they often define or provide clues as to what kinds of hooks they are interested in. For instance, in the European Union, the Horizon 2020 initiative was devised from the start to organize research funding according to specific societal "challenges."

(3) Your specific research question as a way into the broad issue you identified in the hook; this is where you introduce your particular tree(s).

(4) An explanation of why this is a good tree to investigate if you want to understand the forest: is it illuminating, typical, particularly consequential? This explanation needs to make sense to your audience and convince them, so keep them in mind (as you are usually already very fond of your tree at this point).

(5) How you will investigate this tree (usually called "methodology"), and why this is a good way to investigate it. This requires thinking through such details as exactly which sites make sense, how many participants there are and of what kind, what you will do with them and for how long. In this section, you are not usually expected to show your knowledge about methodology. Instead, what they want to know, con-cretely and specifically, is how you are going to conduct your research and how well it fits with your overall design and research questions: will you be able to answer your research questions with the help of this data? The ethical issues are often dis-cussed here, at least when there are issues of consent, vulnerable subjects, etc.

(6) How are you going to make sense of the data you have acquired in your investi-gation, or how are you going to make sense of this particular tree. Here you are expected to show your methodological decisions and arguments: what kind of methods you need to use in order to analyze your data so that you will be able to provide answers to your questions.

(7) How are you going to engage in the conversations relevant to the broader gen-eral issue, or not only this tree, but the forest it is part of. In the guidelines this is often discussed in terms of social impact. This means that you needed to look

a bigger picture: why does this issue or topic that you are going to examine through this data and with help of this method matter?

(8) Why you are the most suitable person to carry out this project, including your skills and training in the field.

(9) Why you have the means to carry this project out, i.e., support from colleagues, the department, labs, resources or additional funding to provide for it. Often the research environment will be assessed as well, e.g., in terms of how much and what kind of support and know-how there is for your research.

(10) Knowledge exchange or dissemination. One important aspect of your research is its potential for social impact. This can mean for example the contribution your research will do not only to the field of research you are working on (e.g., conceptual or methodological development) but also how the findings of your research can be applied or be useful, e.g., in teaching, in developing better practices with stakeholders and perhaps even facilitating innovations related, e.g., to language teaching, multilingual practices or sustainable tourism. Funding agencies may also be concerned whether the investment in research brings about tangible gains in society and the economy. Further, funding agencies expect you to be explicit about how you will communicate your findings and to whom. Usually the key audiences are the academic community, stakeholders and general public. First, you may lay out your publication plans: conference papers that you plan to give as well as publishing articles and/or monographs for academic audiences. This is usually the easy part (see Moment 5). Secondly, you will need to explicate your plans for knowledge exchange with stakeholders. They typically are those people, institutions, organizations or companies that have taken part in your research or that your research is about. They may also include any other social grouping or organization that may be interested in the knowledge that you are producing, e.g., policy makers or politicians. You will also need to describe the means of communicating and collaborating with them (via leaflets, press articles, round tables, meetings, seminars or specific events). Thirdly, you will need to also say something about your plans to make your research and the findings available for the "general public," e.g., through social media activity (e.g., blog, Twitter), project website or media interviews.

(11) Timeline. Here you need to factor in not only how long it will take to do the observations, interviews, focus groups and documentation that you would like to do, but also how long it will take to transcribe and code, if you are planning to do so, and to do the analysis and writing, thinking and redrafting. Also the time needed to carry out the knowledge exchange plan needs to be counted in. Usually it is good to present a timeline or similar kind of visual representation of the time needed for the various parts of your project. You need to be realistic here—one element of the assessment of your proposal is how plausible the plan is.

(12) Data management plan: researchers are increasingly required to make explicit how they store data for use during and after the research. This should specify:

(a) organization of metadata that will define the forms of conceptual access to the data items (see Section 4.2 below); (b) how will you organize the sharing of the data amongst team members if applicable; (c) whether the data will be made publicly accessible and (d) how will you guarantee anonymity and security and other possible ethical issues.

(13) Budget. Do you need to move around? Where will you sleep? How will you eat? Do you need to buy any equipment or software? Will you need to pay anyone for any services? How about your salary? Check carefully the guidelines of the funding agency: there might be rules specifying that costs they will or will not cover, i.e., what costs are eligible (e.g. yes, they will cover your salary and travel expenses but not equipment or no, they will provide you a grant but that money cannot be used to hire anybody else).

6.2.2 Ethical Review Board Applications and Procedures

In this section we assume that doctoral students and researchers must have their projects formally vetted by some form of an ethics committee. Even your institutional criteria may vary, we believe that you should address the ethical issues that we describe here even if you are not institutionally forced to do so, simply because it allows you to think through what it means to do research ethically. Additionally, it is worth bearing in mind that, in many countries, scholars are required to vet their projects with relevant authorities even if these projects are led, financed by, and mostly conducted by staff employed at foreign universities. Formal processes of all kinds may take time, so be prepared for that.

Where formal processes exist, they are usually conducted by universities, and often as well by institutions like hospitals and school boards. You might look at the websites of your professional associations for their statements on ethics. The American Anthropological Association and the Linguistic Society of America both post their statements online, for example. Many universities also conduct workshops for researchers regarding what their boards expect.

What Goes Into Ethical Review Forms?

Typically, ethical review boards want the following:

- A brief, succinct description of the goals of the project. Review board members do not need to be convinced that your research is worth spending money and resources. They need to know only what it is about the nature of the project that makes it make sense to negotiate your research relationships the way you propose to.

- A statement of which agencies, if any, are providing funds for the project.

- An account of any other kinds of permissions you may need, and whether or not you have them already.

159

- What kinds of risks this work involves, and what are the potential benefits that may outweigh the risks. This usually also includes a discussion of how you plan to address the risks: are there ways you can mitigate them? Do you have a plan for what you would do if something bad or unexpected happens?

- The criteria that you will be using to decide whom to approach and include as participants.

- How you will approach the participants. This is often called a "recruitment script," but resist the pressure do it in an overly mechanical, scripted way; here you just need to provide the information that you will be sharing with the people you approach, e.g., consent forms and project descriptions.

- A description of what activities you plan to engage in, and what that means for what you are actually asking from your participants. Often these sections are framed in ways that are conceptualized for positivist approaches, which make little sense for the kind of work we are discussing here. You are unlikely to be able to submit "survey instruments" or "interview schedules." You **can,** however, explain what topics you want to cover in your interactions with people, one way or another.

- An explanation of how you will safeguard the privacy and well-being of your participants. This is usually where issues of participant anonymity and data confidentiality are discussed, including plans for what you will do with the data once this project is over. Will you anonymize them in reports? If so, how? Will you erase identifiers in data records? Will you ensure access to raw data only to your supervisors and/or research team members for the purposes of the project?

- What your plans are for involving participants in analysis, if applicable.

- What, if anything, you are offering to them in return for their participation.

- A detailed description of how you will negotiate consent with research participants, their mentors, guardians, superiors or representatives.

- What specific ways you are planning on sharing your account with participants once you have it.

- How you plan to manage and store the data, for how long and why.

- A copy of the brief project description you will use to explain what your project is about, in plain language.

- A copy of the consent letters you will use to explain what you are asking of potential participants, and what it means for them to agree to participate.

- Any security concerns that you as a researcher may encounter.

The last four items warrant some further discussion.

Data management and storage: Here you need to think not only about minimizing risks to your participants, but also about minimizing the risk that data will be lost, destroyed, or used for unethical or unprofessional purposes. Make sure all team members follow the same procedures.

- Make sure you have a system for indexing your data set, so you can see at a glance what kinds of data you have, who generated it, which participants were involved, where and when.
- Set up a method to immediately and securely handle and classify any piece of data (particularly recordings) from the moment that you produce them. Have specific bags, specific places to store it, secure locations nearby that do not require long delays between data production and storage. Use a simple system to identify the nature of the data (e.g., date, researcher name, place, participant name, nature of the data).
- Plan to copy, photocopy, scan or make digital copies as soon as possible of all data items.
- Make sure you have different devices in different locations for data backup.
- Make sure you have a filing and storage system so that your list of contacts is only connectible to pseudonyms by team members.

Project descriptions: These should fit on a maximum of one page. They can be used to explain what the project is about to potential participants or other possible interested parties, including the media, or your department; they can be used on a website or in a report as well. They should:

- Describe the goals of the project.
- Explain what it is for (a thesis? a funded research project? a film?).
- Which institutions or agencies are involved.
- Who you (and your supervisor or research team) are.
- How to contact you.
- Your website, if you have one.

Consent forms: The "consent form" is the textual representation of the ethical process of gaining *informed consent*. By this we mean making sure that people agree beforehand to participate in your research, and that they know, to the fullest extent possible (because no one can ever know everything beforehand), what they are getting into when, for example, they agree to let you live with them, come to their meetings, talk to you about your subject or photograph their property.

Many institutions ask for signed and dated consent forms. However, such bureaucratic forms may not make sense to your participants, or they may find them frightening, as is often the case with people who have been victims of state violence. Some people may not be able to write, or write in your alphabet of choice. Most institutions are at ease with alternatives if you explain why they are necessary; these often include verbal consent, especially when you audio record the conversation in which you provide the kinds of information necessary to it.

The participants will need to know most of the things you include in your ethics review board proposal. They need to know whom to contact if they have concerns; if you are a university student this might be your supervisor, or it might be the university ethics office. They should be told that they can change their minds if they have said either "yes" or "no" to you at the outset. You should think about what happens to the data if they first agree, and then later decide to withdraw. Normally, the expectation is that you will destroy data connected to them, but this depends on whether the withdrawal is simply due to no longer wishing to participate, or due to regret at having done so in the first place.

Some people feel that under some circumstances it is fine to be deceptive about your goals initially, as long as you tell people afterwards what questions you were really asking. Many review boards are open to arguments that doing so provides benefits that outweigh the risks to which you are subjecting the participants. This is often the case for research in psychology where, for example, you want to know precisely what people remember even when they are actually paying attention to something else. Our own view on this is that it is hard to confidently predict how people will feel upon learning that they have been misled. The conditions under which misleading them is acceptable are extremely restricted. We recommend telling the participants in advance exactly what you are up to, why and what this means for them. The questions that you ask may or may not coincide with your participants' understanding of an activity, and you will need to take that into account. You will probably have to repeat your account a number of times as your project unfolds, but you need to think first about how to do so as part of negotiating the mutual expectations of your relationship.

You also need to be clear about the practical dimensions of what you are offering and what you are asking. This will include such information as how much time you want to spend with the participants, what kinds of activities you plan to engage in, and whether you want people to set aside time exclusively for you or not. You may want to ask for some flexibility, since relationships and questions shift over time. It will also include what you might be offering, whether in the form of an exchange or not. Will you be offering language lessons in exchange for an audio-recorded interview? Will you pay people for their time?

You should spell out how you plan to engage people as you move through different stages of analysis. Do you intend to ask them to talk with you about the sense you are making of things as you go along, or later, once you have a first version of whatever product you plan to produce (thesis, article, report, film, photo album, blog post)? Will you wait until the final version is ready, reviewed, published and out there in the world? What rights over the product will you give people: can they ask you to remove things, modify your text, ask you not to publish it? How will you handle the possibility that you might disagree with them about an analysis or the value of what you produce?

Practical Tips

When you are asking potential participants for their consent, make sure to:

- Have double copies of the forms you want people to sign, in case they want to keep a copy.
- Decide if you want to co-sign as a sign of mutual commitment.
- Get people to print their names in ways that are legible to you in addition to their signatures.
- Record how to find them again in case you have follow-up questions or want to (or have committed to) sharing data, drafts or products.
- Find out if they prefer you to drop in, phone, send an email, contact them via social media, another person or some other way.
- Date the document, even if it is a verbal consent and record where it occurred if you are working in different places.
- Think about how to archive the forms so you can find them again.

Researcher security: Assess whether you may incur any risks that are new to you and think of how to minimize them. Think about whether risks you usually take need to be re-assessed for a new activity and environment. Find out what your institution's procedures are for registering with them; in any case, make sure that you are always traceable by your family and/or colleagues, e.g., that they know where you go and whom you meet. We are usually very traceable in our everyday life; but people may lose track of us when we move to an unfamiliar environment.

In addition, let us comment on two other issues: *use of the data* and *anonymity*.

Use of the data: Participants may want to know what kinds of records you intend to make: fieldnotes, film, audio recordings, artefact collection and so on, and what you will do with them after the data collection period is officially over. In some disciplines it is expected that you will destroy the data right after the project is over, in order to reduce the chances that it might fall into the wrong hands, or simply even be used for purposes other than those for which permission was granted. In any area where longer-term processes may be of interest, destroying data makes little sense. In some places, there is pressure to make data publicly available after a certain point, or colleagues may ask to have access to it in order to address other kinds of questions.

In our view, the only way to make this possible is to make sure that consent is given for such other purposes, whether as part of your consent process or in a separate, possible retroactive one for which the other researchers have to be responsible. We think, however, that it is unethical to permit uses of ethnographic data for other purposes than those for which permission was acquired. As we mentioned, you may run into the overlap between legal and ethical considerations here as well. The upshot of all this is clearly that you need to think about, and be clear with your participants about, what are the limits on the scope of use as far as you can control it, and thereafter what will happen to the data in the long run, after this phase is officially over. This includes their own social media (or other) accounts, and any project website you might have set up.

Anonymity: People will also want to know if other people will know that they have participated or not. Ethical review processes tend to assume that individuals want anonymity, but this may or may not be the case, and it might not be possible to provide. It is, however, something you should at least discuss. If people do wish to have their identity remain confidential, then you have to think about how to accomplish that: will you ask them to choose a pseudonym? Will you refrain from identifying them in published reports only, or does the data also need to be archived in a way that removes identifiers?

Although seemingly straightforward, anonymization can be a highly complex practice. Since ethnography focuses on how people live, experience and act in very particular situations, often carefully selected, removing identifying information may also remove contextual information that has potential value to the research and would be helpful in making sense of the results, especially to the reader. In certain circumstances, however, anonymization is not possible, or for some participants, not even desirable. In other circumstances, informants may want to be identified by their real names, because it is either their preference, they do not see anonymization as useful or possible, and they want to claim or promote issues important to them. This situation can occur, for example, when researching activists, artists, politicians and businesspeople.

The basic guideline regarding anonymization is that you always need to honour the commitments of confidentiality made to participants at the time the data was originally gathered. However, if at a later point in the research you think it useful to include some identifying information, then you need to contact the participant again and ask for his or her permission.

Here are some examples from some of the projects Joan and Monica have been involved in within Figure 6.1.

In the three examples that we provide here in Figures 6.2, 6.3 and 6.4, you will be able to appreciate the difference between the "heavy" approach of Monica's research team and Joan's "light," more user-friendly adaptation. Notice that, often, you may need different consent forms for individuals or institutions or other categories of participants.

OFFICIAL UNIVERSITY LOGO
Mr./Ms. XXXX

ADDRESS DETAILS   **Barcelona, 19 October 2016**
Dear Mr./Ms. XXXX,

This letter is to request your consent to allow our research group access to your Barcelona campus to conduct fieldwork. We are a team of sociolinguistic researchers working at the Universitat Oberta de Catalunya, in Barcelona, in a research project funded by the Spanish Ministry of the Economy and Competitiveness. The activities of data gathering of this research project will mainly consist of those practiced in conventional ethnography: participant observation, interviews and focus group discussions. We abide on principle by the AAA Committee of Ethics Principles of Professional responsibility (http://ethics.americananthro.org/category/statement/) and we are also open to attend to whatever guarantees IES Abroad wishes to be held in terms of security, privacy, confidentiality, respect and accessibility.

I understand that the matter must be brought to the attention of your central office in XXXX, although some concrete aspects of this collaboration will be finally decided and agreed with the director of the Barcelona campus. In any case, we provide here with a summary that we hope will be sufficient for all parties to reach a decision (in the understanding that INSTITUTION always has the option of cancelling the collaboration at any time).

Project description:

This project is part of a line of research aimed at understanding how speakers develop their linguistic repertoires throughout their lives and the social implications of this. After our earlier NEOPHON project, this new project (NEOPHON2) proposes to focus on the processes called "linguistic mudas" that is, the moments in life in which these changes of repertoire occur, usually because the person adopts a new language variety (dialect, language, register) in their social life. [. . .]

Research team

Director: Dr. Joan Pujolar, Associate professor at the Universitat Oberta de Catalunya

Dr. XXXXX, Associate professor at the Universitat Oberta de Catalunya

XXXX, doctoral fellow at the Universitat Oberta de Catalunya

Person yet not hired, research assistant at the Universitat Oberta de Catalunya

Data collection activities:

As is common in ethnographic studies, data collection activities can be negotiated with the research participants. We are interested mainly in the experience of students; although that of tutors, teachers and administrators is also relevant to the study. What we are actually requesting is that we get granted permission to

Figure 6.1 Presentation Document Used by Joan in the NEOPHON2 Project

ask anyone at the Barcelona campus to participate in the study and that they can individually agree or not without any pressure or instructions from their superiors. We assume that the students are over 18 and that they can provide informed consent by signing a document describing the aims of the study and their rights (right not to participate, right to impose limits on the presence and activities of researchers, right of withdrawal and of data cancellation, right to privacy and confidentiality, right to learn about the results of the study).

This list of possible activities expresses our priorities in terms of the types of evidence that we are interested in:

(1) Personal interviews: a private conversation inside or outside the campus premises, recorded via audio or in writing, at the discretion of the subjects. Between 10 and 20 in number.

(2) Participant observation: participation in curricular, time-out or extra-curricular activities (with or without a role assigned by the school, e.g. as "help" in class, as teaching assistant).

(3) Focus groups: a small group inside or outside the campus premises, recorded via audio or in writing, at the discretion of the subjects. Between 10 and 20 in number.

(4) Intensive engagement with 3-4 participants. Should students (or tutors) find our project interesting, we may propose some of the following possibilities:

  (a) Shadowing. Following someone during periods of time to record everyday linguistic practices.

  (b) Diaries. Subjects can run diaries on specific topics of relevance to the project.

  (c) Self-recording. Subjects can record conversations (with due guarantees) deemed relevant to the project without supervision.

  (d) Social network practices. The behavior of specific subjects can be recorded with their permission and those of other participants in social networks who are willing to consent.

(5) Documentation that the IES Abroad is willing to share of any kind relevant to the project: marketing material, yearly reports, course syllabuses, etc.

Copies of documents attesting to the informed consent of participants can of course be shared with INSTITUTION in the form you see fit. The research team is bound to act in accordance with the regulations issued by the University's ethic commission and is willing to uphold any other regulations demanded by INSTITUTION or the staff of the Barcelona Campus.

We look forward to collaborating in this project. Our contact details are in the signature.

Barcelona, 19 October 2016.
FORMAL SIGNATURE WITH DETAILS

Figure 6.1 (Continued)

Mobility, Identity and the New Economy: A Multi-Site Ethnography

Madam,
Sir,

We would like to invite you to participate in our research project titled *Mobility, Identity and the New Economy: A Multi-Site Ethnography*. This project is funded by the Social Sciences and Humanities Research Council of Canada (SSHRC); it is a university-based research project and not a privately sponsored study or evaluation.

The landscape of the Canadian job market is changing rapidly. We are interested in understanding how these changes are experienced by people in terms of their job training, their attempts to establish and maintain themselves in the workforce, the nature of their current work, and their plans for the future. We are particularly interested in the ways in which, or to what extent, these experiences relate to the languages you speak and write and/or to your geographic mobility (have you relocated for work, or are you planning to?)

To answer these questions, we would like to invite you to participate in the following research data collection activities:

(1) Interviews (usually recorded) focused on:
- your educational and work experiences, past, present and future
- the links between these experiences and the places you have lived/live
- the role of your language abilities in these experiences

(2) Observation and possible recording of work or training activities you are currently involved in

The interviews would last approximately one hour. A member of our research team would also spend time with you during your work or training-related activities, with the permission of the institution or workplace. Depending on the type of activities this will involve, this participation could be either selective or could involve observation over a period of time from one to four weeks, over the next two years. We will negotiate with you the best times to visit with you.

We assure confidentiality, and will do our very best to maintain your anonymity (in published documents, your name, the name of your organization and individual's names will be modified). However, there remains a very small chance that people from your environment could identify you in quoted excerpts. The data collected will be kept under lock and key at CREFO (www.oise.utoronto.ca/CREFO/). Once you give your consent to participate in our research, you remain at liberty to withdraw from the project at any time, in which case we will destroy all of the data

Figure 6.2 Consent Form for Individuals Used by Monica in the Project "Mobility, Identity and the New Economy: A Multi-Site Ethnography" (2008–2012)

collected from you. So that you are aware of the results of the research project, if you wish, we will forward you a copy of the final report. The results of the research will also lead to publications and presentations, largely of scientific nature, as well as university theses by our research assistants.

We hope that you will accept our invitation to participate in our research, which will give light to some the realities of current social processes and changes. Do not hesitate to contact us if you have any questions. We thank you in advance for your participation and collaboration.

Sincerely,

Monica Heller,
Principal Investigator

We have read the explanation of the project *Mobility, Identity and the New Economy: A Multi-Site Ethnography* and we accept to participate.

Name of organization:

Date:

Authority giving the organization's consent:

Name of the person authorized to sign for the organization (in CAPITAL LETTERS):

Signature on behalf of the organization:

Address:

Telephone number:

E-mail:

☐ YES, we would like to receive a copy of the final report.
☐ NO, we do not wish to receive a copy of the final report.

Figure 6.2 (Continued)

Mobility, Identity and the New Economy: A Multi-Site Ethnography

Madam,
Sir,

We would like to invite your organization to participate in our research project titled *Mobility, Identity and the New Economy: A Multi-Site Ethnography*. This

Figure 6.3 Consent Form for Institutions Used by Monica in the Project "Mobility, Identity and the New Economy: A Multi-Site Ethnography" (2008–2012)

project is funded by the Social Sciences and Humanities Research Counsel of Canada (SSHRC); it is a university-based research project and not a privately sponsored study or evaluation.

Your organization plays an important role in the reorganization of Canadian identities under new economic conditions. Given the goals of the research (see the attached summary), we are looking to understand the nature, history, functioning, market, personnel and the networks related to your organization. More specifically, we seek to understand the role of your organization in financing and planning of community economic development or francophone-related activities.

To answer these questions, we would like to ask you to permit us to carry out an ethnographic study in order to collect different types of data, including:

(1) Interviews (usually recorded) conducted with people occupying leadership positions within your organization;
(2) Interviews (usually recorded) conducted with employees or other active members of your organization;
(3) Documentation from your organization intended for internal distribution;
(4) Documentation from your organization intended for external distribution;
(5) Observation and possibly the recording of activities, internal meetings and public events (approximately ten).

The interviews would last approximately one hour. They would be related to the questions mentioned above as well as to the personal experiences that interviewees have had at work which relate to francophone organizations. A member of our research team would also spend from one to four weeks within your organization, over the next two years, in order to carry out the observation. We will negotiate with you the best times to visit you.

We assure confidentiality, and would do our very best to maintain your anonymity (in published documents, the name of your organization and individual's names will be modified). However, there remains a very small chance that people from your environment could identify you in quoted excerpts. The data collected will be kept under lock and key at CREFO. Once you give your consent to participate in our research, your organization remains at liberty to withdraw from the project at any time, in which case we will destroy all of the data collected from your organization. To be knowledgeable of the results of the research project, if you wish, we will forward a copy of the final report to the direction of your organization. The results of the research will also lead to publications and presentations, largely of scientific nature, as well as university thesis by our research assistants.

We hope that your organization will accept our invitation to participate in our research, which will give light to some the realities of current social processes and

Figure 6.3 (Continued)

changes. Do not hesitate to contact us if you have any questions. We thank you in advance for your participation and collaboration.

Sincerely,

Monica Heller,
Principal Investigator

_____

We have read the explanation of the project *Mobility, Identity and the New Economy: A Multi-Site Ethnography* and we accept to participate.

Name of organization:

Date:

Authority giving the organization's consent:

Name of the person authorized to sign for the organization (in CAPITAL LETTERS):

Signature on behalf of the organization:

Address:

Telephone number:

E-mail:

☐ YES, we would like to receive a copy of the final report.
☐ NO, we do not wish to receive a copy of the final report.

Figure 6.3 (Continued)

Contact: Dr. XXXX / XXXX@XXXX.EDU/ Tel: 12345678

Tionscadal
Proxecto
Projecte
Projet
Proyecto
Project

NEOPHON

◆☐UOC Universitat Oberta de Catalunya
Estudis d'Arts i Humanitats
Universitat Oberta de Catalunya
Av. Tibidabo 39-43
C.P.08035
Barcelona (SPAIN)

In the Project we investigate the **experience** of people who use or have used **several languages** in their everyday lives in different contexts. We seek to understand the ways in which people adopt different languages in their early socialization, the circumstances involved, the conditions that make it easier or more difficult, and the consequences for everyone.

I have received the information on my rights through this document:	↻ INTERVIEWS LAST BETWEEN 20 AND 40 MINUTES.
	↻ WE NEED TO AUDIO RECORD THEM.
	↻ WE DO NOT OFFER ECONMIC COMPENSATION.
Name:	↻ PARTICIPATION IS **VOLUNTARY**. YOU CAN DECLINE AND DO NOT NEED TO JUSTIFY IT.
Signature:	↻ THE INTERVIEW IS **CONFIDENTIAL**. THE IDENTITY OF PARTICIPANTS GETS PROTECTD THROUGH **PSEUDONYMS**.
	↻ YOU CAN TAKE BREAKS OR END THE INTERVIEW AT ANY TIME.
	↻ YOU CAN ASK US TO DELETE THE INTERVIEW BY WRITING TO XXXXX@XXX.edu or to the University.
	↻ YOU CAN PROVIDE YOUR CONTACT DETAILS HERE IF YOU WISH THAT WE KEEP YOU INFORMED ABOUT THE RESULTS OF THE PROJECT.

Figure 6.4 Multilingual Consent Form for Individual Interviewees Used by Joan in the NEOPHON Project (2011–2015)

Tionscadal
Proxecto
Projecte
Projet
Proyecto
Project

NEOPHON

·]UOC Universitat Oberta
de Catalunya
Estudis d'Arts i Humanitats
**Universitat Oberta de
Catalunya**
Av. Tibidabo 39-43
C.P.08035
Barcelona (SPAIN)

En este proyecto investigamos la **experiencia** de personas que utilizan o han utilizado **varias lenguas** en su vida cotidiana en distintos contextos. Nos interesa entender como las personas pueden adoptar el uso de lenguas diferentes a las de su primera socialización, las circunstancias en que esto se produce, los condicionantes que lo facilitan o dificulta, y las implicaciones que tiene para cada uno/a.

He sido informado de mis derechos mediante copia de este documento	↻ LAS ENTREVISTAS DURAN ENTRE 20 Y 40 MINUTOS.
	↻ NECESITAMOS GRABARLAS.
Nombre:	↻ NO SE OFRECEN COMPENSACIONES ECONÓMICAS.
Firma:	↻ SU PARTICIPACIÓN ES **VOLUNTARIA**. PUEDE DECLINAR LA INVITACIÓN SIN NECESIDAD DE JUSTIFICARSE.
	↻ LA ENTREVISTA ES **CONFIDENCIAL**. LA IDENTIDAD DE LOS PARTICIPANTES SE PROTEJE CON **PSEUDÓNIMOS**.
	↻ PUEDE TERMINAR LA ENTREVISTA EN CUALQUIER MOMENTO.
	↻ PUEDE PEDIRNOS QUE LA BORREMOS ESCRIBIENDO A jpujolar@uoc.edu o la la UOC (ver datos arriba)
	↻ PUEDE DARNOS DATOS DE CONTACTO PARA QUE LE INFORMEMOS DE LOS RESULTADOS DEL PROYECTO.

Contacto: Joan Pujolar / jpujolar@uoc.edu / 622136745

Figure 6.4 (Continued)

6.3 Moment 3: Generating Your Data

6.3.1 Fieldnote Examples

Fieldnotes come in different forms and shapes, as they correspond to the multiple ways in which you encounter events and materials in the fieldwork that you feel a need to make a record of, or make a record of the thoughts that arise from them, so that you can revisit them later. As such, they are very dependent on both the specific goals of your project and your own personal ways of handling note taking, not just in research but also in study, at work or at home. They can be short, almost incomprehensible jottings, wordlists, drawings; they can also be verbatim accounts or extensive narratives. Also their temporality varies: some are, and can be done on the spot (e.g., in a café, in a classroom), some right after the interaction or event (e.g., after a conversation), or only at the end of the day. It is best to try to write them up as soon as possible.

On-the-spot fieldnotes: These usually go through at least two stages: (1) first jottings and words written in haste that you are able to do on the spot or almost right away to help (at least) to keep track of what happened so that you can (2) write more elaborate notes or memos later.

Aide-mémoires: Monica prefers not to write anything down in front of the participants (if possible) and waits until the end of the day. However, she will collect a variety of other *aide-mémoires*, such as photos, programs of events she has attended, maps or other material traces. If possible, Sari takes lots of photos that later, after the event, help her to write the fieldnotes.

Posterior note taking: After the moment of observation, perhaps in a space of a café or your room you will have time to write your account of what happened, in as much detail as possible. It may be helpful for you to organize your notes according to the sequence of events, perhaps by date and time of day (see Monica's example in Figure 6.5) and include as much detail as you can, including your sensorial memories

Monday 17 October

14h AB tells me about a group called 160 which puts up little posters with messages on street posts in St. Boniface, including the one at the corner of Aulneau and Provencher and the one at the corner of Aulneau and Cathédrale in front of the university entrance. The first one now has nothing on it; I took photos of the other: (1) C'est pas clair mais c'est compris [It isn't clear but it's understood]; (2) do you can boost my car toé-là? [you there] (3) à moitié caché: (le cent soi)xante vous salue. [half hidden: (the one hundred si)xty greets you]

Wednesday 19 October

In the evening we go eat at La Chaise. On Blvd. Provencher; on the way there we go up Langevin Street next to Provencher Park, and we find some of the 160 little posters. AB had told me to look on this side. He also gave me the link to the film he made about them. He gave me permission to put the link on our website (see email of 16 October 2016).

Thursday 20 October

In the morning I find more 160 posters on Langevin in front of Mme C's house, but on the park side, as well as in front of the café on Ave. de la Cathédrale.

I do a tour along Ave. Aulneau between de la Cathédrale and Provencher; the post next to the post office that AB had told me about but which I had confused with a different (empty) post and therefore missed entirely, and Ave de la Cathédrale near Taché. Many posters found, including one in front of the cemetery and one in front of the archbishop's residence « Je ne pense pas que Dieu puisse nous aider » [I don't think God can help us].

Afterwards I continue my 160 tour: I find some all along Ave. de la Cathédrale, in front of Louis-Riel School, and on St-Jean-Baptiste. My phone shuts down at the

Figure 6.5 Fieldnotes Monica St. Boniface (October 2016) From the Project "Un Canadien Errant: Mooring, Mobilities and Transformative Restructurations of National Identity" (2015–2020)

Note: We provide first the translation, then the original. These fieldnotes have been edited to remove identifiers.

moment I am trying to take a photo of the poster on the post of the big electronic sign of Louis-Riel School, which says something like « pas de fautes d'orthographe. Promis » [no spelling errors. Promised]. So back tomorrow – but I already have about 20 posters, just in the zone Provencher-Aulneau-Cathédrale (and I have yet done Provencher between Taché and Aulneau, or between Aulneau and St-Jean-Baptiste ; nor the rest of St-Jean-Baptiste between Cathédrale and Provencher, not to mention the area of the sans CCFM [Centre culturel franco-manitobain/Franco-Manitoban Cultural Centre).

----

lundi 17 octobre

14h AB me signale aussi l'existence d'un groupe qui s'appelle 160 et qui affiche des petites affiches à message sur les poteaux de St. Boniface, dont celui à l'angle d'Aulneau et Provencher, et celui à l'angle d'Aulneau et la Cathédrale devant l'entrée de l'USB. Le premier poteau est vide maintenant; j'ai pris des photos de l'autre : (1) C'est pas clair mais c'est compris; (2) do you can boost my car toé-là? (3) à moitié caché: (le cent soi)xante vous salue.

mercredi 19 octobre

Le soir on sort manger à La Chaise, sur le blvd Provencher; en cours de route on monte la rue Langevin à côté du Parc Provencher, et on repère quelques affichettes du groupe 160. AB m'avait indiqué de regarder de ce côté. Il m'envoie aussi le lien à son film à leur sujet. Il nous donne la permission de mettre le lien sur le site web (voir courriel 20 octobre 2016).

jeudi 20 octobre

Le matin je trouve encore d'autres affichettes 160 sur la rue Langevin devant chez Mme C mais du côté du parc, ainsi que devant le café dans l'avenue de la Cathédrale. Tournée avenue Aulneau entre avenue de la Cathédrale et Provencher; le poteau à côté du bureau de poste dont AB m'avait parlé mais que j'ai confondu avec un autre poteau (vide) donc loupé, et Ave de la Cathédrale vers Taché. Plusieurs affichettes trouvées, dont une devant le cimetière et en face de l'archevêché « Je ne pense pas que Dieu puisse nous aider ».

Après je continue ma tournée 160 ; j'en trouve encore le long de l'avenue de la Cathédrale, devant l'école Louis-Riel, et sur la St-Jean-Baptiste. Mon téléphone se ferme au moment où j'essaie de prendre une photo d'une affichette sur le poteau de la grande signe électronique de l'École Louis-Riel, qui dit qqch comme « pas de fautes d'orthographe. Promis » Donc retour demain – mais là j'ai déjà une vingtaine d'affichettes, juste dans la zone Provencher-Aulneau-Cathédrale (et je n'ai pas encore fait le Provencher entre Taché et Aulneau, ou entre Aulneau et St-Jean-Baptiste ; ni le reste de St-Jean-Baptiste entre Cathédrale et Provencher, sans parler de la zone CCFM).

Figure 6.5 (Continued)

(what did you see, hear, feel, touch, taste). This takes a lot of time, indeed if you are attending to detail it can take as long as the time that you spent observing.

Fieldnote checklist: When writing fieldnotes, we recommend that you consider including the following information:

(1) Date, time and place of observation and name of observer.

(2) Description of the setting (perhaps draw—even stick figures and general outlines—or take a picture).

(3) Description of the participants and resources and their role in the setting, including your own.

(4) Activities and their order.

(5) Movement of participants, changes in their participation in the activity.

(6) Sensory impressions: sights, sounds, textures, smells, taste.

(7) Specific words, phrases, gestures, practices, verbatim renditions or summaries of conversations or exchanges.

(8) Relevant linguistic forms, sequences and metacommentary.

(9) Linguistic contrasts (languages, varieties, genres).

(10) Reflections/comments: write down how you interpret what happened, your ideas and insight. What did you find interesting? What was similar to other sites of your observations? Surprises? What do you need to know next/more? (You may want to put this in a column parallel to the rest of the notes).

Teamwork: When you work with others, it can be helpful to either draw up fieldnotes together, or share them among partners and debrief daily. You may want to develop a template together that everyone tries to follow, to ensure you all cover the same things and can easily compare across note sets. Below in Table 6.1 is an example of a template for observation used by Sari in a multi-sited team ethnography. More details can be added if needed, e.g., related to persons taking part in the event. Within the team, the fieldnotes are at times written together, or one of the researchers takes the lead and others add on and comment.

Paper or laptop: This partly depends on what is situationally appropriate, especially if you are taking notes while observing either in real life or on line. You can always type up handwritten notes in order to facilitate sharing among team members, searching, data backup and storage, as well as the inclusion of visual material.

And once you gain access to people's social media spaces and cloud exchanges, you have the advantage of quick reproducibility. For instance, to record a WhatsApp chat you just have to get to the functionality "Send chat via email" and you get it. Qualitative analysis software is increasingly capable of saving Facebook or Twitter interactions. This means that you are likely to have the power to record ten times as much material as any sociolinguist or anthropologist could just a few years ago. But you will also have an added problem: how much material can you handle? In

Table 6.1 Example of a Basic Fieldnote Template Used by a Multi-Sited Team Ethnography Project "Cold Rush. Dynamics of Language and Identity in Expanding Arctic Economies" (2016–2020)

Name of the project/ID information		
FILE CODE		
Researcher		
Description		
A	Event	
	Place	
	Length	
	Keywords	
B	Summary of the event	
C	Fieldnotes	
E	Reflections	
G	Follow up	

what ways can you associate your notes and your reflections to it? You will need a far more systematic and powerful way of organizing your data now than you would have needed a few decades before.

6.3.2 Recording Tips

Digital data and corpus size: Participants' digital exchanges and online visual materials (photos, videos) can be quite easy to save digitally, and you may want to scan print files and save them digitally. You may also want to record interaction via audio or video recorders. It is easy to generate a lot of data, so think about how much you can handle.

How recording shapes activities: When physically recording, think about how the positioning of the mike or camera shapes the event, and what it signals about what you are interested in. You can retrieve some of this information from how people interact with the recording device or with you in your role of recorder, as well as from any (dis)continuities in talk and behaviour across recorded and non-recorded activities.

Whole group talk (for example, in classrooms, bars or meetings): It will be hard when you transcribe to follow what everyone is saying, and to distinguish among speakers as well as who is talking to whom, especially if some speakers have soft voices. There is likely to be significant background noise. In large spaces there may be echoes.

Talk while walking, driving or otherwise moving through space: You will have to solve the problem of getting the equipment to move along with the participants; and figure out how to keep track of constant aural changes (who is closer or further from the microphone, who has the microphone).

Using pre-recorded public material: You will need to take into account that it was not you who decided the way in which the event was going to be recorded or edited.

6.3.2.1 Cold Shower List

Even under the best of circumstances (everyone loves you, they think recording is a great idea, you have top-of-the-line equipment), be prepared to encounter problems, and to fall back to your memory and fieldnote writing. Here are a few things to consider (think of this as the Cold Shower List).

Basic Tips:

Before you go:

- always check your equipment before you record to make sure it is working and has recently been charged or has new batteries;
- make sure it has enough memory space left on it for a new recording;
- keep track of power sources, whether plugs or batteries;
- carry extra batteries and charging devices.

When you start:

- make sure to plug the mike into the right place (notably, do not plug it into the earphones outlet);
- make sure to set the recording level at the right volume;
- turn on the mike and the recorder (we know, it seems obvious, but it isn't);

When you are done:

- turn the recorder off;
- immediately back up copies in safe places; this helps prevent accidental erasure of data;
- stay alert; something important is going to happen, or someone will say something particularly relevant.

In addition, think about the following:

Ethics of recording: There may be people who are not happy about being recorded in certain circumstances. Personal conversations, for instance, usually deal with private matters that people want to keep to themselves; institutional ones may have imply pressure due to unequal relations of power. You should always respect your participants' desire to pause or shut off the recorder, or erase material. Think about what it means for your project that some things may be recordable and others not (not at all, not always, not now). Always make sure that you have free and informed consent.

Suitability of the equipment: At time of writing, just for audio recording we can choose among personal radio microphones, environmental microphones and smartphones. In a few years, other devices will be available. Think about what you really need in the way of technical quality, and about what is situationally possible and appropriate. You should think about your degree of comfort with such devices, and whether you might find them distracting. Always practise first.

Noises: In natural settings, there are always background noises; we tend not to notice them when we are focusing on something else. When you transcribe, things like paper wrapping, tableware use, coughs and sneezes, and table tapping can interfere in your ability to make out what people said. You can minimize the effect of these background noises by putting something absorbent, like a sponge, under the mike.

Voices: Pitch and loudness vary, so be aware of how your participants speak, and take that into account. Don't force them to shout, though. It's your problem, not theirs.

Note taking: It is helpful to note any elements of context that will facilitate later transcription, especially for audio recordings. This includes where participants are located with respect to each other and to the mike, as well as any objects people may refer to or handle.

Should you be present during the recording? You may think that, once the participants have agreed to being recorded, it makes no difference if you are present or not. However, social interaction does not really work like that. First, if you are present, it may well be that the participants feel that you cannot remain silent and that you have to talk as well. So if you stay, you should probably act as a participant too because, if you refrain from talking, you will be a constant reminder that the situation is being recorded. If you leave, you are likely to miss a wealth of contextual information that you could have noted down. You will have to consider whether a participant can control the recorder and how.

6.3.3 Designing Interviewing

Conventional ethnographic interviewing usually involves engaging participants in a conversation for which we have done some preparation. There are many subcategories for ethnographic interviews. *Semi-structured interviews* refer to interviews with a concrete agenda about the issues that need to be discussed but yet allowing the interviewees ample room to address additional issues, or to frame topics in the way they wish. Another category is *in-depth interviews*, ones in which we encourage elaborate reflection on the themes discussed. *Narrative interviews* emphasize events where the informants are given considerable time to tell their accounts: stories from childhood, memories and experiences related to turning points or events relevant to the issue examined.

Interview Guides

We do not think it makes sense to heavily script an interview; instead, start out with a list of the topics you know you want to cover. You will find as you go along that people bring up topics that you had not considered before, but that should then be incorporated. You may also find that some of your topics make little sense, and need to be dropped or reformulated. Certainly, you cannot predict exactly how the actual conversation will go, and so it helps to organize the document visually so that you can see at a glance that you are not forgetting anything. Trying out these questions and topics early on can help you sort some of these things out.

We have used more or less elaborate guides. Here we provide some examples in Figure 6.6, so you can get an idea of what ours look like.

In this example of an interview script, it is noticeable that it contains instructions that take into account the fact that the document is going to be used by the whole team.

Beyond these details, there are no general rules that can be applied as to **how to exactly phrase the questions and in which order**. Thus, Joan has always started

---

ESBORRANY GUIÓ ENTREVISTES NEOPHON

Hi ha un cert consens a favor del concepte de trajectòria, per bé que orientada en dife[...] consens de què les entrevistes constitueixin històries de vida amb atenció específica als temes lingüístics. Luisa i Rosi[...] ntifiquen aspectes del procés migratori entre la preparació, el desplaçament, l'establiment i perspectives futures. A [...] star vigilants a les fases de la trajectòria educativa, la incorporació al mercat laboral i la creació d'una nova llar.

(General instructions for interviewers)

Entenem que les preguntes que orientin el diàleg han de variar segons el perfil d'entre[...] revistador. Els entrevistadors han de conduir el diàleg de manera que se sentin el màxim de còmodes. En tema de llen[...] s força habitual que els entrevistats s'enrotllin bastant espontàniament. Preguntant simplement "quines llengües ha parlat en la seva vi[...] (se'n poden proposar més de dues], podem posar l'entrevista en marxa. Si no és així, es pot utilitzar la llista de temes com a guió per anar g[...] nyant temps de forma senzilla i relaxada.

En tot cas, jo proposo que totes les entrevistes i grups de discussió incorporin els ítems d'a[...]. Encara que alguns punts molt concrets no són d'aplicació a tots els contextos, cada quadret crec que és pertinent a tothom.

(Specific instruction column for interviewers)

*CHECKLIST	Asp[...] trevistadors
INTRODUCCIÓ *(Presentation for the participants and consent issues)*	
En aquest projecte [...] cia de persones que utilitzen o han utilitzat diverses llengües e[...] na. Ens interessa entendre com les persones poden adoptar l'ús d[...] ngües diferents a les de la seva primera socialització, les circumstàncies en què això es produeix, els condicionants que ho faciliten o dificulten, i les implicacions que té per a cadascú/na. La participació en el treball de camp és voluntària i requereix la conformitat dels subjectes. La universitat ens demana que presentem proves que hem informat i obtingut el seu consentiment. Per això li agrairíem que signés aquest paper informatiu.	En ca[...] prefereixi no signar papers, es recoman[...] gir (i gravar) aquests 3 paràgrafs al principi de l'entre[...] ta.
Els entrevistats tenen dret a interrompre l'entrevista o demanar que s'esborri a qualsevol moment. A tal fi, ho podeu demanar per correu electrònic a Joan Pujolar (jpujolar@uoc.edu). Les dades personals són eliminades de les transcripcions i substituïdes per pseudònims. En cap cas es publiquen.	
DADES BÀSIQUES	btem aquestes dades básiques[...] rfils de participants. Poden pr[...] veu alta, o posar-los per escrit[...] Hauran d[...] ci de la transcripció.
☐ Sexe: ☐ Edat: ☐ Ll[...] de naixement: ☐ Ll[...] al de residència: ☐ Oc[...] al: [...] fills, amics, etc.)	
PR[...] Tra[...] als progenitors o tutors (importa no estrictament els progenitors biològics, sinó els responsables de la seva manutenció i educació en la infància): A: En relació als progenitors: ☐ Lloc de naixement: ☐ ~~Llocs de~~[...] ☐ Ocupacions: ☐ Nivell educatiu: ☐ Projecte educatiu i social en relació als fills (això és, **en relació a l'entrevistat** : aquest és el tema important): ☐ Llengües que parlen/parlaven els progenitors:	Aquest punt és molt **important** per al projecte. Dedicar un temps al principi i al final per construir la trajectòria familiar de **mobilitat social** i especialment per veure **quins pro**[...] **genitors en relació a l'entrevis**[...] És una m[...] a de la classe social

Callouts: "Each section is visually salient. Interviewers "see" the structure at first glance." — "First questions are easy and factual: age, birthplace, etc." — ""Covered" issues can eventually be checked"

Figure 6.6 Interview Script from Joan's NEOPHON Project in 2013

<table>
<tr><td>

TRAJECTÒRIA PERSONAL

B: Detalls per controlar:

- ☐ Estudis: explorar la inversió en capital cultural; què va estudiar i per què; si està satisfet/a amb els resultats; quines coses ha estudiat fora de l'ensenyament obligatori/oficial.

- ☐ Mobilitat geogràfica: "mapejar" els canvis de domicili i les seves raons.
  - Justificar el lloc de destí decidit.
  - Detallar el procés d'adaptació (escola, treball, residència, amics)
  - Et sents integrat?

- ☐ Trajectòria professional: anotar l'evolució en les ocupacions i la identificació de la persona amb aquestes.

- ☐ Convivència: Anotar amb qui ha conviscut: p.ex. pares, estudiants, parella, nou nucli familiar, etc.

- ☐ Contacte i relació: explicar com manté el contacte amb persones d'etapes o llocs anteriors de la seva vida.

- ☐ Projectes futurs: quedar-se, tornar, moure's, progressar professionalment, etc.

</td><td>

Aquesta és la biografia de l'entrevistat pròpiament. Es pot combinar amb la trajectòria lingüística.

Assegurar-se que no se'ns escapen els punts detallats, encara que l'entrevistat ho expliqui tot en un altre ordre:

Luisa i Rosina: 4 fases del procés migratori (en cas que solament hi hagi una migració?).

Uns altres:
- Atenció a canvis de centre escolar, de treball i de zona de residència fins i tot dins del mateix país.
- Atenció a si els desplaçaments es fan en solitari o acompanyats.
- Està satisfet amb el resultat del desplaçament?
- Explorar múltiples identificacions: amb el lloc d'origen? Amb nou lloc?

</td></tr>
<tr><td>

TRAJECTÒRIA LINGÜÍSTICA

C: Preguntar, si no sorgeix en la conversa:

- ☐ Llengua(s) de la primera socialització amb pares o tutors.
- ☐ Altres llengües presents en la primera infància.
- ☐ Repertori lingüístic actual: llista de llengües (o altres varietats).
- ☐ Per a cada llengua/varietat incorporada posteriorment:

  Com es va aprendre: formalment (estudiant) o informalment, en quant temps, amb quina fluïdesa/comoditat.
  Com va començar a usar-la: en quins espais, amb quines persones, en quines circumstàncies [aquesta és una de les qüestions més importants, deixar parlar, demanar detalls, animar a explicar anècdotes i exemples].
  Quina actitud presenten els parlants de cada llengua enfront dels *nous parlants, aprenents, etc.
  Com la usa en l'actualitat: en quins espais, amb quines persones, en quines circumstàncies, amb quina freqüència. Barreja llengües? Realitza converses bilingües? Parla les llengües correctament? Cal parlar-les correctament? En quin sentit?
  Relació afectiva (*lligam, attachment*): quina llengua(es) consideren que és/són "la seva(es)" llengua(es), quins sentiments té cap a ella(es), quins conflictes i frustracions ha tingut amb elles, quines alegries, amb quines llengües s'identifica?
  Comparació: la seva experiència és compartida per persones del mateix perfil?

</td><td>

- Assegurar que sabem quina llengua(es) es van ~~~ primerenca i com.
  ~~ llengua, preguntar detalls
  ~~ ines activitats es feien

  [Speech bubble: Never ever forget these points!!! They make the key issues of the project.]

  ~~ antes llengües, sinó ~~ n un entrevistat que ~~ i argentí).

- ~~ tificació de varietats i estils, especialment els de "neofalantes": contrast entre estàndard i dialectes, autenticitat o artificialitat.
- Especificar llengües en l'ensenyament, com a mitjà i estrangeres.

- **Els primers moments d'ús social són un tema clau en el projecte.**

- **Quines facilitats i obstacles ha tingut per aprendre/usar la llengua x? Recursos o temps per a classes, etc.**

- **IMPORTANT: Acceptació per part dels locals, etc.**

- Els patrons d'ús poden haver variat amb el temps.

- Atenció a temes de purisme, contrast entre parla de nadius i no natius

</td></tr>
<tr><td></td><td>

- Animar a explicar situacions i anècdotes. Ens interessen les històries.

</td></tr>
<tr><td>

ASPECTES SOCIALS I POLÍTICS
- ☐ Què és un *nuevofalante, euskaldunberri*? [en contextos on la categoria estigui popularitzada] Quin rol poden tenir els neofalants, euskaldunberris, etc. en el futur de la llengua local? (1)
- ☐ Quines llengües hauria volgut aprendre o vol encara aprendre? (2)
- ☐ Quins beneficis creu que ha obtingut pel fet d'usar/dominar diverses llengües? Com influeix el coneixement de llengües en les oportunitats a nivell laboral? (3)
- ☐ En quina mesura les llengües o varietats són un símbol d'identitat nacional? Què en pensa dels que deixen de parlar "la seva" llengua, i/o deixen de parlar-la als seus fills/es? (4)
- ☐ Què opina de la política lingüística local? (5)
- ☐ Què opina de la gestió lingüística en les organitzacions on ha treballat? (6)
- ☐ Com creu que evolucionarà la situació lingüística en el seu context local i al món en general? (7)

</td><td>

Aquestes preguntes poden haver sortit fàcilment de forma espontània en la conversa. Algunes preguntes no tenen sentit en contextos que no són de minories territorials (Madrid, Londres).

(3) és molt important. Si no ha sortit, buscar diverses maneres de preguntar el mateix.

(5) i (6) segurament poden formular-se de forma diferent en cada context. Es tracta de veure com se senten tractats per les institucions en matèria lingüística. A Catalunya es pot preguntar si estan d'acord en què tothom hagi d'aprendre els dos idiomes, si s'insisteix suficientment en l'anglès, etc. Els llatinoamericans a Londres o a Madrid tindran segurament cuses molt diferents que dir. A Irlanda, Galícia, el País Basc o Quebec sortiran altres temes.

(7) Pregunta de prospectiva sociolingüística: futur de les llengües, del gallec, del català, del gaèlic, del castellà, etc.

</td></tr>
</table>

Figure 6.6 (Continued)

with an easy first batch of factual questions about age, birthplace and occupation. To him, this ensures that the interview gets a good start: (1) interviewers can answer them and become more confident and relaxed, (2) the questions implicitly display a certain formality and professionality that invites people to focus and take the moment seriously and (3) they also provide information that we usually need. However, other researchers may have objections to these reasons. For instance, they may wish to create or maintain a more informal atmosphere. Monica finds that many people find such questions intimidating; they feel they are being interrogated. You will have to find what works for you.

Below in Figure 6.7 is the guide Monica's team used for a project looking into the mobility histories of francophones in Canada. They hardly ever asked questions in

---

Interview guide

- Birthplace
- Training:
  - Schooling
  - Extracurricular
  - Post-graduation
- Work history
  - Type of work
  - Job seeking strategies or recruitment experience
  - Paid and unpaid
  - When?
  - Where?
- Education, training and work history of family members, and of closest relatives and friends
- Geographical mobility
  - Who
  - Where
  - Why
  - For how long
  - Impact on social relations
- Importance and role of language proficiency for education, training and work
  - Spoken, written
  - Importance of bi- or multilingualism

Figure 6.7 Interview Guide for Monica's Project on "Mobilité, identité et la nouvelle économie politique" (2008) (Translated from the original French)

this order, starting instead with whatever aspect of their biographies had caused them to encounter each other in the first place.

In a project on language biographies, Sari used (with a team) material prompts for eliciting narratives related to languages in a person's life history. They asked the interviewees to bring along a material artefact they felt themselves is somehow relevant or important to their language repertoires. Informants brought, e.g., photographs, a Sámi dictionary and a text written by them in Sámi. The interviews started with a discussion about the artefact, and then moved on to discussing languages in their life. As we were interested in memories and experiences around languages through the life trajectory of the informants, we tried to facilitate the narrative mode by providing verbal prompts like "Could you tell more. . . ." "How do you remember. . . ." "Do you remember when. . . ."

6.3.3.2 Interviewing Tips

Use all the tips we gave you about notes and recording, In addition:
Phrasing of questions:

(1) Ask mostly open-ended questions. Closed questions are the ones that allow for just "yes" or "no" or a very restricted set of answers. How and why questions can be especially helpful.

(2) Avoid leading questions. It is important not to phrase questions in a way that indicate how they should be answered, or that imply that the interviewee is at fault: e.g., "but shouldn't you speak French to taxi drivers?"

(3) Avoid politically loaded or biased phrasings of questions. It is best to see which way participants choose to politicize the issue themselves (or not). (Though in extreme cases, you may find this ethically impossible.)

(4) Bear in mind that human communication is complex and that you can exploit this complexity to your advantage. For instance, you can phrase a question with your own voice or with other people's voice, e.g., you can ask something directly or claim that other people would ask this something.

Managing the interview:

(5) Make interviewees feel comfortable, making clear that they are not being judged and evaluated and also that you are genuinely interested in learning what they have to say.

(6) Display interest throughout the interview: use back-channelling (yeah, hmm), react to prompts or jokes, repeat what they said and reflect on it or invite them to reflect further.

(7) Ask for clarifications and elaborations. This shows that you are listening with interest and it also allows the interviewee to explain his points better.

(8) Control your willingness to talk. Unexperienced interviewers tend to talk a lot in interviews, often because they find silence uncomfortable. Give participants space, and mobilize your understanding of the kinds of pacing and sequencing they are comfortable with.

(9) Do not interrupt the interviewees even if you think that they are running off topic. Topic associations are a valuable source of clues about how people feel about things.

(10) Do not worry if you feel that the interviewee has misunderstood your question. Wait until you can rephrase it at an appropriate moment.

6.4 Moment 4: Analyzing Your Data

In this section we cover the tasks of transcribing, archiving, coding and peer deliberation.

6.4.1 Transcribing

Transcribing is extremely labour intensive, so before assuming you must transcribe everything you record, ask: (1) What is the point of transcribing? (2) Which aspects of the data will you need to use for your analysis? (3) How much work can you put into this?

What Is the Point of Transcription?

Transcription involves turning any form of talk into a **written** form. Despite the fact that this is not easy to do, it is helpful for data analysis. In particular, it forces you come to grips with what actually went on, not what you thought happened at the time, and it allows you to really own the data, that is, to really know where things lie so you can check your hypotheses, find anomalies or identify telling examples.

On the downside, transcription forces a written representation of what is usually spoken data, and it is difficult to always provide the contextual information necessary for analysis, like all the subtleties of tone and speed of voice, of accent, of visual information like position of participants or colour of clothing. You can certainly incorporate any aspect of this information in your transcription but never all aspects, and transcription will never retain the feel and liveliness of the situation as we and the participants experienced it. It is not a substitute for the raw data, but a representation of it, and in many ways an analysis. The best scenario, when it is possible, is to combine transcription with tagging and indexing video and audio files.

What Do I Need to Transcribe?

Transcription requires **decisions about the level of accuracy** and the kind of information that you will need to have at hand while you are working on your analysis. It is therefore a theoretical and political as well as a technical decision. It is *theoretical* because the form must be **consistent with the types of claims** that you wish to make, and with the ontologies of the phenomena that you are studying. For example, if you wish to analyze linguistic variation, your transcription will have to include all the features of variation that you intend to address, and these will have to be represented in consistency with the linguistic model that you are working with. If you want to get at people's ideas about something, transcription allows you to get at how they express or construct their ideas; in such cases, you need a clear unedited verbatim form **in the original language** (for sociolinguists, there is hardly a context imaginable where it is acceptable to provide a translation without the original version). Or you may simply be satisfied with a brief summary of topics covered, with some key quotes more carefully transcribed.

And here the theoretical blends again into the political in complex ways. Sociolinguists, for instance, generally expect research to make visible forms of speech that are commonly disparaged or stigmatized, such as dialects, slang, minority languages or working-class registers. However, it has also been noted that the accents of upper class individuals are less likely to be depicted in transcriptions than those of disadvantaged groups. Given the social standing of the less prestigious forms of speech, an accurate translation may at times get dangerously close to condescending mimicry. So a researcher may have good reasons to play down an accent in a transcription to make sure that readers will pay attention to the character's reasoning and not to the colouring of his or her speech. **The politics of transcription** (Bucholtz, 2000) is one more aspect to bear in mind when reflexively addressing the ethical and political implications of the research process.

Here are a few options you have in terms of format:

- Reproducing what the voices of a recording literally say (as if it were a dictation) without any or with very little additional detail on pauses or intonation (this allows us, for instance, to do word searches).

- Reproducing verbatim accounts or exchanges that included indications about some of the following features: pauses, pitch, intonation contours, durations, phonetic features, overlapping turns of speech, gestures, position, morphological or lexical tagging, proxemics, scenery (this level is normally the one required in published material).

- Carefully edited audio or audiovisual material enriched with subtitles, pointers, commentary, etc. (commonly, only done in small stretches of data for specific presentations).

How Much Can I and Must I Transcribe?

Generally speaking, you can perform the second type of transcriptions in the order of five hours per hour of original recording for conversations involving two people. However, if you need a reasonably neat transcript you will need a minimum of seven hours per hour. And if you are transcribing people talking and joking informally you should count on spending a minimum of nine hours per hour according to audibility conditions, how well you master the language(s) used, how good the quality is, and how much detail you need to include. In any case, different people type at different speeds. But you may want to transcribe only part of your data, or different aspects of your data to different degrees of detail.

Transcription software, with or without transcription foot pedals, help speed up the process. Pedals allow you to move back and forth in the document without tying up your hands for that purpose: one pedal stops the playback and moves back the recording one or two seconds, and the other one starts the playback again. Without pedals, the same function can be achieved via conventional keyboard shortcuts.

For the transcription of written documents you can also try Optical Recognition Software (OCR) contained in all commercial scanners or buy specific software packages for the purpose. This software "reads" what is written in a piece of paper and, ideally, turns it into a computer text file. Invariably, you must review the transcription manually, because the software makes mistakes.

Stay attentive to technological innovations. At the time this book was written, Voice Recognition software (VR) was generally not good enough for the kind of spontaneous speech found in interviews and informal conversations. However, it may do the trick if you have formal speeches, radio broadcasts, even films. As the programming of these tools gets better, you may find that you need less and less time to revise the transcriptions that they produce. However, if the software does it for you, then you are not going to get to know the data as intimately as you would if you did by yourself.

Transcription Conventions

Transcriptions usually combine conventional written language with some added signs. The use of the common punctuation conventions of written language is normally avoided, because they largely do not correspond to the intonational and rhythmic patterns found in spoken language. In transcription, other types of punctuation and diacritic signs are used to represent pauses, silences, pitch, etc.

Again, the amount of features that need recording depends on the specific purposes of each project. The writers of this book generally subscribe to the simplest of possible forms for representation. See Tables 6.2 and 6.3.

Table 6.2 Example of Transcription Conventions: Minimalist Model (Heller et al., 2015)

AB:	speaker (named)
?:	unidentified speaker
/	a short pause
//	a pause
(x)	inaudible utterance
[. . .]	section excerpted

Table 6.3 Example of Transcription Conventions: Conversational Analysis (Seedhouse, 2004)

[	Point of overlap onset
]	Point of overlap termination
=	(a) Turn continues below, at the next identical symbol
	(b) If inserted at the end of one speaker's turn and at the beginning of the next speaker's adjacent turn, indicates that there is no gap at all between the two turns
	(c) Indicates that there is no interval between adjacent utterances
(3.2)	Interval between utterances (in seconds)
(.)	Very short untimed pause
word	Speaker emphasis
e:r the:::	Lengthening of the preceding sound
_	Abrupt cutoff
?	Rising intonation, not necessarily a question. Animated or emphatic tone
!	Low-rising intonation, suggesting continuation
.	Falling (final) intonation
CAPITALS	Especially loud sounds relative to surrounding talk
° °	Utterances between degree signs are noticeably quieter than surrounding talk
↑↓	Marked shifts into higher or lower pitch in the utterance following the arrow
< >	Talk surrounded by angle brackets is produced slowly and deliberately (typical of teachers modelling forms)
> <	Talk surrounded by reversed angle brackets is produced more quickly than neighbouring talk
()	A stretch of unclear or unintelligible speech.
(guess)	Indicates the transcriber's doubt about a word
.hh	Speaker in-breath
hh	Speaker out-breath
→	Mark features of special interest

Transcription Conventions (1): Minimalist Model

This is intended basically for cases in which the linguistic features are not the most salient forms of data, but rather the interactional, discursive and substantive features.

Transcription Conventions (2): Conversational Analysis

Conversational analysis is a specific field of language studies that focuses on the details of (largely) spoken interaction sequences. Its tradition of transcription notation has been widely used in sociolinguistics when the mechanics of turn-taking or the organization of utterances are important to attend to.

Transcription Conventions (3): Multilingual Data

Some researchers have developed conventions for bilingual or multilingual data (see the addition of @language tag) analyses by teams using different languages, hence the preference for combinations of common punctuation or accent marks. See Table 6.4.

Table 6.4 Example of Transcription Conventions: Multilingual Data (Codó and Moyer, 1997)

@	Language tag
-'	Falling intonation
-´	Rising intonation
-'	Fall-rise intonation
-^	Rise-fall intonation
-,	Level intonation
#	Pause
##	Longer pause
:	Lengthened sound or syllable
+^	Latching (quick uptake)
+/	Truncation
/	Stressed syllable
()	Omitted material
.	Turn terminator (statements)
?	Turn terminator (questions)
xxx	Unintelligible material
$	Symbol to introduce codes
	Scoped symbols
< >	Indicates scope of any given phenomenon (if no scope is indicated, it applies to previous word)
[/]	Retracing

@	Language tag
[!]	Stressing
[=! q]	Quick rhythm
[=! sl]	Slow rhythm
[=! l]	Loud voice
[=! s]	Soft voice
[$in]	Insertion
[$al]	Alternation
[$cl]	Congruent lexicalization

6.4.2 Data Coding

Coding makes data more accessible. It amounts to tagging pieces of your data so that you can later select specific subsets to examine them in detail to test specific hypotheses. It is an analytically driven form of data organization (see, e.g., Barnett et al., 2000).

In your research, you are supposed to be the creator and the master of your own coding set, because codes represent your analytical categories or are closely linked to them. Not everyone uses the terms "code" and "coding" in exactly the same ways; we use it here to refer to the labels that we create to organize our data set and retrieve sections of it at will.

What are Codes?

Coding, like transcription, helps you to deepen your acquaintance with your data, to recall details that you had forgotten, revisit experiences in a new light, maybe reinterpret events that you saw or things you were told. Coding your whole data set, or most of it, helps you gain some control over your data, to make you more aware of what it includes and what it does not. At the same time, it helps you gain some distance from the material, the people and the experiences that you are dealing with, so that you can start talking about it in more abstract and systematic ways.

Some researchers, drawing on grounded theory, believe that codes emerge from the data without any prior assumptions on the part of the analyst. We believe that we always work with a set of assumptions, or hypotheses; so although we feel strongly that we should always be open to discovering that we were wrong, or to noticing things we had not noticed before, we cannot and should not try to explore the data without a specific analytic framework and a set of questions for which we are responsible.

Not everyone codes in the same way. But here is an example of how coding fundamentally works:

- Imagine that you are interested in a specific issue that your participants often talk about: what makes someone a "good Catalan." You have videos and audio recordings of spontaneous conversations, interviews and many newspaper articles about different issues in addition to this aspect.

- Imagine that you stick a label on each point in a video, audio or newspaper clip in which people say something that is connected to the idea of "being Catalan" (your theoretical and methodological frame will have led you to decide what the criteria for identifying those ought to be).

- Later, imagine that you have a magical machine from which you can ask: can you please show me all the places where I stuck label 1? And boom! There you have all the video, audio and print media clips in front of you. Now you can comfortably start your analysis on ideologies about what it means to be Catalan.

In other words, codes link categories of data to categories of analysis. In any case, when it comes to coding your data set to address the complex social process that you are trying to understand, the million dollar questions are:

- Which labels/codes like the "being Catalan" one do I need to analyze in my data?

- How do I decide exactly what the codes should index, e.g., how do I assign the codes to specific data items, paragraphs, etc.?

Codes are very similar to the items of the conventional indexes that you find at the end of academic books. As with indexes, one major affordance of coding is that any section of data (no matter how large or small) can be linked to different analytic categories via different codes at the same time. To explain it more palpably: if you have an interview in which you discuss issues connected with different hypotheses or questions, you can assign a different code to each section of the interview, and even assign more than one code to particular sections. Through indexes, you can find out the pages where each term or topic is mentioned or discussed inside the book. Through codes, you can find the pages/paragraphs/phrases that relate to each question. Of course, in both cases, it is essentially the author/researcher who must decide in advance which stretches to flag with what codes, and it is best done manually.

How is Coding Done?

We highly recommend **keeping coding simple, in quantity (try not to exceed a total number of 20 basic codes) and in quality (they should be easy to understand)**. Define them as clearly as possible and establish very simple relationships between codes. Do not let the trees obscure the forest. Stay in your forest, but be prepared to alter your codes as you proceed, because you may find that some themes that you were not expecting, and had not previously noticed, consistently recur. Whether you code manually or using software is up to you; small data sets usually can be manually coded.

Whatever decisions you take as to which codes, how many, how to apply them and so on; what is essential to bear in mind is this: **when you retrieve a piece of data you must be able to know its context**, i.e., who says what, when and where, and in response to what. For instance, in conversational data, if one person says something interesting, it is best to assign a code to its whole turn and at least to the previous and following turns. If it is a paragraph in a text that you wish to assign to a code, consider including the same assignation to the previous paragraph and the following paragraph.

It certainly makes sense to do trial coding sessions. Whether you work alone or with others, it is good to estimate whether your codes can be used across the whole data set (if one gets applied only to sections of only one document or one interview, then it will possibly not be useful). It is good to pick a small sample of different types of data, code them, and later review them to see whether you have used all the codes and whether you have assigned the codes in a consistent manner. Indeed, the very process of checking how one's codes work often provides the first useful hypotheses of interpretation of your data and of responses to your research questions.

We provide below in Figure 6.8 an example of a code set for the NEOPHON research project:

What Software Tools Are There to do this?

At the moment of writing this book the Wikipedia entry for "Computer-assisted qualitative data analysis software" listed 33 programs, of which the authors are familiar with Atlast.ti, Ethnograph, MAXQDA, NVIVO and Transana (more commonly used for transcribing)— but this information is likely to be useless in five years, because the functionalities and possibilities of these programs are constantly evolving as new versions are released. The most important thing is that you should be able to use software to achieve your goals, and not to be driven by what the software wants. Choose the program that requires the least time to learn to use, and for which trouble-shooting help is readily available.

6.4.3 Data Sessions

Data sessions constitute a genre that is increasingly used in social science departments and doctoral schools. They are very simple events or short meetings in which one researcher tries out her preliminary hypotheses before friendly audiences: team members, fellow students, close colleagues. Generally, it consists of:

- briefly reminding the audience of the aims of the project;
- showing them raw data (transcriptions, artefacts, pictures), with an explanation of why you chose to present this bit;
- stating the first thoughts about the significance of the data;
- letting attendants openly discuss and come up with objections, questions for clarification, alternative routes of interpretation and new references.

MANUAL ANÀLISI NEOPHON (VERSIÓ 2)

Culpable: Joan Pujolar 10/01/2014

Codis	Detall
(sense accents)	Metacodi
	ETAPES
PROGENITORS	Descripció del projecte dels progenitors, especialment en relació a llengües, educació i mobilitat econòmica.
INICIAL	Inclou: a) Descripció de la socialització primària amb pares o tutors en època infantil (=FAMÍLIA d'origen); b) Descripció de situació lingüística de partida i llengües "inicials" prèvies a canvis o mudes: c) En el cas de migrants, descripció dels plans previs, vincles i xarxes socials prèvies a la migració.
MOBILITAT	Detall de desplaçaments geogràfics a) Necessitats o projectes que impulsen la migració o canvis de residència. b) Nota: referències a mobilitat social s'hauria d'incloure en el concepte ACCES).
INSTALL	Inclou: a) En el cas de no migrants, descripció de les experiències d'educació primària, secundària o universitària (EDUCACIÓ =ESCOLA); b) En el cas de migrants, descripció procés de migració i ...centamiento); primeres impres... lingüístiques i/o ... experiències a la ...
MUDA	Inclou: a) Adopció ... cials en qualsevol moment en la ... pció d'algun canvi significatiu en els patrons o freqüència d'ús de les llengües inicials o adoptades després. c)
ADAPTACIO	Inclou: a) Descripció del procés d'incorporació al mercat laboral i trajectòria laboral; b) En el cas de migrants, descripció de la trajectòria posterior a la instal·lació (estabilitat o precarietat)
FUTUR	Inclou: a) Anticipació de futures trajectòries i llengües; b) Nova família; c) Plans acadèmics i/o laborals; d) Possibles noves movilitats (també=ACCES); d) Herència i/o impuls lingüístic per a la descendència (=FAMÍLIA en construcció o futura).
	CONTEXTOS I PRÀCTIQUES
PLINGÜÍSTIQUES	Descripció/narració de pràctiques lingüístiques concretes de la pròpia experiència en situacions o tipus de situacions concretes.
PCULTURALS	Descripció/narració de pràctiques que es presenten com a formes de construir, representar, expressar identitat cultural o
MEDIA	...re consum cultural: lectura, cinema, ...levisió, etc.
CIVIL	...ació en col·lectius de caire voluntari: ...ons culturals, grups veïnals, ...grats, associacions de pares i mares, clubs esportius, partits polítics.
ACCES	Inclou: a) esments a processos d'aprenentatge lingüístic de tot

Callout (Labels of the codes)
Callout (Instructions on how to apply each code (jointly developed by the team))
Callout (In this project, we divided the codes in 3 different groups (optional))

Figure 6.8 Example of a Code Set for Joan's NEOPHON Research Project

	tipus; b) esment d'estratègies d'accés a espais o persones associats a varietats lingüístiques; c) referències a mobilitat social (accés a persones, ocupacions, sectors); d) aspiracions de mobilitat social, imaginari social.
IDIOMA	Esments de llengües diferents de la dicotomia bilingüe local; p.e. llengües estrangeres.
	IDEOLOGIES I IDENTITATS
VALOR	Valor associat a les diferents varietates lingüistiques (en funció del mercat lingüístic): a) dialecte vs. llengua; b) percepció d'exigència (obligatori per a progressar; per a integrarse)
MONOLINGUISME	Explicacions que pressuposen que parlar una sola llengua és o hauria de constituir la normalitat. Per exemple: "si estamos en España..." o "La lengua de aquí es el inglés" o equivalents.
MULTILINGUISME	Adhesió a la idea de parlar més d'una llengua, per les raons que siguin.
TRANSLINGUISME	Inclou: a) casos de celebració de fenòmens de transgressió o imprecisió de fronteres lingüístiques: code-switching, code-mixing, hibridacions; b) casos de protecció d'aquestes fronteres, deslegitimació de la hibridació (correcció, puresa autenticitat); c) Ocurrències de codeswitching en les entrevistes.
INTEGRACIO	Inclou: a) comentari sobre la necessitat d'assumir trets de la societat d'acollida; b) comentari sobre l'actitud de la societat d'acollida davant del nouvingut; c) comentari general sobre model de relació intercultural: assimilació, segregació, altres.
LEGITIMACIO	Inclou: a) percepció pròpia de la capacitat i el dret d'usar una llengua determinada; b) actitud dels altres respecte a la capacitat i el dret d'ús d'una llengua
INJUNCIO	Experiències d'apel·lació explícita a una ideologia lingüística (esp. integració, legitimacio), a una norma d'ús lingüístic. Inclou també: sancions, reforçaments (p.e. felicitacions).
EMOCIO	Experiències afectives esp. en relació a les llengües. Motivacions. Reconeixement de l'esforç.
POLITICA	Valoració de polítiques lingüístiques.
AUTOADSCRIPCIO	Afirmacions a efectes de categoritzar-se un mateix especialment des del punt de vista de la pertinença ètnica, nacional, cultural, ciutadania, classe social, orientació política, gènere, sexualitat.
HETEROADSCRIPCIO	Testimoniatge en les narracions de definicions dels altres: a) marcar l'aparició de categories de caire ètnic, nacional, cultural o racial, incloent-hi les ad-hoc o recents (p.e. ""castellans", "los sin papeles"), categories de parlants, o altres implícites (nosaltres/ells); b) casos d'esment explícit a diferències de gènere o sexualitat; c) casos de designació de tipologies de col·lectiu jove.

Figure 6.8 (Continued)

Data sessions are effectively work-in-progress sessions focused on the data, and they usually work well to draw doctoral students out of their isolated cogitations, to let researchers begin articulating their thoughts in a communicative fashion, detect what aspects seem to raise more interest or connect one's research with people working in other fields. Data sessions are easy to organize, ideally involve no more than half a dozen people, can be set up autonomously by students on their own initiative, and should of course be reciprocated (e.g., you should attend other people's data sessions too).

6.5 Moment 5: Making Your Story

In Moment 5 we covered the principles of what it means to project one's identity and one's argument in a text, and we visited the rationale behind the most common structure of academic genres in theses and journal articles. Here we discuss questions of time management when writing in a context with many competing professional duties, and a list of tips that touch upon specific procedural implications of the principles discussed in the related chapter.

6.5.1 Finding Time for Writing

Everyone has to find a path that works for him or her, but here are some things that have worked for us.

Know the time of the day you write best and save it for writing. Hardly any of us can or wants to write for days on end. Usually what is plausible in the course of everyday life, while balancing other commitments, is to find a few hours in which we can think and write. You can try to reserve an hour or two per working day in that moment when you think and write best (cf. Belcher, 2009). For example, if you write best early in the mornings, you can try to keep these early hours free on most working days.

Set up a writing plan. This is for people with a degree of self-discipline. Once you have some experience with writing, you can split the text in parts and assign time to each part, and then distribute the plan in your work schedule between lectures, meetings and administrative chores. You should treat every stretch of time scheduled for writing as a meeting during which you cannot receive calls, attend to other matters or respond to emails. Once you get practiced in this, there is the significant advantage that you will become more aware than most people about how much you can actually commit yourself to writing every semester or every year; which in turn may be helpful in negotiating with colleagues with whom you work or with your heads of department about workloads.

Organize writing retreats. Writing retreats are events involving from two to half a dozen people that may last a whole day, a weekend or even a few days. They involve time and space exclusively dedicated to writing. Students working on their theses can help each other advance, as can co-authors finalizing an article or a book manuscript. The basic requirement of such an event is an agreed moment of time and accessible space (which can be the public library, a café or your living room). But it can also entail applying for funding and perhaps even bringing in writing experts to comment on your writing. The event is typically organized around writing, which means making a schedule for composing, reading each other's text and exchanging feedback.

Find a writing partner. A writing partner is somebody who is willing to share her time with you, make a pact with you about the deadlines, is a good listener and remains unconvinced by your excuses. A writing partner is not your co-author, but rather a fellow writer who has the same struggles as you do (finding the key argument, keeping deadlines, deciding what to include, not over- or under-writing). Sharing deadlines with someone else with mutual obligations can be instrumental in making you stick to your program.

6.5.2 Tips for the Text

Use your voice in the first person. Historically, academic texts have favoured hiding the voice of the writer through such devices as the use of a vague "we," agentless passives ("it was found that"), or according agency to the research or the text ("this study has shown"). However, much social science has now shifted to a more clearly personal note in which the author's (or authors') voice is clearly identifiable. We prefer this, in keeping with our constructivist position. So in this book, "we" is used because we are three authors; but any of us would have used "I" on our own. Having said that, remember that your readers are not primarily interested in you, but in the story you are telling. Reflexivity is important, but not to the point where the researcher takes over the stage.

Make sure that all sources of evidence and ideas are clear. Your text is in some ways like a play in which all characters have their lines, and turn up at the right moment in the scene. You should make sure that readers understand who pronounced each statement, notably when you are referring to concepts or analyses or information that you owe to others. If you want to use a specific set of concepts circulating in the literature, you should provide examples of texts which use it in the ways you do, or when relevant, cite the text which introduced the concept to the field in the first place: "I will use the concept of vampire-talk, first discussed by AB (2063), in order to describe xyz"; or "Vampire-talk has been addressed in the following ways by AB (2063) and CD (2062)." At the same time, you don't always need say what you think by quoting what others say, when it is a matter of identifying your position. You don't need such statements as: "As AB (2063) says, interviews must be analyzed as socially situated events." You might say something like: "Like AB (2063), I take the position that interviews must be analyzed as socially situated events," though only if you absolutely believe that you really need AB getting your back here. Statements, principles and methods that are arguably universally known in the discipline need not be traced to the authors that all readers are familiar with.

Quotations. Some novice researchers have the instinct to fill their text with quotations from other authors as a way of displaying the breadth of their readings and also, more problematically, to support their arguments. Generally speaking, you should never use a quotation from an authoritative source as proof that your opinion or your reasoning is correct. It is the formulation of your own argument that should convince readers, not the quotations.

Qualify (and highlight) your own interpretations. Flag what you want to present as description, what is interpretation and what is a claim. You need to help the reader to see what you see, e.g., "I understand this excerpt as representing one form of teacher control over classroom talk."

And then there is the step of moving from "showing" to "interpreting" in which it is crucial to "shake up" the reader to the fact that you are changing gears. So a change of section or chapter should occur, accompanied with a strong flagging of your appearance as the thinking subject. So you might use something like the following:

- I argue that . . .
- My contention is . . .
- I show that . . .

Help your reader all along the way to recognize how you are building your argument. Working your way through these conventions in academic genres helps to ensure that readers understand the text and the key parts of it. Importantly, they also help you find your own voice as a member of the academic community.

Organize your paragraphs. While writing this book, Monica and Sari were impressed by a specific form of editing that Joan used. He took a finished text draft and turned it into a text plan by giving each paragraph a number and a title. By looking at each title in the order in which they appear, this exercise alone helped identify weaknesses and inconsistencies in the overall structure: points that get repeated (unnecessarily), diversions or digressions from the argument, issues missing, issues that are raised out of place, paragraphs that include too many points or paragraphs that mention issues that have not been previously presented.

Use respectful language. Think about the assumptions behind the conventions you use. One that has attracted a lot of attention is the generic masculine: e.g., "a researcher should substantiate his argument" or "no man would believe this." At present, it is expected that you write either in generic feminine ("should substantiate her argument") or in the double form ("his or her argument"). Think carefully about your category labels, and what they might signal about unexamined relations of power or ideologies of language, race, gender, sexuality or anything else. Terms like "minority language," "small language," "traditional speaker" or "native speaker" are contentious. Take your own speaking position into account, and be clear about it. Clearly, much of our work requires references to such labels, since we examine the role of language in the making of social difference and social inequality; all the more reason to think carefully about how you want to write about it.

Go back and cut, cut, cut. Although novice researchers usually fear that they have little to say, in practice the problem of learners in academic publishing is that they produce excessively lengthy texts that tend to be too much about the description and less about the actual claim they want to make. Nowadays almost all academic genres involve length limits, particularly journal articles. Most of the time, first drafts are very long and contain arguments that, upon inspection, are evidently peripheral to the main argument. It is also common to provide too much detail on the context, theoretical issues or aspects of the analysis. Often, writers run into a problem that we call "writer exhaustion" or "reader blindness," which means that they have worked so much on it that they can no longer read it from the perspective of a first-time reader; they cannot see what works and what does not. It is at this stage when colleagues are often necessary, as well as leaving the text "to rest" a few days and going back to it with a refreshed perspective.

6.5.3 Peer Review

When you are aiming at publishing, take a look at the journal or series you are aiming for; look at what they publish, and what genre structure they prefer. Many journals publish detailed guidelines as well as narrative commentary on what they are looking for (this is true, for example, of the *Journal of Sociolinguistics* and *American Ethnologist*). Many editors or associate editors are happy to respond to your questions; they are actively interested in mentoring novice writers.

However terrifying the peer review process may be, it really helps sharpen writers' arguments and make them accessible. With very few exceptions, reviewers are actually trying to help.

Here are a few things to keep in mind:

(1) Reviewers must read your article more carefully than the average reader, but they will be very busy scholars with time constraints too. Whatever they fail to see is likely to be missed by other readers.

(2) English-speaking populations commonly expect commands and reproaches to be expressed indirectly; but indirect language requires more thinking and more time and more complex grammar, and often leaves assertions too open and vague. Reviewers may have good reasons to prefer clarity and directness. They may also be asked to do so by the editor of the journal, who ultimately has to make a decision.

(3) Reviewers may detect things that do not work but very rarely know your data set and your overall agenda enough to come up with solutions. They should detect problems, but have no obligation to solve them (though often they will point you to helpful literature).

(4) Once you get your reviews, sleep on them before responding. Often the comments make (better) sense after you have had some time to think. You should take reviewers' comments very seriously, even if the texts that they produce may not be very elegant or you are having hard time figuring out what they actually are suggesting. Do not be afraid to ask the editor for clarification if necessary.

(5) Next you will need to make some decisions and a working plan for your revision processes. If the reviews suggest only minor revisions, usually the process is quite straightforward and manageable in terms of time and recourses. In case of major revisions, you will need to assess the plausibility of the suggestions by the reviewers, e.g., in terms time available to you (usually the journals set a deadline for resubmission), as well as resources and skills that you have. You might also need to come to terms of the possible differences in their suggestions, and possibly contact the editor for advice or clarification. At the end of the revision process, you will need to defend your decisions carefully, usually by writing a set of responses to reviewers' specific points. Depending on the journal, this response is read at the minimum by the editor, but often your responses and revised article go back to the reviewers for the next round of review.

(6) Because the most widely read journals are in English, journals require transcriptions of other languages, or multilingual transcriptions, to be accompanied by an English translation (in many European academic traditions in other languages, this is not always the case). This adds another layer of decision-making regarding how to represent the material.

Epilogue

The final drafts of this book were completed in early 2017, a moment that felt like a crisis of democracy and capitalism, like a deep questioning of the social and political order set up after World War II. Manifested around the world in electoral surprises, populism, rejection of established political élites, xenophobia, and protests against increasing wealth gaps, against a backdrop of climate change, the Zeitgeist is vigilance, action, expression. Suddenly everyone is paying attention to how Donald Trump speaks and to his body language; images and language combine and collide in demonstrations, graffiti and street art; speaking something that sounds to someone like Arabic can get you kicked off a plane or turned away at a border. While we would argue that language has always mattered, as we wrap up this book this seems more evident than ever.

And therefore so does honing the skills to investigate them, and to engage in the dialogue necessary to understanding them, and the interests they represent. We all need to come to grips with how deeply social life is constituted through particular discourses and through the strong investments people have in discourses that legitimate those interests and give them meaning and moral valence: that help us explain how it comes to pass that we can disagree so passionately on what the nature of our problems are, and on how to address them, and that help us come to grips with the contradictions of liberal democracy and of capitalism. Language and discourse must cease to be "transparent," since meaning is inextricably linked to the situations and the trajectories of events in which social actors get involved.

It is by recognizing this (social) materiality of language that we can further investigate how the symbolic relates to the economic. For many inhabitants of the planet, the turn of the millennium has brought about better life conditions and rapid growth, particularly in Asia. However, the overall figures point towards an increase of inequalities globally, and a greater accumulation of wealth amongst those who are already rich. In a parallel way we have seen a rapid spread of neoliberal discourses about how business and social life should be conducted and regulated. These discourses consistently claim to be the recipe for growth and stability; but in fact industrial and post-industrial economies are slowly and consistently stagnating, and major wealth gaps are spreading. This has not prevented most of us from getting ruled by targets and indicators, even as the very master narrative in which these procedures are based was clearly failing to meet its own targets. How is it that our societies still *invest* in these ideas a way of formulating what counts and what does not?

Critical Sociolinguistics and Critical Discourse Analysis constitute in many ways an intellectual reaction to these processes. In the Introduction we revealed our experience of the profound transformation that our field of study had undergone. The type of political critique that we advocate here has been with us for a while, from some of the work on decolonization which first emerged in the 1960s, and which gathered renewed momentum in the mid-1990s with numerous publications on the discourses of racism, language and gender, or the politics of multilingualism. But clearly we are now facing a set of conditions which both reinvigorate politicized approaches to language (that is, ones which interrogate the workings of power) and which seem to require a different combination of theories and methods, as well as perhaps a different set of conversational partners.

Along with the rest of the social sciences and humanities we are asked now to think carefully about the evidential bases for our claims, and to reflexively understand our own stakes in the game. We have the tools, however, to discover how ways of communicating are ways not only of making meaning, but also of making the meaning that constructs or contests social difference and social inequality. We can adapt those tools to the conditions we now find ourselves in. It is clear that it is not enough to say that ways of speaking are linguistically equivalently complex or that diverse social practices need to be respected as distinct, not deficient; there is enough anger around the backlash to those arguments, and enough continuity in the persistence of discourse the field has tried to contest, to make it clear that we need a different approach. We have been assuming that scientific knowledge will prevail because of its rigour and its internal validity, but this is probably just a dream of the Enlightenment from which we have not fully woken up. The question is: why should our stories make sense to people living in specific social conditions? And in what ways are we to share it with them?

In this book, we have suggested two main ways to address this problem. One is through interdisciplinary work, that is, by placing language and discourse in the social sciences and thus bringing down a boundary that keeps the socioeconomic, the political and the linguistic/symbolic artificially separate; the second is by diversifying our conversational partners well beyond academic circles, and doing a better job of accounting for how and why anyone should pay attention to what we have to say.

We have resorted to many examples of our own work in order to illustrate points and share our experience; but it is very important for readers not to take these portrayals as examples to follow but rather as points of departure or stepping stones to go further. During our research careers we have sought to query our inherited ideas and we have done away with a few boundaries attempting to delimit what language is about and what questions can be asked. However, with regard to interdisciplinarity and outreach, we have barely begun to scratch at walls that we hope that younger researchers will at some point finally bring down.

References

Albury, N. J. (2016). Māori language revitalisation: A project in folk linguistics. *Journal of Sociolinguistics* 20 (3): 287–311.

Aracil, L. V. (1982). *Papers de Sociolingüística*. Barcelona: Edicions de la Magrana.

Bailey, A. J., Canagarajah S., Lan, S. and Powers, D. G. (2016). Scalar politics, language ideologies, and the sociolinguistics of globalization among transnational Korean professionals in Hong Kong. *Journal of Sociolinguistics* 20 (3): 312–34.

Bakhtin, M. (1981). *The Dialogic Imagination* (M. Holquist, Ed.). Austin, TX: University of Texas Press.

Bakhtin, M. (1986). *Speech Genres and Other Late Essays* (M. Holquist, Ed.). Austin, TX: University of Texas Press.

Barnett, R., Gardner-Chloros P., Turell, M. T., Codó, E. and Van Hout, R. (2000). Coding language interaction data. *International Journal of Bilingualism* 4 (2): 181–97.

Belcher, W. L. (2009). *Writing Your Journal Article in 12 Weeks*. Los Angeles, CA: Sage Publications.

Bourdieu, P. (1982). *Ce que parler veut dire*. Paris: Fayard. English version: (1991). *Language and Symbolic Power* (J. B. Thompson, Ed.). Cambridge, MA: Polity Press.

Bourdieu, P. and Wacquant, J. L. (1992). *An Invitation to Reflexive Sociology*. Chicago, IL: University of Chicago Press.

Briggs, C. (1986). *Learning How to Ask*. Cambridge: Cambridge University Press.

Bucholtz, M. (2000). The politics of transcription. *Pragmatics* 32 (10): 1439–65.

Codó, E. and Moyer, M. G. (1997). LIDES and the analysis of bilingual conversation: A proposal for analyzing Spanish-English conversations from Gibraltar within the language interaction data-exchange system. In Seminario de Sociolinguistica (Ed.), *Actas do I Simposio Internacional Sobre o Bilingüismo*. Vigo: Universidade de Vigo. 488–503. ssl.websuvigo.s/actas1997/index.htm

Deleuze, G. and Guattari, F. (1980). *Mille plateaux: Capitalisme et schizophrénie*. Paris: Les Editions de Minuit. English version: *A Thousand Plateaus: Capitalism and*

Schizophrenia (B. Massumi, Trans.). Minneapolis, MN: University of Minnesota Press.

Foucault, M. (1971). *L'ordre du discours: Leçon inaugurale au Collège de France*. Paris: Editions de Minuit.

Frekko, S. (2016). *Academic Writing (Course Module)*. Barcelona: Universitat Oberta de Catalunya.

Goldstein, T. (1997). *Two Languages at Work: Bilingual Life on the Production Floor*. New York and Berlin: Mouton de Gruyter.

Heller, M. (2011). *Paths to Post-Nationalism: A Critical Ethnography of Language and Identity*. New York: Oxford University Press.

Heller, M., Bell, L., Daveluy, M., McLaughlin, M. and Noël, H. (2015). *Sustaining the Nation: The Making and Moving of Language and Nation*. Oxford: Oxford University Press.

Labov, W. (1966). *The Social Stratification of English in New York City* (2nd ed.). Cambridge: Cambridge University Press.

Lafont, R. (1979). La diglossie en pays Occitan, Ou le réel occulté. *Bildung and Ausbildung in der Romania* 2: 504–12.

Mason, J. (2002). *Qualitative Researching*. London: Sage.

Mougeon, R. and Heller, M. (1986). The social and historical context of minority French language education in Ontario. *Journal of Multilingual and Multicultural Development* 7 (2): 199–227.

Pietikäinen, S. (2000). *Discourses of Differentiation: Ethnic Representations in Newspaper Texts*. Jyväskylä: Jyväskylä University Press.

Pietikäinen, S. (2013). Heteroglossic authenticity in Sámi heritage tourism. In S. Pietikäinen and H. Kelly-Holmes (Eds.), *Multilingualism and the Periphery*. New York: Oxford University Press. 77–94.

Pietikäinen, S. (2015). Multilingual dynamics in Sámiland: Rhizomatic discourses on changing language. *International Journal of Bilingualism* 19 (2): 206–25.

Pujolar, J. (1991). *Patterns of Language Choice in Equal Encounters among Bilingual University Students in Catalonia*. MA Thesis, Lancaster University.

Pujolar, J. (2001). *Gender, Heteroglossia and Power: A Sociolinguistic Study of Youth Culture*. Berlin: Mouton de Gruyter.

Pujolar, J. (2007). African women in Catalan language courses: Struggles over class, gender and ethnicity in advanced liberalism. In B. McElhinny (Ed.), *Words, Worlds, and Material Girls: Language, Gender, Globalization*. Berlin: Mouton de Gruyter. 305–47.

Seedhouse, P. (2004). Transcription conventions. *Language Learning* 54 (1): 267–70.

Wee, L. (2016). Language policy, homelessness and neoliberal urbanization: The case of San Francisco's Union Square. *Journal of Sociolinguistics* 20 (3): 263–86.

Woolard, K. A. (1989). *Doubletalk: Bilingualism and the Politics of Ethnicity in Catalonia*. Stanford, CA: Stanford University Press.

Further Reading

Agar, M. H. (1996). *The Professional Stranger: An Informal Introduction to Ethnography* (2nd ed.). San Diego, CA: Academic Press.

Atkinson, J. M. and Heritage, J. (1984). Transcription notations. In J. M. Atkinson and J. Heritage (Eds.), *Structures of Social Action: Studies in Conversation Analysis*. Cambridge: Cambridge University Press. 9–16.

Austin, J. L. and Urmson, J. O. (1962). *How to Do Things With Words*. Oxford: Oxford University Press.

Barth, F. (1969). *Ethnic Groups and Boundaries: The Social Organization of Culture Difference*. Boston, MA: Little, Brown and Co.

Cameron, D., Frazer, E., Harvey, P., Rampton, M. B. H. and Richardson, K. (1992). *Researching Language: Issues of Power and Method*. London: Routledge.

Carr, W. and Kemmis, S. (2004). *Becoming Critical: Education, Knowledge and Action Research*. London and New York: RoutledgeFalmer.

Cicourel, A. V. (1988). Elicitation as a problem of discourse. In U. Ammon, N. Dittmar, K. J. Mattheier and P. Trudgill (Eds.), *Sociolinguistics. Soziolinguistik. An International Handbook of the Science of Language and Society: Ein Internationales Handbuch Zur Wissenschaft von Sprache Und Gesellschaft*. Berlin, New York: Walter de Gruyter. 903–910.

De Fina, A. (2003). *Identity in Narrative: A Study of Immigrant Discourse*. Amsterdam: John Benjamins.

Emerson, R. M., Fretz, R. I. and Shaw, L. L. (2011). *Writing Ethnographic Fieldnotes*. Chicago, IL: University of Chicago Press.

Fairclough, N. (1992). *Discourse and Social Change*. Cambridge: Polity Press.

Fairclough, N. and Chouliaraki, L. (1999). *Discourse in Late Modernity*. Edinburgh: Edinburgh University Press.

Gee, J. P. (2014). *An Introduction to Discourse Analysis: Theory and Method* (4th ed.). London: Routledge.

Geertz, C. (1988). *Works and Lives: The Anthropologist as Author*. Stanford, CA: Stanford University Press.

Goffman, E. (1959). *The Presentation of Self in Everyday Life*. Garden City, NY: Doubleday.

Goffman, E. (1974). *Frame Analysis: An Essay on the Organization of Experience*. Cambridge, MA: Harvard University Press.

Goffman, E. (1981). *Forms of Talk*. Philadelphia, PA: University of Pennsylvania Press.

Graff, G. and Birkenstein, C. (2006). *They Say, I Say: The Moves That Matter in Academic Writing*. New York: Norton.

Gumperz, J. J. (1982). *Discourse Strategies*. Cambridge: Cambridge University Press.

Hannerz, U. (2003). Being there . . . and there . . . and there! Reflections on multi-site ethnography. *Ethnography* 4 (2): 201–16.

Heller, M. (2002). *Éléments d'une sociolinguistique critique*. Paris: Didier.

Heller, M. (2008). Doing ethnography. In M. Moyer and L. Wei (Eds.), *Blackwell Guide to Research Methods on Bilingualism*. Oxford: Blackwell. 249–62.

Heller, M. (2011). *Paths to Post-Nationalism: A Critical Ethnography of Language and Identity*. New York: Oxford University Press.

Heller, M. and Pujolar, J. (2010). The political economy of texts: A case study in the structuration of tourism. *Sociolinguistic Studies* 3 (2): 177–201.

Hua, Z. (2016). *Research Methods in Intercultural Communication*. Chichester: Wiley-Blackwell.

Jackson, J. E. (1990). I am a fieldnote: Fieldnotes as a symbol of professional identity. In R. Sanjek (Ed.), *Fieldnotes: The Makings of Anthropology*. Ithaca, NY: Cornell University Press. 3–33.

Litosseliti, L. (2010). *Research Methods in Linguistics*. London: Continuum International Publishing Group.

Machin, D. (2011). *Introduction to Multimodal Analysis*. London: Bloomsbury.

Marcus, G. A. (1995). Ethnography in/of the world system: The emergence of multi-sited ethnography. *Annual Review of Anthropology* 24: 95–117.

Michrina, B. P. and Richards, C. (1996). *Person to Person: Fieldwork, Dialogue, and the Hermeneutic Method*. New York, NY: SUNY Press.

Narayan, K. (2012). *Alive in the Writing*. Chicago, IL: University of Chicago Press.

Nash, R. J. (2004). *Liberating Scholarly Writing: The Power of Personal Narrative*. New York: Teachers College Press.

Ochs, E. (1979) Transcription as theory. In E. Ochs and B. B. Schieffelin (Eds.), *Developmental Pragmatics*. New York: Academic Press. 43–72.

Pietikäinen, S. (2016). Critical debates: Discourse, boundaries and social change. In N. Coupland (Ed.), *Sociolinguistics: Theoretical Debates*. Cambridge: Cambridge University Press.

Pietikäinen, S., Kelly-Holmes, H., Jaffe, A. and Coupland, N. (2016). *Sociolinguistics from the Periphery: Small Languages in New Circumstances*. Cambridge: Cambridge University Press. 263–81.

Scollon, R. and Scollon, S.B.K. (2004). *Nexus Analysis: Discourse and the Emerging Internet*. London: Routledge.

Scollon, R. and Scollon, S.B.K. (2007). Nexus analysis: Refocusing ethnography on action. *Journal of Sociolinguistics* 11 (5): 608–25.

Van Maanen, J. (1988). *Tales of the Field: On Writing Ethnography*. Chicago, IL: University of Chicago Press.

Wei, L. and Moyer, M. G. (2009). *The Blackwell Guide to Research Methods in Bilingualism and Multilingualism*. Malden, MA: Blackwell Publishing Ltd.

Wortham, S. and Reyes, A. (2015). *Discourse Analysis Beyond the Speech Event*. London: Routledge.

Index